INSTRUCTOR'S MANUAL WITH TESTS
AND TRANSPARENCY MASTERS
Joyce S. Osland
Susan Mann
Both at University of Portland

ORGANIZATIONAL BEHAVIOR: AN EXPERIENTIAL APPROACH

Seventh Edition

Joyce S. Osland
David A. Kolb
Irwin M. Rubin

Prentice
Hall

Upper Saddle River, New Jersey 07458

Acquisitions editor: David Shafer
Associate editor: Michele Foresta
Production editor: Leah Crescenzo
Manufacturer: Integrated Book Technology, Inc.

ISBN 0-13-030880-3

10   9   8   7

CONTENTS

Introduction

APPENDICES

INTEGRATIVE CASES—TEACHING NOTES

TRANSPARENCY MASTERS

INTRODUCTION

Thank you for choosing our textbooks: *Organizational Behavior: An Experiential Approach*, which we refer to as the workbook, and its companion volume, *The Organizational Behavior Reader*. We hope that teaching this course will be as pleasurable and rewarding for you and your students as it has been for us. We continue revising these books year after year because we strongly believe an experiential approach is the most effective way to teach this material and to create a productive learning environment.

In addition to major revisions in the textbooks, this instructor's manual explains in greater detail how we teach the course and avoid or handle potential tricky bits. Professors always put their individual stamp on this course. Many of them are kind enough to share their innovations with us, which we then incorporate into the texts or the manual. Please take the suggestions in this manual in the spirit we offer them—not as the "one best way" to teach these classes but merely lessons professors have learned over the years that you may find helpful.

With a few exceptions that are noted in the beginning of each chapter in the instructor's manual, the other chapters contain all the materials you will need for the group exercises.

I. About The Seventh Edition

Three decades have passed since the two original authors of the textbook started what they believed was an experiment in teaching the beginning Organizational Behavior course at the Sloan School of Management, MIT. That beginning resulted in seven editions of these textbooks.

We have made major revisions in the workbook and the reader, in response to both developments in the field and feedback from professors who use these books. Specific changes include more information on cross-cultural material, creativity, both rational and intuitive decision making, virtual teams, e-commerce structure, and integrative cases at the end of the workbook. There are several new exercises. The workbook format remains the same, but the content has been totally revised, and you will find new material reflecting recent research findings in every chapter. Two-thirds of the *Reader* are new articles that capture current thinking in the field. The reader now contains chapter introductions that set the stage for each selection.

II. Overall Intent of the Text

Our stated intent in writing the workbook is to provide students of management with a course that engages not just their intellect, but their behaviors and feelings as well, so that they may actually experience in the classroom many of the issues associated with organizational life. In doing this, students work toward a second goal: learning how to learn from experience. The experiential learning model found in the third chapter explains the authors' assumptions about this type of learning; please read this chapter before beginning to structure your course. You may also wish to read David Kolb's book, *Experiential Learning*, (Upper Saddle River, NJ: Prentice Hall, 1984).

The chapters are designed to take the student through the experiential learning cycle—concrete experience, reflective observation, abstract conceptualization, and active experimentation. The chapters begin with a **Vignette** that emphasizes the practical importance of the topic. The **Premeeting Preparation** not only outlines the "homework" for each session, but also attempts to ground students in their own experience and encourages them to focus on what they want to learn. The ubiquitous question "What are the significant learning points from the readings?" nudges students to analyze what they've read and come prepared to integrate those points with the experiential exercise. The **Topic Introduction** presents what we see as the essential content information. Each chapter has an experiential exercise, described in **Procedure**

for Group Exercise, that includes both instructions and debriefing questions. The **Follow up** either elaborates on what occurred in the exercise or contributes additional content material. The **Learning Points** summarize the key points, and **Tips for Managers** provide practical advice. Each chapter ends with the **Personal Application Assignment,** which helps students analyze a personal incident by guiding them through the entire learning cycle.

III. Role of the Instructor

Experiential learning requires a very different role for the instructor than the standard lecture or seminar format. It helps to think of yourself as a coach who should be modeling good supervisory or managerial behavior. Each chapter includes an exercise (role play, simulation, case) that is designed to involve all students in a variety of ways. The teacher's role becomes less one of purveying information and more one of managing the class and classroom as a learning organization. Some units require you to do very little other than keep track of time, a chore you may wish to delegate anyway. There are many times when the instructor should play an unobtrusive role and let the students take the major responsibility for the learning that goes on. The primary task of instructors is to develop a good climate for learning; this means modeling respect, curiosity, and a nonjudgmental attitude. Some of the most common interventions that instructors make are: bringing a discussion back on track, ensuring that students are not avoiding or overlooking certain types of behavior, and clarifying points about research findings. With the exception of the opening lecturette, the instructor contributes knowledge on an "as needed" basis and always attempts to let the students get there first.

Given the experiential nature of the course, it's a great advantage if instructors can "read" group and individual behavior and skillfully handle whatever situations arise. Occasionally, they must gently help students see the negative effects of their behavior on other people. If you want to develop these process skills, it helps to observe an experienced instructor or read more about group facilitation. When you first begin teaching this course, you often come up with your best responses to questions and what occurs in class as you are driving home ("What I really should have said was..."). You just have to trust that all that revisionist history and delayed brilliance in the car will eventually find its way into the classroom. Students learn from the exercises and each other, in spite of our fumbles.

Because of the emphasis placed on self-awareness in this course, students often come to instructors or teaching assistants with questions about personal issues relating to the course topics. It's neither necessary nor advisable to set yourself up as a therapist, but if you develop an open environment and demonstrate a willingness to be helpful, students are more likely to voice important concerns or issues, either in class or afterwards. There are many opportunities to use coaching or counseling skills when you teach this course, which students seem to appreciate.

Students, especially undergraduates, sometimes ask the instructor for permission to behave in a particular way during a simulation ("Can we...?"). You don't want to become the arbiter or authority figure in this way. Therefore, simply tell them that as long as they follow the rules established for the simulation, they can do whatever comes naturally. There is no predetermined right or wrong behavior in a simulation; we try to learn from whatever behavior emerges.

When instructors debrief a session, the emphasis is on what students have learned. The art of debriefing lies in finding a happy medium between a meandering laissez-faire approach at one extreme and, at the other, pushing students to see a point that only the instructor thinks is important. We are open and enthusiastic about whatever students key in on and find important; not only is this the essence of experiential learning, but it is also what makes it possible to teach this course year after year without becoming bored. As an instructor, you never know what will happen with different groups of students, and there is always something to learn from them.

However, we also go into a debriefing session prepared for things that could and even should emerge. This preparation comes from past teaching experience, our stated goals for the chapter, and from observing what's occurring during the group exercise. After students mention a key concept, we try to highlight it ("Let's analyze this a bit more. Why did your group react like this? Is that what typically happens in a work setting?"). We have tried to create debriefing questions that will elicit good discussions after each exercise. However, if by the end of the debriefing, students have not mentioned something that is an important OB concept, we ask another prompt question to get at it. Nevertheless, instructors should avoid asking questions in a way that causes students to feel as if they are guessing an obscure answer that the instructor is looking for but won't tell.

The role of the instructor is to teach students to think like an organizational behavior expert. This means modeling and explaining your own approach to situations and how you perceive them. It also means asking questions in class (and on exams if you use them) that will elicit this type of critical thinking.

We suggest that you take a few minutes at the end of each class to set the stage for the next session by briefly telling students about the articles they will be assigned in the *Reader* and explaining the premeeting preparation for the next chapter.

IV. Ways of Organizing

Sequencing. The four sections of the workbook progresses from the level of the individual to the level of the organization in its environment:

Part I   Understanding Yourself and Other People at Work
Part II Creating Effective Work Groups
Part III Leadership and Management
Part IV Managing Effective Organizations

We think the order of the chapters promotes group development and personal growth. In addition, later chapters build on concepts and skills covered earlier in the course. The initial chapters focus on different mental maps in order to help students see and appreciate individual differences. This sets the stage for different ways of viewing behavior. The second section, Creating Effective Work Relationships, begins with basic interpersonal skills that are a prerequisite for subsequent chapters like conflict management and performance appraisal.

We encourage instructors to modify the sequence of chapters in whatever order best fits their particular objectives and circumstances. For example, some professors prefer to cover Career Development and Stress Management at the end of the course. Others, especially those who teach in schools that emphasize macro courses, begin with the last section because topics like organizational analysis and design are more similar to what students have received in other courses. Regardless of the order you choose, we do, however, recommend that you begin with the first chapter, "The Psychological Contract," followed by either Chapter 2, "Theories of Managing People," or Chapter Three, "Individual and Organizational Learning." The first chapter sets the stage for experiential learning and focuses on the process of joining an organization where it is most relevant. The second chapter describes the evolution of management thought and provides a conceptual ground from which to build. The third chapter establishes the learning methodology for the course and helps students understand some of the ways individual differences will be accepted and used. If you wish to use Chapter 2 later on in the course, or to omit it, we suggest you begin with Chapter 1, followed by Chapter 3. This ensures a good beginning to the course.

Chapter Times and Flexibility. The chapters in the text are designed for two-hour class sessions, but can be easily adjusted to shorter or longer class sessions. The transition is usually a simple one of splitting the unit up for shorter sessions or expanding the times listed for longer sessions.

In each unit, there are limited times for each step and the time if often tight. These times are not cast in stone; they are merely guidelines.

One-hour class sessions constitute the greatest challenge because some exercises are so lengthy that the debriefing time may be too limited to gain the maximum learning. One solution is to leave out certain steps in the exercises; another is to have students bring their written reactions and answers to the debriefing questions to the next class. We have included sample course designs in the appendix for both short (A) and longer (B) class periods. It is not impossible to use this course in a 50–60 minute format, but it is easier if the sessions are at least 80 minutes in length.

The debriefing time is the most important portion of the class, so avoid scrimping on debriefing time. You may not be able to cover all aspects of an exercise and you certainly don't have to use all the debriefing questions, but make sure students have the opportunity to reflect on what they learned and pull these lessons together. Otherwise, instructors could leave themselves open to charges that experiential learning is just "fun and games."

Saturday Sessions. We strongly recommend including a longer Saturday session in your course design. The expanded time format permits more comprehensive examination of a particular chapter and a synergistic presentation of several chapters. These sessions are like a workshop, and students appear more relaxed in these sessions and welcome the change of pace they bring.

Saturday sessions can be used in various ways. Some professors have one eight-hour session near the beginning of the course to help students become acquainted with their learning group and move quickly through the beginning stages of group formation. Students "bond" much more rapidly in a Saturday session than they do in class. Make sure you do Chapter 3 on learning either before the Saturday session or as the first event. Others have two four-hour sessions—one in the beginning of the course for these reasons mentioned previously and one towards the end. One of the authors incorporates outdoor challenge course activities into these Saturday sessions, which students see as the highlight of the course. The hours in the Saturday sessions replace regularly scheduled class meeting times, which means that the course usually ends early, another advantage in the eyes of students.

To avoid scheduling problems, it works best if the Saturday sessions are listed in the course descriptions provided at the time of registration. This way students realize what is involved and can clear their own schedules ahead of time. When it is not possible to set the date as part of the course description, professors can ask the students if they agree to a Saturday class and give them three dates from which to choose. In our experience, students have always been willing to attend a Saturday class, even though it meant juggling work schedules, etc.

Learning Teams. Learning teams or groups are one of the most important features of the course because they provide an opportunity for students to work in a successful team, receive feedback on their behavior, and learn to get along with people who may be quite different from them. Because students work in the same group throughout the course, they come to value the belonging and friendship these groups provide. In some schools, the organizational behavior course is strongly recommended for entering MBA students because it helps them quickly form relationships with other students. It is not uncommon for both undergraduate and MBA students to remark that their learning group was the most successful group experience they have ever had. Chapter 3 contains advice on forming the learning teams.

V. Evaluation Methods

The Personal Application Assignment. Some professors have difficulty with the issue of grading in experiential courses that are ideally driven more by student learning than the professor's evaluation requirements. For example, grading class participation may introduce a power and authority dynamic into the exercises that could potentially have a negative effect on the interaction. However, some form of systematic feedback is an essential element in the learning process. The grading assignment that is most in keeping with the philosophy of the course are PAAs (personal application assignments), because they model both the learning cycle and organizational behavior thinking. PAAs allow students to write on topics that are relevant to them and provide them with a framework they can use throughout their career when they face problematic situations. Some instructors use the brief PAA format found at the end of each chapter, others require longer versions. Examples of the longer PAA format are included in the appendix, along with instructions, entitled "The Personal Application Assignment," which we hand out to students along with the Grading Criteria ("What We Look for When We Grade...") found in the appendix.

Other professors prefer a less-structured approach to this assignment and use them as homework assignments. For example:

"Each week following our in-class experiences each student will write a 3–5 page paper called a PAA. These PAAs will be your way of reflecting and commenting on the class experience and applying some personal interest or experience of yours to the class lesson. Each PAA should:
a.   summarize what you learned from the in-class exercise(s) including your opinions, feelings, and thoughts;
b.   demonstrate some of the knowledge gained from the articles in the reader;
c.   show how you experienced in the past or plan to apply the acquired knowledge to a real situation of your own;
d.   demonstrate what you learned about yourself from partaking in the exercise; and
e.   demonstrate wit, humor and be delightful to read."

When we grade the PAAs, we take a developmental approach that both models good coaching and demonstrates how an organizational behavior person thinks.

With MBA students, we require four PAAs unless they opt for a take-home mid-term and final or a learning journal. Students respond well to being given a choice in the way they are evaluated.

Undergraduates have less life experience and sometimes have difficulty finding PAA topics. Therefore, we require one or two PAAs for undergraduates in addition to other evaluation methods.

Exam Questions. The instructor's manual includes various types of exam or review questions that cover material from both the workbook and the reader. We use these questions almost exclusively with undergraduates. Some of the questions merely test whether students have learned the key points; others are geared more towards applying knowledge. We also ask students to contribute exam questions, which they put on the board at the beginning of each class. We would caution you against the exclusive use of multiple-choice tests, because this test format is not entirely compatible with the overall philosophy of the course.

Term Papers. Students have the option of writing a personal analysis of their role as a manager (a journal can be used to record and keep track of their daily activities) and/or an analysis of an organization.

Thought Pieces. These are short 1–2 page reactions to the readings or what has occurred in class. They are an excellent device for understanding where students are. Requiring that these thought pieces by sent via E-mail promotes Internet use and allows the professor to make an immediate quick response. This has been particularly effective with international students who feel more comfortable with this medium than speaking up in class.

With undergraduates who need to develop critical thinking skills, we sometimes require a certain number of reaction pieces on reader articles. Students are asked to summarize the gist of the article in the first one or two paragraphs and follow up with their own reaction to the article and a real-life example of this concept.

Journals. Journals are a good way to see how students are responding to and learning from the course. Some professors use the brief PAA forms at the end of each chapter; others simply have students describe their reactions and learning from each class. It's a good idea to vary the journal assignment so that it does not become stale. For more information on using journals, please see Toby Fulwiler, *The Journal Book* (Portsmouth, NH: Boynton/Cook 1987).

Group Projects. Group projects provide an opportunity for students to practice group dynamics and learn from their experience. The major complaint about group projects, both in class and at the workplace, is that some members do not carry their share of the workload. For this reason, we aim for both individual accountability and a group grade. The percentage of the group grade that an individual receives is determined by peer evaluations. We have feedback sessions on group projects so that students have the opportunity to learn from and improve their performance as a group member.

With MBA students, one possible assignment is to ask that each learning group present, in the most creative way possible, what they see as the common threads or integrating themes found throughout the course (appreciation of differences, contingency theory, analyzing the situation before choosing a certain behavior, management as a developmental approach, etc.). This assignment helps them integrate the material and by the time each group has made their presentation, the learning has been strongly reinforced. Their presentations are made in the last class session, which then takes on the air of a celebration.

Group projects with undergraduates can be designed to expose them to OB issues in real organizations; they involve interviews, surveys, and analyses of local businesses or a university process or department that is trying to make improvements. For example, one class researched and made improvements on course registration in the business school, teaching the need for continuous improvement in processes.

Another effective use of group projects is to have groups take the responsibility for leading a class session or a portion of the class. For example, groups can be assigned to investigate and report on outstanding companies that can be used as benchmarks in the area of career development, managing diversity, performance appraisal, etc.

Peer Evaluation. A small percentage of the grade can be determined by the students' learning group. We have them assign 0–5 points to the students' class preparation (reading and homework assignments) and in-class contributions and participation in the group exercises. Please see the Peer Evaluation Form in Appendix C, which also includes a section on group project contributions. We warn students to take these evaluations very seriously and to keep their personal feelings (positive or negative) about other students from biasing their evaluations. It's a good idea to check these forms while the students are still in class to make sure they have filled them out correctly.

VI. Participation

One of the advantages of beginning the course with the group exercise in Chapter 1 is that it models participation and gets students involved and talking right away. If your first classes are more lecture than group work, it is more difficult to break out of this mold. Active participation is seldom a difficulty at the MBA level; indeed, the greater problem may be tactfully managing people who talk too much and bore the other students or make it difficult to complete the exercises without rushing.

Encouraging participation may be more of a challenge at the undergraduate level or with international students who are less comfortable with English as a second language and with this type of classroom expectations. One way to get undergraduates talking is to have them write on the board at the beginning of class both a significant point from the readings and a question. Undergraduates may be more likely to speak up if they have been asked to do a "quick-write" response to the exercise before a general debriefing. We recommend cooperative learning techniques, especially for classes that have difficulty participating. If you only have time to read one book on this subject, try D. W. Johnson & R. T. Johnson's *Learning Together and Alone: Cooperative, Competitive, and Individualistic Learning* (Upper Saddle River, NJ: Prentice Hall, 1987).

VII. Midcourse Evaluation

It's always helpful to utilize a midcourse evaluation form, like the one shown in Appendix E. This allows you to see what students are thinking and, if there are problems to be rectified, you will have time to do so before the course is finished. This models the lesson from Sherwood and Glidewell's Pinch Model (Chapter 1) to look for "pinches" before they become "crunch points."

VIII. Teaching Assistants

If you have the luxury of teaching assistants, you could consider following the method Dave Kolb used with great success for teaching doctoral students how to teach. He had two three teaching assistants for a class of 45 MBA students. Kolb met with the teaching assistants before every class to debrief and evaluate the last session and plan the upcoming session. Each teaching assistant was assigned two three learning groups; during the group exercise they would observe these groups, answer their questions, and occasionally make a process intervention. They graded the PAAs written by their learning group members; Kolb would check their grading in the beginning of the course to make sure it was consistent. The TAs eventually assumed some of the teaching responsibilities—the lecturette, the debriefing, or the design of a new exercise. This was a wonderful learning experience.

IX. Integrative Cases

For the first time, we have included integrative cases, which contain the following concepts.
The Donor Services Departmen—managerial style, motivation, job redesign, supervision, conflict, organization design and effectiveness, change, and global diversity.
Custom Chip, Inc.—managerial role, leadership, communication, conflict, organization design, and meeting behavior.
Rudi Gassner—work teams, global diversity, compensation, anxd decision making
Women and Global Leadership at Bestfoods—global and domestic diversity, change, organization design, and leadership.

X. Chapter Format

-Materials needed
-Learning objectives
-A sample design for a two-hour session
-Setting the stage—suggestions about beginning the class and the lecturette
-Issues to consider in leading the experiential exercise
-Transparency Masters (at the end of the manual)
-Exam or review questions from both the workbook and reader
-Reader articles that can be used with the workbook chapter

More extensive PowerPoint Electronic Transparencies are available. Visit our custom site at www.prenhall.com/osland for these PowerPoints. This site also offers the downloadable Instructor's Manual files.

Chapter 1
THE PSYCHOLOGICAL CONTRACT

Materials Needed: Name tags or name tents and chairs or desks for representatives in the front of the class. Some instructors hand out Appendix K, "How to Succeed in Organizational Behavior by Really Trying" in this session.

Objectives: After completing this chapter, students should be able to:

A.   Define the terms *psychological contract* and *self-fulfilling prophecy* and explain their importance
B.   Describe the external influences that affect workplace expectations
C.   Explain the *pinch model*
E.   Make a psychological contract with their professor
F.   List the characteristics of the field of organizational behavior

Sample Design Schedule

6:00–6:25	Icebreaker and Introduction
6:25–6:45	Students prepare to be interviewed in groups
6:45–7:05	Instructor interviews students
7:05–7:15	Students prepare to interview instructor
7:15–7:40	Students interview instructor
7:40–8:00	Summary and Debriefing (Pinch Model)

Preparing the Classroom

❑   We write the class schedule on the board, these questions (what, why, how, when) and the quotation from Confucius from the workbook preface:
> I read and I forget
> I see and I remember
> I do and I understand.

❑   To save time, instructors can have both syllabus and name tags or tents available as students enter the classroom.

Setting the Stage—Lecturette

Our first concern is helping students enter a new situation so they feel comfortable enough to participate. Therefore, we begin with a 15-minute icebreaker, usually Name Bingo (see Appendix J) which is adapted for each class. This exercise works well because it provides students with a task and an excuse to approach people they don't know. In the process, they learn more about the other students and also begin learning names. It also serves a frame-breaking purpose and signals to students that they have entered a different type of course where the traditional expectations do not apply. The person who has gathered the most signatures wins a prize (bag of Goldfish crackers or something else that is edible and easily shared). The instructor asks what an exercise like this accomplishes so they have their first taste at analyzing organizational behavior. This also helps students see that there is a purpose behind the instructor's actions, which builds credibility.

If you talk at great length in the first class, this reinforces the norms of a more traditional classroom; the longer they sit without talking, the harder it is to gain their participation. Therefore, the next step is providing just enough information to let students know what organizational behavior is and your objectives for the course (WHAT), its benefit to students and organizations (WHY), the methodology used in the course (HOW), and when special Saturday sessions will be held if that's applicable (WHEN).

1

WHAT For the "what" section, we use the "Course Objectives," (see Transparency T1.0) the "Characteristics of Organizational Behavior" section, (T1.1) and p. 15 of the workbook. We put the objectives on a transparency (see Appendix I) that we show the students again at the last class session as a check that we did indeed do what we set out to accomplish.

WHY Instructors, like good managers, have a motivational role, and enthusiasm for one's subject is crucial. In discussing the "why" aspect, they can tell students why it's important to study organizational behavior in whatever way is most persuasive to students. We stress the necessity of mastering people skills and organizational behavior knowledge in order to advance and create work environments that are productive as well as rewarding and fun.

HOW The "how" part should be a quick description of experiential learning and why it's appropriate for this course. We usually write the Confucius quotation on the board, "I hear and I forget, I see and I remember, I do and I understand." You can either explain your role at this point or during the interview process.

WHEN If you do a Saturday Special, explain that we do this because groups can develop more rapidly if we have a large block of time. The exercises build on one another and we can take advantage of the resulting synergy in a way that is not as feasible with a regular class schedule. In some schools, the Saturday class appears in the registration information; in others the professor ask students if they are willing to trade a Saturday for an equivalent number of regular class and provide some alternative dates. (See the section entitled Saturday Special, p. xv. for more details.)

We quickly define the psychological contract and why it's important, provide a current example, and ask whether any of them have seen examples of broken contracts. What was the aftermath? Read the instructions on page 10 to the class and begin the exercise.

Alternative Approaches

An innovative method for going over the syllabus is to give them a group quiz on the syllabus. This forces them to discuss the key aspects and ensure that they have really read it.

Issues to Consider in Leading the Experiential Exercise

A. This unit is designed to let students get to know you and exchange expectations. By encouraging them to think about what they want out of the course, they are more likely to take responsibility for their own learning. It's useful to think about your answers to the interviewer questions ahead of time. Try to put yourself in their place and envision the key issues for them. If your syllabus is clear and detailed, you can avoid devoting all the interview time to the mechanics of grades, paper length, etc.

B. The key issue is the initial negotiation of a psychological contract between you and the class, which legitimizes the renegotiation of that contract during the course as either you or the students feel what Sherwood and Glidewell call a "pinch." (See Chapter 1 in the workbook and Transparency T1.2 for the Pinch Model.) This is not intended to be just a simulation of how the socialization process might take place in a real organization. Rather, it is designed to be a real contracting activity that clarifies how you and your students are going to work together in the real organization of the class for the entire term. It is a genuine attempt to avoid a violation of the contract wherein expectations are transgressed and parties to a relationship eventually become psychologically disconnected from each other.

C. Your own behavior in this class may strike many students as rather surprising (unless they are familiar with your reputation as an experiential professor). They may be unaccustomed to interacting with professors in this way. Consequently, you may well find some signs of disbelief, e.g., sighs, cynical looks. This is the first sign of a "pinch" in that some of their implicit expectations are undoubtedly being violated. You should try to be sensitive to these signs and confront them as much as possible in this session. In doing so, you will be modeling a very important norm of openness and directness that should elicit comparable behavior on their part. This also makes it easier for people to raise their own "pinches" with classmates or with you later on in the course. Incidentally, we've never had students complain about serious pinches; having a vehicle in place for dealing with problems is merely a safeguard.

D. The questions that you ask the students will be of your own choosing. Unless you instruct them otherwise, they can concentrate on the four general areas outlined in the workbook when preparing to be interviewed by you. We suggest you take notes on their responses (or have a teaching assistant take notes). You can also put their goals on a transparency that can be reviewed along with the course objectives in the last class session when you evaluate the course.

The following issues may arise in regard to the workbook student interview questions:

1. <u>Goals</u>. Within the larger framework of the learning goals established by you and the textbook, what specific things do people want to get out of the course? There will be different responses and they will, for the most part, be reasonable ones. Occasionally students will ask why we bother seeking their input if the syllabus is already laid out. One response is to note that although organizations always have both goals and constraints, they must also integrate individual goals. Another response is to mention that an understanding of student goals helps the instructor know what types of examples to use in class and how much emphasis to place on different areas. If possible, the instructor can also make some modifications in the syllabus. Some professors prepare a short syllabus for the first segment of the course and incorporate the results of the interview in a complete syllabus handed out later on.

2. <u>Attitudes and Reservations</u>. These questions allow students (especially those who are simply taking the course as a requirement) to examine their feelings about their new association with what is often regarded as the "soft-touchy-feely," less-rational area of either organizational behavior or the business school curriculum. Students are usually struggling more with the stereotypes about the discipline rather than with a prejudice that they themselves hold. You can stress the importance of both the hard and soft subjects or approaches and provide examples of the latter. We'd avoid getting into an argument with students or pushing your own point of view too strongly. The intent with these questions is to get the issue out in the open and acknowledge their concerns so that the focus can be on learning.

If there are fears about experiential learning, they often concern being forced to do role plays or disclose more of themselves than they want. We reassure students that participation in role plays in front of the entire class is strictly voluntary (and fairly rare in most courses). Other role plays occur in their learning groups with everyone participating, so no one feels under much performance pressure. Concerning self-disclosure, we point out that no one is ever pressured to talk about themselves and this is not a T-group atmosphere. Nevertheless, it is true that the more they invest in the course and the more they open themselves up to examining their own behavior and receiving feedback from others, the more they will learn in the course. They themselves will determine their receptivity and openness without pressure from others. We point out that this course is like a laboratory. It's a safe place to see how your behavior affects others and vice versa and to make mistakes and learn from them. Better to learn these things in a course among people whom most students come to see as friends than at work.

Students who have little or no work experience sometimes worry that this is a serious constraint in a course like this. You can honestly reassure them that lack of experience has never proved to be a major drawback. Even if they cannot contribute work examples or lessons, they can participate in the class exercises and tease out the learning from them as well as other students. This particular concern usually vanishes after the first few classes. It helps that the PAAs can be written on incidents that have taken place outside a work setting.

3. <u>Resources</u>. With this question, we are modeling our belief that adults bring skills and expertise to the classroom that can benefit everyone. This allows students to establish themselves as people with knowledge to contribute. It also alerts the instructor that there are extremely capable students in the class who can be used as a resource or who may be likely to "compete" with the instructor. You can defuse the latter situation by sincerely welcoming their expertise ("I'm glad to hear we have someone in the class with experience in that area.") and requesting their opinions in class ("Sam, you've had experience with self-managed work teams. What do you think are the main difficulties with implementing them?").

4. <u>Reputation</u>. This is a good opportunity to learn about your reputation as a teacher or a department, although you are more likely to hear the positive side than the negative. If you seem open, they will mention negative things they have heard. This gives you a chance to explain or to note that you have made changes in assignments, etc. Sometimes, it can be an impetus to change your ways.

5. <u>Ground Rules</u>. We've found that asking this question in the beginning of both courses and seminars eliminates most negative behaviors and gives the participants a sense of ownership over the environment we are creating. If someone exhibits a behavior that was talked about here, another student is likely to point that out to the offender, saving the instructor from taking on the role of authoritarian. If the students fail to mention it, the instructor can refer back to the ground rules in a low-key manner. If you happen upon an especially unruly group, you can post the ground rules on the wall or provide each student with a copy.

E. The students also have the opportunity to interview you. You can set the stage here and signal what type of questions you are willing to take. ("I'll answer any question except those you might hear on a daytime talk show.") Students seem to appreciate being able to question instructors about their background and life. They typically ask us about our educational history, work experience, family, hobbies, biggest work mistake or success, life goals, why we teach rather than consult full-time, pet peeves about students, etc. Afterwards they always comment that they like having this understanding of our personal context. However, if you are a very private person, you may wish to limit them to the questions pertaining to the course like those in the workbook.

This will probably be such a new experience for them that you may see a whole range of behaviors, from currying favor to outright hostility (a very rare occurrence, but it's good to be prepared). How you deal with these behaviors is, of course, a function of your own personal style and teaching style. Humor is helpful. Being honest about your feelings ("It feels as if I'm under attack" or "Feels like I'm being buttered up") usually helps to clear the air and allows the entire group to share the problem and hopefully, the solution to it as well. **The most important thing to remember here is that your behavior should model the behaviors (openness, respect, non-defensive reaction, curiosity) that will set a solid foundation for the rest of the course.**

The reference in the book to self-fulfilling prophecy and the role of expectations is a perfect opportunity to tie in your own high expectations of the students. If you like, you can hand out "How to Succeed in Organizational Behavior by Really Trying" (Appendix K) either at the first or the second class session.

F. The **debriefing** questions, "What differences do you see when you compare this method to the traditional way other courses begin?" and "What is the impact on you as a student?" models how we will examine the results of behavior throughout the rest of the course. Students often comment that it's easier to speak up and participate in a course that begins using an exercise like this and that they feel more motivated to work as a result of the interviews. This provides an opportunity to bring up the "decision to join versus decision to participate" concept, which is exemplified in the different goals students give for taking the course.

G. We ask for examples about broken psychological contracts in real life as a lead-in to the Sherwood-Glidewell Model.

H. We make the link between the importance of expectations in the pinch model and the effect of expectations on behavior described in the self-fulfilling prophecy. Then we relate this to ourselves as teachers who have high expectations of students in the hopes that they will meet them.

I. We finish the class by going over the learning points and the tips for managers. **Make sure you explain to students how to use the workbook**. For every chapter, they read the objectives and opening vignette and do the premeeting preparation. Their before-class assignments are always in the premeeting preparation instructions, rather than in the syllabus.

Transparency Masters

T1.0   COURSE OBJECTIVES
T1.1   CHARACTERISTICS OF ORGANIZATIONAL BEHAVIOR
T1.2   MODEL FOR MANAGING PSYCHOLOGICAL CONTRACTS
T1.3   COMMON SOURCES OF CONTRACT VIOLATION
T1.4   HOW TO MANAGE GENERATION XERS
T1.5   COMMITTED EMPLOYEES
T1.6   EARNING EMPLOYEE COMMITMENT

Workbook Exam and Review Questions

1. The psychological contract is
    a.   a written notarized document.
    b.*   an individual's beliefs regarding the terms and conditions of a reciprocal exchange agreement.
    c.   irrevocable.
    d.   solely a statement of the employers' expectations.

2. Which two classes of decisions do individuals make when approaching a new organization?
    a.*   The decision to join and the decision to participate
    b.   The decision to be socialized and the decision to participate
    c.   The decision to join and the decision to cooperate
    d.   The decision to join and the decision to be socialized

3. Which of the following is not an aspect of the current psychological contract?
    a.*   Long-term employment
    b.   Employment determined by business needs
    c.   Employee rewards for skills and performance
    d.   Employee responsibility for maintaining their employability

4. What percentage of the workforce will be made up of women by the year 2020?
    a.   64 percent
    b.   23 percent
    c.*   50 percent
    d.   15 percent

5. The average high school or college graduate will hold (13) different jobs in their working life.

6. Give an example of the self-fulfilling prophecy.

7. Supervisors and managers who have high expectations of their employees will be more likely to be disappointed.
    _____True or __X__False
    Why?

<u>Answer</u>: Due to the self-fulfilling prophecy, supervisors and managers will be more likely to have their expectations met. Employees will live up to these expectations.

8. What's the difference between a psychological contract and an employment contract?

    <u>Answer</u>: Psychological contracts, unlike employment contracts, are usually not written and are often not even explicit. Psychological contracts focus on a dynamic relationship that defines the employee's psychological involvement with their employer.

9. The <u>(Pinch Model)</u> describes the process by which psychological contracts are established, disrupted, and renegotiated.

10. What impact do broken psychological contracts have?

    <u>Answer</u>: loss of trust and good faith in the employee-employer relationship, disillusionment, lower employee satisfaction, lower productivity, increased desire to leave the company.

11. What are the external influences and changing expectations that have influenced psychological contracts in the last decade?
    <u>Answer</u>:
    - Rapid rate of change in the business environment
    - Global economy
    - Changing economic conditions
    - More uncertainty and decreased job security for workers
    - Increased demands for performance, flexibility, and innovation
    - Less full-time jobs and core employees and more contingent and temporary employment for peripheral employees
    - Downsizing
    - Reengineering
    - Mergers and acquisitions
    - Outsourcing and subcontracting of work
    - Relatively low union representation
    - Technological change
    - Demographics
    - Switch from high- to low-unemployment
    - Nomadic nature of the workforce
    - Changing complexion of the workforce
    - Changing value trends

12. Why is employee commitment such a concern for employers at present?
    <u>Answer</u>:
    - Broken psychological contracts resulting from massive terminations reduced employee loyalty and forced them to worry about themselves first
    - Low-unemployment conditions means employers are competing for workers who have more than one job option open
    - Unhappy employees can readily find work elsewhere

13. How can managers successfully manage the psychological contract?

    <u>Answer</u>: See tips for managers on page 16 of the workbook.

Reader Exam and Review Questions

Psychological Contracts: Violations and Modifications **by Rousseau**

14. Rousseau in "Psychological Contracts: Violations and Modifications" states contract violation usually results in the employee's exit from the company.
_____True or __X__False
Why?

Answer: Contract violation is common. Contract fulfillment is a matter of degree and is affected by the attributions made about motives, the behavior of the violator, and the scope of the losses.

15. Which of the following is not a source of experienced violations according to Rousseau?
a.   Breach of contract
b.   Disruption
c.*   Human rights
d.   Inadvertent

How 'Gen X' Managers Manage **by Conger**

16. According to Conger in "How 'GenX' Managers Manage," which of the following is not a prominent character trait of Generation Xers?
a.   They desire work/life balance.
b.   They want workplaces that feel like communities.
c.   They are independent masters of their own fate.
d.*   They are comfortable with hierarchy.

17. Conger calls the generation born between 1925 and 1942 (the silent generation).

18. "To understand how generations differ from one another, we have to see each as a product of (historical events) that profoundly shaped its members' values and views of the world." (Conger)

How to Earn Your Employees' Commitment **by Dessler**

19. According to Dessler, what's the advantage of having committed employees?

Answer:
❏ Current focus on teamwork, empowerment, and flatter organizations puts a premium of self-control or organizational citizenship behavior that results from commitment.
❏ Committed employees act instinctively to benefit the organization and are willing to help
❏ Commitment is associated with employees' and organization's ability to adapt to unforeseeable occurrences
❏ Better attendance records
❏ Longer job tenure
❏ Work harder at their jobs and perform better

20. Which of the following is not one of Dessler's recommendation for earning employee commitment?
a.   Guarantee organizational justice
b.*   Guarantee employee job security
c.   Commit to people-first values
d.   Clarify and communicate your mission

Reader Articles

1. PSYCHOLOGICAL CONTRACTS: VIOLATIONS AND MODIFICATIONS by Denise M. Rousseau
2. HOW 'GEN X' MANAGERS MANAGE by Jay A. Conger
3. HOW TO EARN YOUR EMPLOYEES' COMMITMENT by Gary Dessler

Chapter 2
THEORIES OF MANAGING PEOPLE

Materials Needed: Transparency of old lady/young lady or Escher's Angels and Devils from Chapter 8.

Objectives: By the end of the chapter, students should be able to:

A.   Describe six theories of management and their "ideal" manager
B.   Explain the competing values framework and what constitutes a master manager
C.   Explain why it's important to identify their personal theories about management and organizational behavior
D.   Describe their personal theory of management
E.   Identify the managerial skills they need in today's environment
F.   Distinguish between Theory X and Theory Y managers

Sample Design

6:00–6:30	Lecture: Theory X and Y
	Evolution of Management Thought
	Quinn's Competing Values Theory
6:30–7:00	Groups prepare speeches and select speaker
7:00–7:30	Manager of the Year speeches
7:30–8:00	Summary and Debriefing

Setting the Stage—Lecturette

This is the first of four chapters that are integrated by the idea of mental maps (management theories, learning styles, motivation, and values) that leads to an understanding of individual differences. If you wish, you can ease into mental maps by using a perception figure that contains two images, like Escher's angels and devils (T8.0). Assure students that it is not uncommon for people to fail to perceive one of the images and have other students help them find it. A lesson from a figures like this is the need for humility when arguing with people who see things from a different perspective or mental map.

Theory X and Y are examples of different mental maps about human nature. We go over the theory and their scores on the test and comment on cultural differences relating to this theory. The majority of U.S. students that we have seen in recent years categorize themselves as Theory Y, so you can bring the theory home to them and provoke an interesting discussion by asking them what percentage of their fellow students are Theory Y or X students. How would a Theory X or Y student behave? Is their own test score consistent with the way they behave as students? Why? Usually someone mentions that they act like a Theory X student in some classes and not in others. This leads into a discussion of the contingencies that affect behavior in the classroom and at work. Which type of student or employee would they prefer to teach or supervise and why? We generally mention Lewin's $B = f(P \times E)$ at this point and emphasize that a key job for a manager is creating an environment that fosters Theory Y behavior. The lesson here is that people are more complex than a simple test indicates and that many factors influence behavior.

If you want to go over the evolution of management thought, you can involve the students by putting these categories on the blackboard: (1) theory, (2) historical time, (3) social climate, and (4) concept of the "ideal manager." Then we ask them to fill in the blanks for scientific management, administrative theory, human relations, open systems, contingency management, and Quinn's theory.

Another technique we sometimes use to introduce Quinn's theory is to ask the students, "What's the best way to manage people?" As students contribute their ideas, the instructor places them into the appropriate columns, which are not labeled until the end of the exercise. Often, there is a preponderance of items in one category, e.g., human relations with younger students.

We give a brief recap of Quinn's theory, using the two transparency masters (T2.1 and T2.2) and emphasizing its usefulness to a manager. We make the point that our theory determines what we see and by extension the roles we assume as managers. (Incidentally, Pfeffer sells an assessment instrument developed by Quinn that you may want to use with MBA students to determine what roles they perform relating to each quadrant.)

Another type of mental map that works well with this chapter is the structural, human resource, political, and symbolic framework found in Bolman and Deal's *Reframing Organizations* (Jossey-Bass, 1991).

Issues to Consider in Leading the Experiential Exercise

A. Divide the students into groups of approximately five people; consider how many speeches this will mean in the time you have available before you determine the number of people per group. Too many speeches in a row can become boring. Before students select a group member to give the speech, remind them that your goal is to have everyone participate during the course; encourage them to share the opportunity to get speaking practice in class.

B. When the groups are ready to begin their speeches, explain the coding scheme. It may help to show them the Quinn's Competing Values Model of Leadership (T2.1) again.

C. For shorter classes, you can do the theory one day and the speeches the next. Be careful, though, about having too many lecture classes in the beginning of the course, because this sets a norm of passivity that does not promote experiential learning and participation. For this reason, we included the suggestions on how to make the lecturette more interactive.

D. Barker's video on Paradigms or Mintzberg's video on The Manager's Job: Folklore and Fact could be used in this session.

Transparency Masters

T2.0   QUINN'S COMPETING VALUES MODEL OF LEADERSHIP
T2.1   THE POSITIVE AND NEGATIVE ZONES
T2.2   MANAGERIAL WORK: FOLKLORE AND FACT

Workbook Exam and Review Questions
1.   Taylor's scientific management theory focused on
    a.   maximizing efficiency through time-and-motion studies.
    b.*   maximizing efficiency by matching the capacities of workers to specific, standardized jobs.
    c.   maximizing efficiency by following proven management principles.
    d.   maximizing efficiency by employing rational decision making.

2.   The 1920s solution to the nepotism, favoritism, and unprofessional behavior found in organizations at the time was
    a.   systems theory.
    b.   span of control.
    c.   scientific management.
    d.*   bureaucracy.

3.   Which of these was *not* one of the functions of a manager as defined by Fayol?
    a.   Planning
    b.   Organizing

c.*   Motivating
d.   Controlling

4.   When productivity is improved due to attention to worker's social needs, this phenomenon is known as the (Hawthorne) effect.

5.   The sociohistorical context of a strong union movement, distrust for businesspeople, decreased immigration, and scarce labor served as the backdrop for
     a.   scientific management.
     b.*   human relations school.
     c.   administrative theory.
     d.   open systems theory.

6.   How did the Hawthorne studies affect management theory?

     Answer: They contributed the idea that output was affected by worker's feelings and attitudes. This led to the development of the human relations theory of managing.

7.   What is the basic premise of contingency theory?

     Answer: There is no one best way to manage in every situation. Managers must find the appropriate method to match a given situation.

8.   Successful organizations are characterized by good (fit) among their strategy, structure, systems, staff, style, skills, and superordinate goals.

9.   The contention that our decisions are limited by the amount of variables our brains can handle, the time available, and our reasoning powers is know as
     a.   maximization.
     b.*   bounded rationality.
     c.   entropy.
     d.   interdependence.

10.   Open systems theory maintains that all of an organizations "parts" are
     a.   independent.
     b.   complex.
     c.   Internally focused.
     d.*   interdependent.

11.   Discuss the concept of the open system.

     Answer:
     ❑ Popular during the rapidly changing environment of the mid-1960s
     ❑ Different parts of the systems are interdependent
     ❑ Organizations are embedded in the larger environment
     ❑ Organizations take in resources and transform them into a service or product that is purchased or utilized by a larger system
     ❑ A crucial role for managers is dealing with external entities
     ❑ Three major factors affect organizational effectiveness: individuals in the organization, the organization itself, and the larger environment
     ❑ Organizational success requires the effective management of the interfaces between the individual and the organization, and the organization and the environment

12.   In Quinn's competing values framework, master managers (balance) the competing values of the rational goal, internal process, human relations, and open systems management models.

13. Contrast the assumptions of Theory X and Theory Y. Give an example of a management practice based on each theory.

Answer: Theory X is based on the assumption that humans are inherently lazy, dislike responsibility and prefer to be led. In contrast, Theory Y is based on the opposite assumptions—that humans are responsible, motivated to work hard and develop skills, and capable of self-direction. An example of Theory X is the time clock. An example of Theory Y is comp time.

14. Which management concept could you use to explain to Joe what's going on here?

Your friend Joe works at a grocery store; he's been complaining bitterly about his job and his boss. Because he knows you are becoming an expert on organization behavior, he has come to you for advice. He tells you that his boss is constantly looking over his shoulder and telling him what to do next, even when it's obvious. The boss threatens all the employees that he will fire them if they do anything wrong, and he's always sneaking around trying to catch them in the act. Joe asked if he could learn how to do some of the ordering for his department; his boss replied that Joe is paid good money to do the job he already has and that should be good enough. Joe was excited about a new customer service program that corporate headquarters wanted to implement. However, he overheard the boss tell his supervisor they could forget implementing this program in Joe's store because the employees were lazy and incapable of adapting to change. Joe sees himself as highly responsible and dedicated and wishes the boss trusted him more.

Answer: Boss has a Theory X orientation whereas Joe has Theory Y values.

Reader Exam and Review Questions

The Manager's Work by Mintzberg

15. Which of the following does Mintzberg describe as "folklore" about managerial work?
    a.   A manager's activities are brief, varied, and continuous.
    b.   Managers favor verbal media over detailed, data-filled reports.
    c.*   Management is becoming a science and a profession.
    d.   Managers perform regular duties in addition to handling exceptions

16. According to Mintzberg, managers seem to prefer information from
    a.   large databases.
    b.   regular staff reports.
    c.   trade journals.
    d.*   phone calls and meetings.

The Human Side of Management by Teal

17. According to Teal, managing is not a series of mechanical tasks, but
    a.   a series of creative tasks.
    b.*   a series of human interactions.
    c.   a set of problems to be solved.
    d.   a series of novel conditions to be analyzed.

18. Teal says that Integrity in management means all of the following except
    a.   knowing yourself.
    b.   being responsible.
    c.*   listening to your stakeholders.
    d.   keeping promises.

Mastering Competing Values: An Integrated Approach **by Quinn**

19.   How do "Master Managers" differ from other managers, according to Quinn?

Answer: Master Managers look at situations from various perspectives and have learned to balance competing values. They use whichever theory is most appropriate for a given situation.

20.   The stage of evolution of mastery marked by the emergence of effortless performance is
        a.   the competence stage.
        b.*   the proficiency stage.
        c.   the novice stage.
        d.   the expert stage.

21.   Using Quinn's theory of competing values, which management theory does each person in the following example hold?

There is a problem at the factory. The production figures are way down and employees are grumbling. You have been asked to attend a problem-solving meeting with the managers. **Ellen** thinks the best solution is to set clear production goals and carefully delegate tasks. **Carlos** thinks management should talk to employees to find out what is bothering them and then do team building with the key employees. **Anna** suggests that it's time to put their house in order by coming up with tighter procedures and information systems. **Sung Wu** is advocating an expansion program because he thinks the market is favorable and the challenge will pull everyone together.

        Ellen   =   (rational goal)
        Carlos   =   (human relations)
        Anna   =   (internal process)
        Sung Wu   =   (open systems)

Reader Articles

1.   THE MANAGER'S WORK by *Henry Mintzberg*
2.   THE HUMAN SIDE OF MANAGEMENT by *Thomas Teal*
3.   MASTERING COMPETING VALUES: AN INTEGRATED APPROACH TO MANAGEMENT by *Robert E. Quinn*

Chapter 3
INDIVIDUAL AND ORGANIZATIONAL LEARNING

Materials Needed: Masking tape to make a giant grid on the floor of the classroom or in an adjacent space.

Objectives By the end of the chapter, students should be able to:

A.   Describe the model of adult learning
B.   Identify individual learning styles and their characteristics
C.   Improve the learning organization in this course by sharing learning objectives, available resources for learning, and learning environment preferences
D.   Distinguish between adaptive and generative learning
E.   Describe the characteristics of a learning organization

Setting the Stage—Lecturette

To set the stage for the experiential exercise, we try to link the importance of learning in materials already covered in the course. For example, much of what we've read or studied so far has some relationship to learning. Mintzberg stated that managers have to learn about the job of managing and be introspective. Quinn's article mentioned that people need to learn how to become a master manager, and part of that is learning to identify your own theory of management. Shell tried to accelerate learning; their research concluded that organizations that don't learn simply don't survive. Companies that can adapt quickly to changing rules have a competitive advantage. All of this brings us to today's topic, which is how people learn. No one can teach students everything they will need to know in their career, but we can teach them how to learn—our purpose in this session.

We ask students what's the difference in how children and adults learn. We cover the following points in the lecturette:

- Lewin's model
- The two paradoxical axes (concrete-abstract, active-passive), using transparency T3.0
- The four words that sum up what is happening at each of the four points (feeling, watching, thinking, doing)
- Because of individual differences people tend to put more emphasis on a particular model
- How do the students think that comes about? (personality, education, family, career, current job/ life situation, psychological type)
- We ask students to look at the profiles on page 45 to see where they stand compared to others who have taken the LSI and describe each of the four learning modes
- Help them locate their style on the graph on page 47 and explain the four learning styles.
- Remind students that this instrument measures their perception of the way they learn. Each question in the instrument relates to feeling, watching, thinking, or doing. Do their scores make sense when they compare them to the learning experience they described in the premeeting preparation? How people learn the computer is a good way to point up differences in learning styles.
- The LSI is useful to point out individual differences but shouldn't be used to stereotype people.

There is invariably one student who scores his or her instrument incorrectly. Therefore, we use the transparency (T3.1) of the Learning Style Type Grid to graph an example for the whole class. To check whether they have done this step correctly, they can refer back to the Profile Norms on page 45 to see where their scores were highest. In most cases, you can predict the style from that chart.

When students have a score that is very close to the junction of the axes, this indicates that they have a balanced learning style. Their scores were fairly similar on all four modes. Therefore, they may not fit neatly into one quadrant—they may have characteristics from various quadrants.

A common question is whether your learning style can change over time. A particular type of educational program or job, as well as a concerted self-improvement effort, can develop a learning mode and change your score.

Issues to Consider in Leading the Experiential Exercise

THE LEARNING STYLE INVENTORY
A. Make sure the students understand that no one style is better than the others. The LSI gives individuals some data about which aspects of the learning cycle they may prefer or be good at. For most individuals, however, this approach will vary somewhat from situation to situation. By locating themselves on the LSI grid and discussing their self-assessment with others of similar learning style, individuals get additional data to assess their approach to learning. Finally, future course experiences in the heterogeneous student learning groups will provide additional data about learning styles.

B. Point out that the LSI is not a perfectly predictive instrument. You may wish to raise concerns in the discussion at the end of the like-style group reports about the use and validity of "pen-and-paper" tests describing individual differences. For example, what are some instances where tests such as the LSI might be useful? What are the instances where it might not be recommended? What are the dangers in the use of such tests? The LSI has its critics. Nevertheless, it has a great deal of face validity and many students find it to be a very useful theory.

C. The interesting aspect of this process is that people often act out their learning styles during the discussions. Some will focus on abstract conceptualization issues, e.g., validity of the theory, evaluation of the instrument, what is the "right" score. Others with an active experimentation bent might seize on issues of pragmatic usefulness, e.g., how can the theory or test be used to help a manager? The concrete experiencers may struggle to identify and deal with the feelings they are having, while the reflective observers might be doing just that—sitting back and observing. The accommodators usually finish their discussion questions before the other groups and remark on that.

D. After the groups have presented the results of their discussions, the instructor can direct their attention to the chart on page 65 to see if there is anything that needs to be added. The excess and deficiency categories on this chart explain what happens when there are too few or too many of a particular learning type **in an organization**, i.e., it refers to organizational rather than individual excess or deficiency. The point here is that students understand that each style has strengths and weaknesses and groups benefit from having people with different learning styles. Students like to hear real-life examples of learning style differences and how people learn to monitor their own style-related behavior. We tell them both an academic- and business-related story we've experienced—one with a message about tolerating styles different from ours and the other with a message about the need to adapt training to the audience's learning style.

CREATING A LEARNING COMMUNITY
E. One of the most important steps in the course is the **formation of learning groups** that occurs during this session. Some criteria are stated at the top of page 61, but you can also ask students to determine the criteria themselves. We tell students to go back to the grid and stand in their learning style quadrant. Then we announce that no groups are completely formed until everyone is satisfied with the group they are in. Some instructors warn students not to choose a group based on either friendship or personal attraction. These groups have difficulty getting members to pull their weight or they spend so much time flirting that their grades suffer.

Instructors should consider carefully how many groups they want to have. Too many groups means that too much time will be devoted to repetitious group report-outs during the debriefing section. (If you have extremely large classes, you may want to modify the debriefing instructions to focus more on individual contributions, so each group does not have to speak. It is possible to teach this course with casts-of-thousands style classes; 300 students is the highest we've heard of. One of the authors taught a 100+ student class by delegating the responsibility for group exercises to students on a rotating basis, meeting with them before each class, and evaluating their facilitation efforts.) On the other hand, if your learning groups are too large, students won't have enough opportunity to talk. Eight is probably the maximum number and six or seven is the ideal number. You may also want to take attendance patterns at your school into consideration. If groups are too small, absent members can limit the group's ability to do the exercises.

F. The newly formed groups need time to introduce themselves and do the Creating a Learning Community exercise on page 51. It is not necessary to reconvene the class afterwards if you think the groups can profit more from using this time on their own. When students will be doing group projects outside class, we ask them to establish ground rules for working together. They fill out Appendix I and report their decisions back to the entire class for cross-fertilization purposes. As a result of this preparatory team building, they experience less process-related difficulty on their projects.

G. Please note that Step 2 d. assumes that instructors are willing to adapt their methods to accommodate the suggestions of students. Refer to the characteristics of learning organizations (T3.2) to aid this discussion. How can this be applied to the classroom?

H. In shorter class sessions, instructors may wish to form the learning groups in a separate class session. If the instructor is using a Saturday session, this can also be done in the beginning of such a session. Make sure you have people in their permanent groups for a Saturday session because the groups develop and "form" so extensively on this occasion that students will not want to change their allegiance to another group. Later in the course, it does no harm to modify the group formation for specific exercises (e.g., having them number off by four to create the four groups necessary for a specific exercise). It is good to let students see how other groups or students function later in the course; in the beginning days of their learning groups, however, it is best to keep them in their own learning groups.

I. The end of this session or the beginning of the next one is a good time to explain the PAA assignment in greater depth.

Transparency Masters

T3.0   KOLB'S EXPERIENTIAL LEARNING MODEL
T3.1   LEARNING STYLE TYPE GRID
T3.2   CHARACTERISTICS OF A LEARNING ORGANIZATION
T3.3   ARGYRIS'S TYPES OF LEARNING

Workbook Exam and Review Questions

1.   Which of these is *not* a skill of a learning organization?
        a.   Transferring knowledge
        b.   Acquiring knowledge
        c.*   Departmentalizing knowledge
        d.   Modifying behavior based on new knowledge

2. Identify the modes of the adult learning cycle used in the Learning Style Inventory.

    Answer: The four modes of the adult learning cycle are concrete experience, reflective observation, abstract conceptualization, and active experimentation. The process is both concrete and abstract, both reflective and active.

3. A learning orientation toward (reflective observation) focuses on understanding the meaning of ideas and situations by carefully observing and impartially describing them.

4. A learning orientation toward (abstract conceptualization) focuses on using logic, ideas, and concepts.

5. The four styles in Kolb's learning model are known as
    a.   concrete, abstract, active, and reflective.
    b.*   accommodation, divergence, convergence, and assimilation.
    c.   situational, problem oriented, solution oriented, implementation oriented.
    d.   experience, observation, conceptualization, and experimentation.

6. Terry's boss, Maria, is good at inductive reasoning, creating theoretical models, and planning. Therefore, you think that her learning style is the (assimilator) style.

    The strength of Terry's learning style are learning by trial and error, getting things done, and risk taking. He has the accommodator style.

    Given their different learning styles, what difficulties might Terry and Maria have in working together?

    Answer: Maria may want to take more time planning whereas Terry may want to leap into action and prefer a trial-and-error method. Maria may find Terry to be too pushy. Terry may be uncomfortable if Maria focuses more on ideas than on people issues, and vice versa.

7. Learning communities and organizations profit from having members with different learning styles because
    a.   life consists of concrete, abstract, active, and reflective dimensions.
    b.   diversity provides a greater variety of organization knowledge.
    c.   each style has its particular strengths and weaknesses.
    d.*   All of the above.

8. Argyris claims we have two types of theories. What are they and how are they different?

    Answer: "Espoused theories" are ones we profess to believe. "Theories in action" are theories that actually guide our behavior.

9. Defensive routines prevent people from questioning their
    a.*   assumptions.
    b.   values.
    c.   self-concept.
    d.   learning style.

10. Explain the difference between adaptive (single-loop) learning and generative (double-loop) learning.

    Answer: Adaptive learning has a coping orientation and focuses on solving problems by using or refining the prevailing mental model or way of doing things. Generative learning, on the other hand, has a creative orientation and involves surfacing and reviewing the underlying assumptions about the prevailing mental model or way of doing things. It involves continuous experimentation and feedback in an ongoing analysis of how problems are defined and solved.

11.   Managers should be aware of their personal learning styles so they understand
   a.*   how they approach work issues and how they react to others who have different styles.
   b.   how they appear to people and how they react to problems.
   c.   how they can best learn.
   d.   how they approach people issues.

12.   Managers who are training others have a tendency to assume that everyone learns the same way they do.
   __X_True or ___False

13.   To create a learning organization, managers should do all of the following except
   a.   make time to reflect on work events.
   b.   reward generative thinking.
   c.*   develop an elite group to handle decision making.
   d.   treat failure as a natural part of learning.

Reader Exam and Review Questions

Learning from Experience through Reflection by Daudelin

14.   According to Daudelin, reflection progresses through four distinct stages. What are they?

   Answer:
   ❑   Articulation of a problem
   ❑   Analysis of a problem
   ❑   Formulation and testing of a tentative theory to explain the problem
   ❑   Action (or deciding whether to act)

The Leader's New Work: Building Learning Organizations by Senge

15.   Explain Senge's "Principle of Creative Tension" and provide an example. (essay)

16.   Which of the following is *not* one of the roles of leaders in Senge's concept of learning organizations?
   a.   Designers
   b.   Teachers
   c.*   Heroes
   d.   Stewards

17.   Which of the following is a skill of new leaders according to Senge?
   a.   Building a shared vision
   b.   Surfacing and testing mental models
   c.   Systems thinking
   d.*   All of the above

18.   What is a learning organization according to Senge and how does it function? What are the advantages of a learning organization? How would you evaluate your own organization as a learning organization? (essay)

Reader Articles

1. LEARNING FROM EXPERIENCE THROUGH REFLECTION by *Marilyn Wood Daudelin*
2. THE LEADER'S NEW WORK: BUILDING LEARNING ORGANIZATIONS by *Peter M. Senge*

Chapter 4
INDIVIDUAL AND ORGANIZATIONAL MOTIVATION

Materials Needed: None.

Objectives: By the end of this chapter, students should be able to:

A.   Explain the basic theories of motivation
B.   Understand and recognize McClelland's three needs
C.   Gain insight into their own motive patterns
D.   Explain how managers can direct individual motivation
E.   Identify job characteristics related to motivation
F.   Describe five methods of job redesign

Setting the Stage—Lecturette

One way to begin a discussion of motivation is to ask what happens when people win the lottery—do they quit their jobs or continue working? Approximately 80 percent continue at work, which can lead into the discussion of what meaning work has for people. What needs does it meet, beyond money for basic subsistence?

Our lecturettes usually begin with a definition of motivation and reemphasize that it is not something you do to other people. However, good managers and team members understand what motivates the people they work with and create an environment in which individual motivation is aligned with the organization's or team's goals and rewards. We distinguish between content and process theories and cover the key theoretical points of Maslow, Herzberg, and McClelland before the TAT Motive exercise. We use the transparency (T4.0), "David McClelland's Major Motives." **Be careful not to present some of the three needs as more desirable than the others because this can bias the scoring and cause students to worry about their motive patterns.** Finally, we ask students to figure out how these three theories relate to each other so they can integrate these ideas and remember the theories more readily. We present process theories after the TAT exercise. If we use the Motivated Classroom (and the level of students is high), we don't go over the theories in class as they have to master them in their small groups in order to apply them to the classroom. You can assign the preparation for the Motivated Classroom to be done outside class if you wish.

Another technique to get them thinking about manifestations of McClelland's theory is to have students guess at behaviors related to motivation research results that follow.
- What type of sports do people with a dominant need in the three motives tend to play?
  n-Pow = football
  n-Ach = cross country, tennis, golf
  n-Aff = volleyball (as long as it's not killer beach volleyball in California)
- What type of books would they be likely to read
  n-Pow = Robert Ludlum, James Bond-type mysteries, books that focus on glamour
  n-Ach = science fiction, Agatha Christie-type mysteries where the reader works to figure out "Who done it" self-help
  n-Aff = romance, relationships

McClelland's theory of motives is another type of mental maps—they reflect our preoccupations and the way we see the world.

Issues to Consider in Leading the Experiential Exercise

TAT MOTIVE ANALYSIS

A. The T.A.T. is used as the diagnostic stimulus to let students gain some insight into their own motives and see how differently people respond to the same stimulus. We tell students that our diagnoses will not be as accurate as those made by trained coders in laboratory conditions; we use the T.A.T. as a pedagogical tool for learning about the research on motivation and for stimulating thought about one's own motive patterns. The instructor should make sure that this distinction is made between research and pedagogy and that students understand that this is not being used as a clinical instrument to give them final answers about their motive patterns. The themes that are identified in the stories may be rightfully seen as indicators of motive directions, but the scoring system used here is a simplified one. Students can continue examining their own behavior to better understand their motive pattern.

B. Read the coding criteria out loud to the students. Make sure they understand that you only code actual words, not assumptions or interpretations. This is an exercise in content analysis, not interpretation. The only inferences can be made with n-ach.

C. Offer your services if they come upon a story or sentence they find difficult to code. ("Let me know if you find something that stumps you.") Walk around and listen unobtrusively to the groups at work. This allows you to see whether they are coding accurately and following instructions and, more importantly, you can see interesting events that should be included in the debriefing section. If they don't mention these things in the debriefing of their own volition, you can gently prompt them by saying something like, "Would you mind telling us what happened in your group when you were discussing the second picture?"

D. Some students will be worried about their motive patterns and what it means. While it is true that managers should encourage n-Ach behavior in the workplace, instructors should not convey the idea that people whose dominant needs are either affiliation or power are less valuable. Students may also worry if their stories have no power imagery and they want to be managers. You may need to reassure them that we find successful people with all types of motive patterns. Some are merely more comfortable in certain jobs due to their motive pattern. Others find they have to make a special effort to focus on things that do not naturally grab their attention (i.e., the manager low in affiliation who finds himself in an organizational culture or business that values warm, personal relationships and has to schedule in time to make the rounds and talk to employees).

E. In **debriefing**, students often mention how surprising it is that people can come up with such disparate stories for the same picture. This fits right into the mental map analogy and idea that we are "programmed" differently when it comes to motives. Good managers learn to identify the motive patterns of the people they work with. Why is this important? This is a good place for real-life examples e.g., letting a colleague with a high need for power make the final presentation). How can we figure out motive patterns without administering a test like the TAT?

F. If you as a professor were trying to elicit n-Ach in the classroom, what would you do? Incidentally, don't forget to act like a good manager and tell the class when they're doing well. Students usually work very hard in this course so we compliment them individually and as a group whenever we remember and catch them doing things that warrant reinforcement, like good preparation, getting down to task quickly, respect for others, etc.

THE MOTIVATED CLASSROOM

G. In a long session, we present the process theories (expectancy theory, equity theory, reinforcement theory, and goal setting) after the exercise, using the $T = M \times E \times R$ theory as a link. The transparency on expectancy theory (T4.1) is taken from the *Reader* article and seems to be the easiest way for students to understand this theory. We ask students to analyze their own motivation for this course, using expectancy theory. One way to demonstrate reinforcement theory is to assign one student to throw candy at students who speak in class. This results in a debate about the theory and a timely discussion on class participation. Throwing candy raises the issues of consistency of rewards (someone invariably gets skipped) and the valence of the reward (it's not candy they like; or the valence isn't high enough to change their participation behavior; they think candy is stupid). These same complaints can be found in company incentive programs. Note that there is a transparency for characteristics of effective goals (which does not appear in the workbook).

H. The preparation for the Motivated Classroom can be done inside or outside the class. This is an interesting method for hearing their ideas on classroom incentives. This requires openness on your part and a willingness to empower your students. Make sure you don't agree to more than you can manage.

I. With shorter class sessions, the Motivated Classroom is done in a follow-up class. It works well to ask students to identify all the things managers can do to encourage high performance and a motivated workforce. This helps them integrate the practical implications from all the different theories.

Transparency Masters

T4.0   DAVID McCLELLAND'S MAJOR MOTIVES
T4.1   EXPECTANCY THEORY
T4.2   JOB CHARACTERISTICS MODEL

Workbook Exam and Review Questions

1.   Motivation is
        a.   an external force that directs individuals toward certain goals.
        b.*   an internal state the directs individuals toward certain goals.
        c.   activated by different needs for different people.
        d.   All of the above.

2.   Maslow argued that human motivation can be viewed as
        a.   linear.
        b.   circular.
        c.*   hierarchical.
        d.   curvilinear.

3.   According to Maslow, once a need is (satisfied or met) it no longer motivates.

4.   Herzberg identified factors that cause dissatisfaction or demotivation if they are absent. He called these
        a.   intrinsic factors.
        b.   security factors.
        c.   self-esteem factors.
        d.*   hygiene factors.

5.   McClelland's theory of motivation focuses on three needs that are learned from one's culture and family. They are
        a.*   affiliation, achievement, and power.
        b.   affiliation, challenge, and achievement.
        c.   self-esteem, self-actualization, and power.
        d.   security, affiliation, and self-esteem.

6. People motivated by <u>(personalized power)</u> demonstrate an unsocialized concern for personal dominance.

7. A concern for interpersonal relationships, but not at the expense of goal-oriented behavior, is referred to as <u>(affiliative interest)</u>.

8. What is the difference between the positive and negative need for power? Discuss these different faces of power and provide examples of both faces.

   Answer: People motivated by the positive need for power (*socialized power*) use it for the good of others—to make their organizations better. They are hesitant to use power to manipulate others. People with this need are less defensive and selfish and work to empower others. An example is a coach. People motivated by the negative need for power (*personalized power*) use it to dominate others. They have little inhibition or self-control and they exercise power impulsively. They tend to exploit and manipulate others and often satisfy their needs vicariously. An example is a dictator.

9. According to McClelland, a high need for achievement seems absolutely necessary for
   a.   managers.
   b.   social workers.
   c.   supervisors.
   d.*   entrepreneurs.

10. Which of the following is *not* a characteristic of high need for achievement?
    a.   Like to set their own goals
    b.*   Like to own prestige belongings
    c.   Tend to avoid either extremely difficult or extremely easy goals
    d.   Prefer tasks that provide immediate feedback on their performance

11. What is the difference between the positive and negative faces of a need for affiliation?

    Answer: The positive face of affiliation (affiliative interest) is a concern for interpersonal relationships but not at any expense. Although people with this need value and work at maintaining good relationships, this doesn't prevent them from giving negative feedback or making tough decisions. However, the negative face of affiliation (affiliative assurance) makes people look for assurance about the security and strength of their relationships and avoid rejection. They seek approval from others over achieving work goals and avoid issues and conflicts that might threaten relationships.

12. Which of the following is *incorrect*?
    a.   In addition to internal need states, motivation is also affected by the environment.
    b.   Equity theory maintains that employee motivation is affected by the perceived fairness of what people contribute and receive.
    c.   Social reinforcement theory maintains that people learn to use behaviors that are rewarded and to suppress behaviors that are punished or ignored.
    d.*   When it comes to goal achievement, it makes no difference whether goals are publicly stated or kept private.

13. To motivate employees, managers should
    a.   link rewards to performance even though rewards may not be equitably distributed.
    b.*   reward employees for behaviors that promote the organization's goals.
    c.   be sure that the reward is one that the organization deems valuable and rewarding.
    d.   All of the above.

14. You have acquired a company that has a poorly motivated workforce. Describe what actions you would take to improve motivation and achieve a high performance workplace.

   Answer:
   ❑ Determine what motivates employees by learning about their nonwork activities and what type of work or projects they enjoy. Check your assumptions.
   ❑ Set challenging but attainable goals, establish clear work objectives and standards of good performance, and provide feedback to encourage achievement
   ❑ Link rewards to performance and distribute equitably. Reward employees for behaviors that promote the organization's goals. Be sure the individual employees find the rewards valuable and motivating.
   ❑ Match people to jobs they find rewarding and recognize their contributions
   ❑ Remove demotivators such as politics and favoritism, unproductive meetings, withholding information, etc.
   ❑ Practice gain-sharing
   ❑ Make sure pay and security needs are satisfied

Reader Exam and Review Questions

That Urge to Achieve by McClelland

15. McClelland states that high achievement motivation is
   a.   an inherited condition.
   b.   learned at school.
   c.*   learned from parents.
   d.   partly inherited and partly nurtured.

16. Which of the following is *not* one of the goals of McClelland's training to increase n-Ach?
   a.   Teach participants to think, talk, and act like a person with high n-Ach
   b.*   Acceptance of one's destiny
   c.   Goal setting
   d.   Self-awareness

Motivation: A Diagnostic Approach by Nadler and Lawler

17. Discuss two hypothetical students in this course—one who was motivated to study for this exam and one who was not—and thoroughly explain their motivation or lack thereof using expectancy theory as described by Nadler and Lawler. (essay)

Recognize Contribution: Linking Rewards with Performance by Kouzes and Posner

18. Which of the following is important when recognizing contributions according to Kouzes and Posner?
   a.   Connect performance with rewards
   b.   Have high expectations
   c.   Use a variety of rewards
   d.*   All of the above

19. Using recommendations from Kouzes and Posner, explain how you might link rewards with performance for a manager of a local, nonprofit homeless shelter. Be specific. (essay)

Reader Articles

1. THAT URGE TO ACHIEVE by *David C. McClelland*
2. MOTIVATION: A DIAGNOSTIC APPROACH by *David A. Nadler and Edward E. Lawler III*
3. RECOGNIZE CONTRIBUTIONS: LINKING REWARDS WITH PERFORMANCE by *James M. Kouzes and Barry Z. Posner*

Chapter 5
VALUES AND ETHICS

Materials Needed: None.

Objectives: By the end of this chapter, students should be able to:

A.   Describe how organizations foster unethical behavior
B.   Explain how organizations can promote ethical behavior
C.   Define ethics and values
D.   Better articulate their own values
E.   Distinguish between ethical and non-ethical values
F.   Explain and recognize the stages of moral reasoning
G.   Describe five different ethical models

Sample Design

6:00–6:25	Lecturette
6:25–7:00	Read case individually and come to group consensus (Steps 1–3)
7:00–7:20	Learning groups determine what stages of moral development are reflected in group and individual decisions (Step 4)
7:20–8:00	General debriefing (Step 5)

Setting the Stage—Lecturette

The purpose of this chapter is to get students thinking about their own values and to introduce them to the basic principles of ethics so they can discuss ethical problems. In the lecturette, we highlight the need for ethical behavior in business and present the basic themes in the topic introduction. After a brief overview of Rokeach's model, we discuss the students' scores on the Rokeach instrument in the premeeting preparation. By a show of hands, we see the dominant value orientations in the class.

We present Kohlberg's theory, using the transparency "Kohlberg's Three Levels of Moral Development" (T5.0), and make sure that students understand each level. We give them samples of moral reasoning and ask what level they represent. We ask students to summarize the research findings on Kohlberg's theory. Kohlberg's theory has come under attack; the major criticisms are included in the workbook. We included Kolhberg's theory in the workbook after consulting with several ethics scholars who say some of the criticisms have been answered; they believe it is still the best moral reasoning theory we have at present.

Because I have ROTC students in my classes, I use the example of going or refusing to go to Vietnam with all the stages in Kohlberg's theory. This promotes mutual understanding between students who support and oppose the military.

After the exercise we discuss the role of the organization and practices that foster unethical behavior. We ask them to give examples of unethical behavior observed at work and then ask why this occurred. Then we show them the transparency that summarizes these conditions (T5.1).

Issues to Consider in Leading the Experiential Exercise

A. Try to avoid judgmental arguments in this session. Moralistic students are sometimes offended by "expedient" decisions, whereas worldly students may look down upon the "idealism" of other students. Neither approach makes dialogue easy. The emphasis should be on understanding the different approaches, the values that drive them, and their consequences.

B. We recommend you read James Weber and Sharon Green's "Principled Moral Reasoning: Is It a Viable Approach?" *Journal of Business Ethics, 10* (1991): 328 because it concerns teaching ethics to business students. According to their research, most sophomore undergraduate students (77%) reason below stage 4, so we should not give them the impression that they should be more advanced than they are. As with any developmental theory, there is a concern that people will want to be at the top rather than the bottom of the scale. Instructors should be sensitive to this issue.

C. When you come to question 6 on page 110, you can ask students to do a quick-write about what Roger should have said to the partner. Then ask for volunteers to role-play what they would say in Roger's shoes. Afterwards, create with students a list of suggestions that might work—"avoid a moralistic tone, get the partner to problem solve with Roger, etc."

D. Allow students to read the five models of ethics to answer Step 5, #7 if they haven't already done so prior to class.

E. With a shorter class session, teach values on one day and use the ethics case on another.

F. Undergraduates sometimes have difficulty looking beyond short-term expediency to the long-term consequences of unethical behavior (diminished reputation, loss of business, termination, etc.). They may also mistakenly assume that everyone cheats to get ahead in business. To give students a dose of reality, some instructors take students to prison where they interview white-collar criminals. Whenever you have businesspeople as speakers, ask them for their views on business ethics.

G. One of The Massey Triad videos on values can be used with a values class session, although there is a little overlap with the Conger article in the *Reader*. Massey describes the values of different generations in an entertaining, if condescending, fashion. The Enterprise Trust videos on companies that have been rewarded for their social consciousness are very good.

Transparency Masters

T5.0   KOHLBERG'S THREE LEVELS OF MORAL DEVELOPMENT
T5.1   FACTORS THAT FOSTER UNETHICAL BUSINESS PRACTICES

Workbook Exam and Review Questions

1.   Meeting the needs of present generations without compromising the ability of future generations to meet their own needs is known as
      a.   environmental ethics.
      b.   eco-futurism.
      c.*   sustainability.
      d.   renewability.

2.   The Natural Step program has helped companies to achieve all the following benefits except:
      a.   reduce operating costs.
      b.*   comply with existing regulations.
      c.   enhance the organization's standing among stakeholder groups.
      d.   build brand image.

3.   Ethics refers to standards of conduct that indicate how one should behave based on moral duties and virtues arising from principles about (right and wrong).

4.   Why do ethical practices pay off in the long run?

Answer: Because trusting relationships and well-satisfied customers are the basis of repeat business.

5. Which of the following is a characteristic of companies in which unethical practices are likely?
   a. Sole focus on profit and intense competition
   b. Top management talks about ethical behavior but does little else
   c. Indifference to customer's best interests
   d.* All of the above

6. Companies that want to encourage moral behavior do the following.
   a.* Communicate their expectation that employees will behave ethically and define what that means.
   b. Hire top executives who have been leaders in their respective churches.
   c. Reward ethical behavior monetarily and punish unethical behavior by firing the guilty.
   d. Discourage the discussion of ethical issues because it leads to rationalizing.

7. (Values) are core beliefs or desires that guide or motivate attitudes and actions.

8. According to Rokeach, terminal values
   a. fall into two categories: moral and competence.
   b. are preferable modes of behavior.
   c. are the means to achieving one's instrumental values.
   d.* are desirable end states of existence or the goals people want to accomplish in their lifetime.

9. Which of the following is an ethical value?
   a.* Responsibility
   b. Ambition
   c. Faith
   d. Personal fulfillment

10. Briefly explain Kohlberg's theory of moral development.

   Answer: The theory consists of three levels: self-centered, conformity, and principled. Individuals move through these stages from a self-centered conception of right and wrong to an understanding of social contracts and internalized principles of justice and rights.

11. If a person believes you should not cheat on income taxes solely because you might be put in jail, this is moral reasoning at the (self-centered or preconventional) level according to Kohlberg.

12. There are five basic ethical models or approaches that people use to make decisions. Identify and briefly describe each.

   Answer: *Utilitarian* ethics judge in terms of the welfare of everyone—what does the greatest good for the greatest number of people. Approaches based on *rights and duties* emphasize the personal entitlements of individuals. Approaches based on *justice* are guided by fairness, equity, and impartiality. Approaches based on *caring* focus on the well-being of other people. Approaches based on *environmentalism* extend to consideration of the person-land relationship.

13. A disadvantage of utilitarian ethics is
   a. it engenders a self-centered, legalistic viewpoint.

b.   it encourages a sense of entitlement.
c.   it values the environment over people.
d.*   it can overlook the rights of minorities.

14.   The Ethics Warning System uses all of the following except
a.   Golden Rule—are you treating others as you would want to be treated?
b.*   instrumental vs. terminal values—which type of values are you using?
c.   publicity—would you be comfortable if your reasoning and decision were to be publicized?
d.   kid on your shoulder—would you be comfortable if your children were observing you?

Reader Exam and Review Questions

Changing Unethical Organizational Behavior by Nielsen

15.   According to Nielsen, how does organizational culture affect ethical behavior within an organization? (essay)

16.   Which of the following is *not* one of the ways suggested by Nielsen to handle unethical behavior?
a.   Sabotage or refuse to implement unethical behavior
b.*   Resign from the company
c.   Blow the whistle inside the organization
d.   Blow the whistle outside the organization

17.   According to Nielsen, what are the limitations of the intervention strategies an individual can use to change unethical organization behavior?

Answer:
❑ Individuals can be wrong about the organization's actions
❑ Relationships can be damaged
❑ Organization can be hurt unnecessarily
❑ Strategies can encourage "might makes right" climate

When Ethics Travel by Donaldson and Dunfee

18.   According to Donaldson and Dunfee, there are four ethical approaches used by global companies. Identify and briefly describe the four approaches. (essay)

19.   Hypernorms, as defined by Donaldson and Dunfee, are
a.   culturally specific, legitimate values.
b.   illegitimate norms.
c.   morally neutral norms.
d.*   fundamental values of all cultures and organizations.

Reader Articles

1.   CHANGING UNETHICAL ORGANIZATIONAL BEHAVIOR by *Richard P. Nielsen*
2.   WHEN ETHICS TRAVEL by *Thomas Donaldson and Thomas W. Dunfee*

Chapter 6
CAREER DEVELOPMENT AND WORK STRESS

Materials Needed: Some instructors prefer flip chart paper and markers to the Life Line page in the workbook page 131–2. Otherwise, no additional materials are needed.

Objectives: When this chapter is completed, students should be able to

A. Describe the characteristics of adult development
B. Explain Levinson's concept of life structures.
C. Recognize career anchors and their significance
D. Describe the functions that mentors perform
E. Identify trends in career management and planning
F. Explain the transactional model of career stress
G. Assess your current life-career situation and develop a plan for the future

Sample Design

6:00–6:20	Lecturette
6:20–7:40	Self-assessment and Life Planning Exercise
7:40–8:00	Brief debriefing and lecturette on stress

Setting the Stage—Lecturette

Some instructors prefer to use this chapter at the end of the course when students know each other extremely well and are looking ahead to the future. When instructors use this chapter in the sixth session (after people settle down a bit and have some familiarity with each other), it helps students set goals relevant to the course and can focus their learning. It also allows them to understand each other much better. If you use it in the sixth session, you can check up on their achievement plan progress at the end of the course if you wish.

The purpose of the chapter is to model for students the self-assessment and career planning process and help them identify the aspects that are important for them in planning a balanced, satisfying life. This chapter is extremely useful for MBAs and many undergraduate students. Some undergraduates don't have a felt need for life planning at the time. For this reason one of the authors assigns this unit (including the trio work called for in the career planning exercise) as an outside project for undergraduates—sometimes required, sometimes as an option among several term paper type projects.

We begin the lecture by writing Eisenhower's quotation on the blackboard, "A plan is nothing; planning is everything," and go on to discuss the importance of career planning. There is sometimes a degree of career-related anxiety among students; the trick here is to emphasize the need to be proactive about one's career without overwhelming them. We do a brief overview of the adult development theories in the Topic Introduction, focusing on developmental challenges. We ask the MBA students if these theories seem valid, given their own life experience.

Next, we briefly cover career anchors, balancing dual careers, and mentoring in as interactive a fashion as possible. There is a survey instrument in Schein's book, *Career Dynamics*, that you could use with students if you want to do some self-assessment on career anchors.

The changes in career planning, particularly the shift to employee responsibility for career development and life planning as a continuous process, provide a lead-in to the exercise. We show the transparency (T6.0), "Tripod of Life Plan Perspectives," and note that the premeeting preparation exercise contains aspects of both the present and the future. The class exercises complement the premeeting preparation and are similar to the exercises used in career planning workshops.

Issues to Consider in Leading the Experiential Exercise

A. Tell the students to search for themes as they listen to the people in their trios talk about themselves and their history. Career counselors help people to identify these career anchors and interests; students in learning groups come to know each other so well that, if they are perceptive, they can pick up these themes. For example, one student complained that she had no career and no goals, just a series of jobs. However, when she described her work history, the other students noted that she had always accepted jobs that involved setting up new programs and left when the routine aspect of the job became intolerable. As a result, she decided to capitalize on her creative and entrepreneurial skills.

B. If you have former homemakers or international students without much formal job experience, they may need individual reassurance that their experience as volunteers, Scout leaders, Sunday school teachers, domestic engineers, serious hobbyists, etc., is not insignificant and should be analyzed.

C. The life line exercise is often used in the beginning of team-building workshops to help people understand each other's personal contexts. People tend to appreciate others more after hearing their life history with its ups and downs.

D. We mention the importance of goal setting and publicly sharing one's goals before asking students to share the goals they set in the premeeting preparation exercise with their trio in Step 5.

E. This exercise has no formal general debriefing questions at the end. You can ask for their reactions to the exercises if you wish ("Were the exercises helpful?" "What did you learn from doing this?").

F. We segue to the topic of stress as shown in the beginning of the Follow-Up section (the effect of cultural differences regarding destiny on career planning and the stress that abounds in restructured economies). Next, we define stress and describe the stress response. We walk them through the "Transactional Model of Career Stress" transparency (T6.1). We note the costs of excessive work stress and, if time permits, ask students how they reduce and manage stress. The *Reader* has a stress instrument in the Cooper selection.

Transparency Masters

T6.0   TRIPOD OF LIFE PLAN PERSPECTIVES
T6.1   TRANSACTIONAL MODEL OF CAREER STRESS

Workbook Exam and Review Questions

1.   The disequilibrium of adult development results from new psychological issues that arise from new (internal) forces and/or (external) demands or pressures.

2.   Levinson refers to the pattern of a person's life as
        a.   life lines.
        b.*   life structures.
        c.   life stages.
        d.   life challenges.

3. According to Levinson, major life transitions occur about the ages of
   a. 21, 35, and 50.
   b. 18, 28, and 38.
   c. 10, 20, and 30.
   d.* 30, 40, and 50.

4. (Career anchors) are motivational, attitudinal, and values syndromes formed early in life that function to guide and constrain people's careers.

5. Which of the following is *not* a career anchor?
   a. Service
   b. Managerial competence
   c.* Social competence
   d. Technical/functional competence

6. Discuss the career anchor that appears most appropriate for you. Describe its characteristics and the typical career paths associated with it.

   Answer: See Figure 6.2, pg. 128.

7. Which of the following is *not* a strategy for managing dual careers?
   a. Subordinating one career to the other
   b. Taking turns
   c.* Participating in independent ventures
   d. Limiting the impact of family on work

8. A (mentor) is a senior person within the organization who assumes responsibility for a junior person.

9. According to research, what are the advantages to being mentored?

   Answer: More promotions, higher pay, higher job satisfaction.

10. Which of these is *not* a career function of mentoring?
    a.* Role modeling
    b. Coaching
    c. Exposure and visibility
    d. Protection

11. Why is it so important to set career goals?

    Answer: Those who set goals are more likely to achieve them.

12. Why should managers try to help employees reach their career goals?
    Answer: They are usually rewarded with the employee's loyalty and commitment.

13. Which of the following statements about stress is *incorrect*?
    a. Stress is defined as the nonspecific response of an organism to demands that tax or exceed its resistance.
    b. There are three types of coping mechanisms: direct action, cognitive reappraisal, and symptom management.
    c. People who receive social support from their supervisors, coworkers, or families are somewhat buffered from the effects of stress.
    d.* Individual characteristics that are related to greater susceptibility to stress are hostile Type B behavior and internal locus of control.

14.   (Coping) is the means by which individuals and organizations manage internal or external demands that tax or exceed their resources.

15.   Stress is always bad.
       ____ True or __X__ False

       Explain why or why not?

       Answer: Some types of stress are "good" whereas others are "bad." Examples of bad stress are office politics and bureaucratic red tape. Examples of good stress are challenges that accompany increased job responsibility, high-quality assignments, and reasonable time pressure.

Reader Exam and Review Questions

On the Realization of Human Potential by Shepard

16.   According to Shepard, a "path with a heart"
       a.*   encourages uniqueness.
       b.   promotes conformity.
       c.   emphasizes human similarities.
       d.   encourages people to pursue hobbies and interests outside work.

17.   Which of the following institutions does Shepard identify as the most immediate custodian of society's standards and dogma?
       a.   The church
       b.*   Parents
       c.   Schools
       d.   Work organizations

18.   What does Shepard call the "worthwhile life" indicator that emphasizes feeling good about your relationships"?
       a.   Tone
       b.   Perspective
       c.   Social support
       d.*   Resonance

The New Protean Career Contract: Helping Organizations and Employees Adapt by Hall and Moss

19.   According to Hall and Moss, the new "protean" career contract is
       a.*   self-directed.
       b.   organization directed.
       c.   negotiated and documented.
       d.   All of the above.

20.   The ingredients for success change under the new "protean" career contract according to Hall and Moss. For instance, job security changes to
       a.   job enrichment.
       b.   job design.
       c.*   employability.
       d.   job competence.

21.   Describe what the organization should provide for you under the new "protean" career contract outlined by Hall and Moss.

<u>Answer</u>: The organization should give you challenging assignments, help you develop relationships and provide information and resources related to personal career development. The goal should be psychological success.

The Growing Epidemic of Stress by Cartwright and Cooper

22. Which of the following is NOT a major cause of stress according to Cartwright and Cooper?
   a. Change
   b. Lack of control
   c.* Technology
   d. High workload

Reader Articles

1. ON THE REALIZATION OF HUMAN POTENTIAL: A PATH WITH A HEART by *Herbert A. Shepard*
2. THE NEW PROTEAN CAREER CONTRACT: HELPING ORGANIZATIONS AND EMPLOYEES ADAPT by *Douglas T. Hall and Jonathan E. Moss*
3. THE GROWING EPIDEMIC OF STRESS by *Susan Cartwright and Cary L. Cooper*

Chapter 7
INTERPERSONAL COMMUNICATION

Materials Needed: None.

Objectives: By the end of this chapter, students should be able to:

A.   Understand the transactional model of communication
B.   List common sources of distortion
C.   Identify gender differences in communication
D.   Describe and identify the five response styles
E.   Explain how to create a climate that encourages nondefensive communication
F.   Recognize assertive communication and utilize I-statements
G.   Improve their listening skills

Sample Design

6:00–6:40   Lecturette on interpersonal communication
6:40–7:30   Active Listening Exercise
7:30–8:00   Debriefing and I-statements

Setting the Stage—Lecturette

This is the first chapter in the second module of the course, which is devoted to developing the key skills needed by effective managers and employees. Research indicates that these are among the most important skills needed in the workplace. The first section of the course should have helped students perceive the different mental maps they hold and taught them to appreciate the differences among them. This module will continue the emphasis on self-awareness, but in the context of skill building.

The purpose of this chapter is to give students a basic grounding in interpersonal communication. Consequently, this chapter is best used after several class sessions, but before the chapters on Perception and Attribution, Conflict and Negotiation, Performance Appraisal, and Power and Influence. The Communication chapter lays the groundwork for the remaining chapters in Part II.

The lecturette we use (crafted by a gifted professor, Gail Ambuske) begins with an explanation of why communication is such an important skill for both managers and employees. We define communication as mutual understanding and warn students that communication doesn't happen until the message has been accurately received. Sometimes we use the "Arc of Distortion" transparency (T7.0) at this point and mention that many communications result in partial misunderstanding.

We explain the Transactional Communication Model transparency (T7.1)and then launch into the barriers or distortions in the communication process. We begin by asking students why two people might encode a message differently. This leads to a discussion of the individual differences that affect encoding and decoding. We also cover or elicit from the students the remaining barriers: individual differences in encoding and decoding, noise, defensiveness, self-esteem, gender differences, lack of clarity, emotions, and poor listening skills.

At this point, we go over the Communication Climate Inventory in the premeeting preparation and Gibb's model that underlies it (transparency T7.2).

We emphasize the fact that meaning lies in people, not words, and quote Mehrabian and Weiner's findings that only 7 percent of meaning comes from words, 55 percent from facial expressions and posture, and 38 percent from vocal intonation and inflection. We give an example of a discrepancy between words and posture. We also ask for a student volunteer with dramatic aspirations to read us a sentence ("Why did you come to this meeting?"), accenting different words with each reading to demonstrate the importance of inflection.

After briefly explaining the response styles, we ask for another volunteer who is instructed to initiate a conversation with the instructor, always using the same sentence ("I think I lost the bid" for MBA's and "I think I failed the midterm" for undergraduates). The instructor uses one of the response styles and the rest of the class identifies it. We do this five times in a row until the instructor has modeled all the response styles. We do this in part because it's fun, but mainly because students need practice hearing and recognizing the styles. Instructors can reinforce this learning throughout the course by asking, "What kind of response style was that?" We mention that the only response style that does not involve a one-up, one-down relationship is the understanding response, which introduces the topic of active listening. We explain the importance of feedback and active listening in the communication process.

We distinguish between normal and active listening, using the analogy of a worn-out marriage where the couple reads their newspapers at the dinner table versus the total attention that characterizes the courtship phase. We explain why it's easy to divert your attention from speakers (brain's over capacity to process words) and the competitive nature of many U.S. conversations. People hear a topic and run it through their mental computer, searching for what they will say when the speaker finally stops talking. It's easy to come up with real-life examples of this type of conversation.

It's possible to do the lecture and exercise in 80 minutes if you don't cover the Gibb material and I-statements. Some instructors pick up these topics when they do performance appraisal.

Issues to Consider in Leading the Experiential Exercise

A. To begin the exercise, we recommend either using a training video on active listening or explaining the components of active listening and giving a demonstration with a willing student volunteer. The skill-building exercise works best if they can see what active listening looks like first. If we have a student who is trained in customer relations, we ask them if they want to do the demonstration; otherwise, the instructor does it. Then we use the observer criteria to evaluate the active listener. Sometimes instructors make mistakes when they demonstrate a skill. If this occurs, an admission of error ("I could have done a better job with reflecting possible implications; what else might I have said there?") is a good example for students and reinforces the laboratory nature of the course.

B. Because the feeling part of the message is often the most difficult, make sure students understand why it is necessary to key in on feelings. The instructor can provide personal examples of communications that lacked congruence and their consequences. For example, when a student says, deadpan, "I'm dropping out of school to get married or because I'm being transferred," we don't know whether this is good or bad news without understand the accompanying emotion.

C. Make sure that students can distinguish between "inviting further contributions" and the probing response style. In active listening, we invite further contributions when we don't yet have enough information to understand what the speaker is saying. Our motivation is merely to gain full understanding, not satisfy our curiosity or catechize the speaker.

D. If you want to let students choose a controversial topic of discussion rather than use the scenarios in the workbook, spend a few minutes asking them to identify hot topics, which you then write on the blackboard. They do not have to find a topic on which partners are on opposite sides, as that might take too long. Warn them not to spend too much time settling on a topic—it's better to use their time practicing the skill.

E. The role-playing stimuli are designed to be very realistic and require that students be themselves rather than "making believe."

F. Warn the students who will be speaking that they should pause to let the active listeners paraphrase their meaning before an overwhelming number of sentences has gone by. Remind students that the feedback/discussion phases of the exercise provide yet another opportunity to practice active listening.

G. For many students, the most difficult part of active listening is suppressing their own opinions. Caution them beforehand that this is not a dialogue or an argument; the listener's task is simply to understand and feed back the message they received to ensure it was transmitted accurately and fully. Walk around the room and listen to their communication. If it is not obvious who is the listener and who is the talker, you can politely interrupt and ask the observers what is occurring. As an empowerment strategy, ask the observers to pinpoint the problem before you advise the active listener.

H. In initial efforts at active listening, students usually focus primarily on paraphrasing literal content, sometimes in a stilted or even mocking way. Reflecting expressed feelings is harder for them and may presuppose a certain level of trust and rapport, which is why we do this chapter at this point in the course. Some students are not used to tuning into either feelings or nonverbal cues, and they will need extra help with this. We have run into younger students who cannot distinguish between thoughts and feelings; they mistakenly assume that a sentence that begins with "I feel" is automatically a feeling.

I. In the **debriefing**, a student will invariably say that they feel somewhat silly when they paraphrase. The instructor can explain that we all feel a bit silly when we practice new skills and that it may feel forced in the beginning. However, people who are good at active listening and use it appropriately have a great advantage both in the workplace and at home. The trick is learning to use it naturally and almost unconsciously. Students should be seeing examples of naturally occurring active listening in the classroom when instructors check to make sure that they really understand student questions and comments.

Typical reactions that are mentioned in the debriefing are that it was nice to be "heard" and that active listening was much more difficult and exhausting than it looks. The latter reason is why therapists and interviewers are careful not to overschedule their days. Ask students when active listening should be used (when people are angry or troubled, negotiating, selling, handling complaints, in a fight, or uncertain whether or not they have accurately received the message). You can ask students to practice active listening at home and work during the week and report on their efforts at the next class.

J. At the end of the class, we go over assertive communication and Figure 7.2 and I-statements (T7.3). It is surprising how many undergraduates write PAAs on negative situations with bosses whom they never confronted; they simply became less motivated and eventually quit the job. Therefore, it may be more important to emphasize this with younger students and devote more time to this issue.

We use real examples of I-statements from the class ("When you come to class late. . .") to model that it is possible to give feedback in a nonthreatening way. Then we ask students to write down an I-statement for a personal situation in some realm of their lives where they need to give someone feedback. We ask for volunteers to read theirs out loud and correct them as a group. It takes some practice for people to master I-statements. In collectivist cultures, people are uncomfortable owning the feeling part of the I-statement; they prefer to say "we" or to leave the feelings out altogether. You may want to ask international students whether they could use this format in their country. Students often ask if I-statements always result in getting people to change their behavior and, of course, they do not. Some people are remarkably intransigent, and it takes much more than an I-statement to do the trick. Nevertheless, learning to give feedback in this manner is an especially valuable skill for supervisors, managers, team members, and at home. As you know, young supervisors often have difficulty reprimanding or giving feedback in an appropriate manner.

We also touch upon the importance of seeing communication within a historical context and not merely as individual statements. Covey's idea of an Emotional Bank Account, described in the Follow-up section, highlights the significance of the relational context. Some students fail to perceive that "all that went before" influences reactions.

K. In shorter class sessions, you can present all the content in the first session and the active listening exercise in the next.

Transparency Masters

T7.0   ARC OF DISTORTION
T7.1   TRANSACTIONAL MODEL OF COMMUNICATION
T7.2   DEFENSIVE/NONDEFENSIVE COMMUNICATION CLIMATES
T7.3   I-STATEMENTS

Workbook Exam and Review Questions

1.   Communication is the process by which information is exchanged between communicators with the goal of
        a.   Influence.
        b.   Interpretation.
        c.   nonemotional decoding.
        d.*   mutual understanding.

2.   Describe the transactional model of communication. Use a diagram if helpful.

        Answer: This model describes two communicators who participate equally and often simultaneously in the communication process. Communication occurs within a social system, and each communicator has a personal context or field of experience through which they interpret messages. Mutual understanding is more likely when these fields of experience are shared. The communication relationship and the communicators field of experience may change over time. Noise can interfere with intended communication. See Fig. 7.1, p. 153.

3.   Which of the following is *not* a type of *noise* that interferes with intended communication?
        a.   Emotional
        b.*   Social
        c.   Physiological
        d.   Environmental

4.   Meaning lies in people, not in words.
        __X__ True or ____False
        Why or why not?

        Answer: The potential for distortion in communication is very large because encoding and decoding are heavily influenced by personal factors such as education, personality, socioeconomic levels, family, culture, experience, etc. It is a fact of communication that people perceive messages differently, thus meaning lies in people, rather than in words.

5.   As partial misunderstanding is a fact of most communication attempts, two ways to improve communication are

a.*   feedback and active listening.
b.   defensive and one-up communication.
c.   feedback and defensive communication.
d.   active listening and gender-neutral communication.

6.   (Defensiveness) is one of the most common barriers to communication because people get too caught up in protecting or justifying themselves to pay attention to the message.

7.   Researcher have found five common response styles. Which one is the most common?
       a.   Supportive
       b.*   Evaluative
       c.   Interpretive
       d.   Understanding
       e.   Probing

8.   "So you think your job is on the line and you're pretty upset about it" is an example of the (understanding) response style.

9.   "Why do you think you're going to be fired?" is an example of the (probing) response style.

10.   "You're just saying that because you lost the account" is an example of the (interpretive) response style.

11.   "What a great report" is an example of an (evaluative) response style.

12.   (Assertiveness) is the ability to communicate clearly and directly what you need or want from another person in a way that does not deny or infringe upon the other's rights.

13.   Contrast nonassertive, assertive, and aggressive communication in terms of verbal and nonverbal elements.

       Answer: See Fig. 7.2, p. 157.

14.   One of the members of your study group, Joshua, is constantly goofing off and interrupting you to make wisecracks, which is impeding your group's ability to get work done. Write an I-statement that would give Joshua feedback on the situation. **Label** the three components of your statement.

       Sample Answer: When you goof off and interrupt me during our group meetings, (behavior) I get off track and it takes me time to get refocused (effects), which makes me resentful (feelings).

15.   The components of active listening include
       a.   being nonevaluative, paraphrasing, and reflecting implications.
       b.   reflecting underlying feelings, inviting further contributions, and using nonverbal responses.
       c.*   a & b
       d.   None of the above

16.   Give an active listening response, using as many components as possible, to your harried-looking, tense fellow employee Katherine when she bursts into your office saying,"I didn't get the bid in on time! think I've ruined our chances of getting the Nike account and I'll probably lose my job."

       Answer: See pp. 158–160.

17. Which of these are *not* characteristic of Latin American communication patterns?
    a.   Politeness
    b.*   Direct language
    c.   Frequent gesturing
    d.   Expressive use of language

Reader Exam and Review Questions

Active Listening by Rogers and Farson

18. According to Rogers and Farson, the active listener
    a.*   allows the speaker to say what's on his or her mind and makes sure the message is understood.
    b.   probes for more facts.
    c.   tries to make the speaker feel good.
    d.   focuses only on the content of the message.

19. Rogers and Farson identify the two components of a message as content and
    a.   definition.
    b.*   feelings.
    c.   context.
    d.   structure.

Defensive Communication by Gibb

20. According to Gibb, a nondefensive climate is created when people are
    a.   descriptive.
    b.   egalitarian.
    c.   spontaneous.
    d.*   All of the above.

21. One way to avoid provoking defensive communication is by
    a.   controlling the situation rather than assuming a problem-solving orientation.
    b.*   being provisional rather than certain.
    c.   being neutral rather than showing empathy.
    d.   being evaluative rather descriptive.

The Power of Talk by Tannen

22. Which of these is *not* a characteristic of communication patterns in men according to Tannen?
    a.*   Soften criticism with praise
    b.   Ritualistic fighting
    c.   Blunt feedback
    d.   Display confidence

23. Contrast the differences in communication patterns of men and women as identified by Tannen. Give an example <u>for each gender</u> of how these patterns can be both positive and negative in managerial communication.

    Answer:
    ❑ Women focus on relationships and equality/Men focus on being one up rather than one down
    ❑ Women are less likely to promote themselves/Mean are more likely to take credit
    ❑ Women are more humble and downplay certainty/Men are more confident and minimize doubts

- ❑ Women ask more questions/Men ask fewer questions
- ❑ Women offer more ritual apologies/Men offer fewer ritual apologies
- ❑ Women soften criticism and praise/Men offer blunt feedback
- ❑ Women offer ritualistic exchanges of compliments/Men engage in ritualistic fighting

Reader Articles

1. ACTIVE LISTENING by *Carl R. Rogers and Richard E. Farson*
2. DEFENSIVE COMMUNICATION by *Jack R. Gibb*
3. THE POWER OF TALK by *Deborah Tannen*

Chapter 8
PERCEPTION AND ATTRIBUTION

Materials Needed: None.

Objectives: By the end of this chapter, students should be able to:

A. Define perception and explain the perceptual process
B. Identify the sources of misinterpretation in cross-cultural interactions
C. Understand both the benefits and the drawbacks of the perceptual process
D. Recognize common perceptual errors
E. Describe the Johari Window
F. Explain attribution theory
G. Understand the relevance of perception and attribution for managers

Sample Design

6:00–6:30	Lecturette on interpersonal perception and the Johari Window
6:30–7:30	Perception Exercise
7:30–8:00	Debriefing and attributions

Setting the Stage— Lecturette

The purpose of this chapter is to familiarize students with perception, their own schemas, and how others see them. Although we would not use the group exercise with a work group, it is very effective with learning groups that know and trust one another. For this reason, the chapter occurs when it does in the sequence. Some instructors who have never used this exercise find it threatening or silly, but we have used it for years without any difficulty. In fact, most students really like the exercise and find it both enlightening and entertaining. People are very curious about how others see them.

We begin the lecturette by noting that perception was mentioned in the previous chapter as a barrier or potential distortion in the communication process. Many instructors begin the lecture with a perceptual exercise, like Escher's Angels and Devils figure. We ask students individually what they see and then ask students to help others see what they see in the image.

With perceptual exercises, we emphasize that all the perceptions are partially correct at the same time that they may be partially incorrect. Students are reminded that with the help of others, many of them were able to view the same situation in more than one way; without that help we are likely to assume that what we perceive is what is actually there. Perception is another example of individual differences and yet another way in which we perceive the world in different ways.

We define perception and ask students how the perceptual process works. In the ensuing discussion, we make sure that the following points are covered: selective attention and the internal and external factors that influence what we attend to; the concept of figure and ground; organizing into schemas; evaluation or inference; sources of misinterpretation in cross cultural interaction; and stereotyping. In sum, because of perception, we don't hear or see everything we should; we only pay attention to a part of what we hear; then we usually take that and interpret it subjectively, rather than objectively. Furthermore, stereotyping is always a danger.

However, perception performs a useful function by limiting information, selecting what input we will attend to, and organizing and classifying input. If you want to show students a visual demonstration of perception, you can ask them to position their thumb and index finger in front of their eye, as if it were the lens of a camera. Instruct them to keep your entire body framed inside their fingers and then walk from one end of the room to another. They will have to move their fingers to keep you within that frame. What the naked eye sees is a person becoming bigger and smaller; the perceptual process stabilizes that input and gives us the message that the person's size is really constant. We don't believe the instructor got bigger and smaller even though that is what the naked eye saw.

Next we cover the common perceptual distortions: halo effect, central tendency, contrast effects, projection, and self-fulfilling perceptual defenses. We explain the Johari Window, using the transparency (T8.2), as an information processing model.

Issues to Consider in Leading the Experiential Exercise

A. When introducing this exercise, we mention that it may look silly but if taken seriously it is a good opportunity to see how other people see you and to become more aware of your own perceptual schema.

B. The exercise instructions are very complete. The only addition we make is to give an example, using a learning group of how the process works (e.g., "In this group, say, Sam decides he wants to go first. So Julie reads off all the things she has written down about Sam, and then Martha does the same thing and so on until we have gone around the entire group. Then Sam reads the words he used to describe himself.") We advise students to request feedback by asking why a person came up with a particular word if they are curious. They should accept, however, that people may not always be able to explain their impression.

C. If there is an extremely difficult person in the class, you may want to observe what happens during his or her turn. We've never seen this exercise blow up, but better safe than sorry. (There was the time the MBA group all chose a shark to describe one member. He just grinned sharkishly throughout.)

D. Some groups may finish before others. If that occurs, have them work ahead on the group discussion questions. Eliminate these questions for groups that are very slow. If some groups have more members than others, they will finish at different times.

E. In the **debriefing,** students often mention that they were not comfortable giving negative impressions and they were astonished there was so much agreement (to the extent of several people choosing the same words in several categories) about some people. People who disclose little about themselves are often surprised at the impressions they create. We mention that self-disclosure is a bell-shaped curve—too much frightens others off; too little leads others to "project" their own attributions on the "mystery" person.

F. After the debriefing, we cover attribution theory, as presented in the Follow-Up section, and the Tips for Managers about how to manage perceptions at work.

Transparency Masters

T8-0 CIRCLE LIMIT IV (ESCHER)
T8-1 JOHARI WINDOW

Workbook Exam and Review Questions

1. Which of the following is *not* a step in the processing of stimuli during perception?
   a. Selection
   b. Organization
   c. Evaluation
   d.* Synthesis

2.   (Selective attention) means that people do not see or hear all of the stimuli that is actually present.

3.   Which of these is not an internal factor that affects perception?
     a.   Motives
     b.*   Salience
     c.   Attitudes
     d.   Expections

4.   Give an example that explains how internal factors affect what we perceive.

     Answer: Refer to p. 173.

5.   (Schemas) are cognitive frameworks that represent organized knowledge about a given concept, event, or type of stimulus.

6.   Which of the following is untrue?
     a.   Stereotyping occurs when we attribute behavior or attitudes to a person on the basis of the group or category to which the person belongs.
     b.   The drawbacks to perception are that it prevents us from taking in everything we should and makes our interpretations open to question.
     c.*   Another drawback is that perception limits, selects, and organizes stimuli subconsciously.
     d.   There are numerous perceptual distortions you should try to avoid.

7.   Explain three perceptual distortions that can bias the evaluation process.

     Answer:
     ❑ Stereotyping—attributing behavior or attitudes to a person on the basis of the group or category to which the person belongs
     ❑ Halo effect—our perception of another is dominated by only one trait
     ❑ Central tendency—avoiding extreme judgments and rating everything as average
     ❑ Contrast effects—evaluations are affected by comparisons with other people we have recently encountered who are better or worse in terms of this characteristic
     ❑ Projection—tendency to attribute one's own attitudes or feelings to another person
     ❑ Self-fulfilling perceptual defenses—screens that block out what we do not wish to see and allow through stimuli that we wish to see

8.   The quadrant of the Johari Window characterized by information known by the self and unknown to the other is called
     a.   arena.
     b.   blindspot.
     c.*   facade.
     d.   unknown.

9.   Good communication is most likely to occur when which of the four quadrants is the largest?
     a.   Unknown
     b.   Facade
     c.   Blindspot
     d.*   Arena

10. According to attribution theory, what is the difference between an internal cause and an external cause?

Answer: Internal causes have to do with personal characteristics (intelligence, initiative, hard work, etc.); external causes are factors not under an individual's control (demanding boss, too much work, interdepartmental problems, competitive industry, etc.)

11. If several subordinates agree that their boss does not know how to delegate, this is an example of
a.* consensus.
b. distinctiveness.
c. fundamental attribution error.
d. consistency.

12. Which of the following statements is (are) *not* true?
a. Attribution theory contends that when people observe other's behavior, they attempt to determine whether it is internally or externally caused.
b. The self-serving bias occurs when people attribute their success to personal qualities while blaming their failure on external causes.
c. Fundamental attribution error is the tendency to overestimate the influence of personal failings and underestimate the influence of external factors when judging others.
d.* None of the statements are untrue.

13. The most important lesson to be learned about perception is that no one's perceptions are
a.* ever totally accurate.
b. able to respond to all of the quadrants of the Johari window.
c. ever totally distorted.
d. stereotypical.

Reader Exam and Review Questions

Communicating Across Cultures by Adler

14. According to Adler, when are stereotypes helpful?

Answer: When they are:
❏ Consciously held
❏ Descriptive
❏ Accurate
❏ The first best guess about a group
❏ Modified after further experience and observation

15. Which of the following is *not* a source of misinterpretation in cross-cultural interactions according to Adler?
a. Subconscious cultural blinders
b. Lack of cultural self-awareness
c.* Contrast effects
d. Projected similarity

16. "Latinos must be lazy—they're used to taking naps in the middle of the day for gosh sakes," is an example of what source of cross-cultural misinterpretation?

Answer: Subconscious cultural blinders

***When Bias Begins: The Truth about Stereotyping* by Murphy Paul**

17.　　We all use categories—of people, places, things—to make sense of the world around us. (Stereotypes) are categories that have gone too far.

<u>Reader Articles</u>

1.　　COMMUNICATING ACROSS CULTURES by *Nancy J. Adler*
2.　　WHEN BIAS BEGINS: THE TRUTH ABOUT STEREOTYPING by *Annie Murphy Paul*

Chapter 9
GROUP DYNAMICS AND WORK TEAMS

Materials Needed: Two concentric circles of chairs for each pair of groups. It's helpful to have the chairs located by blackboards or flip charts with markers but not absolutely necessary.

Objectives: By the end of this chapter, students should be able to:

A.   List the benefits of self-managed teams
B.   Identify what organizational requirements must be in place to set the stage for successful work teams
C.   Describe two models of group development
c.   Distinguish between group content and group process
D.   Explain and diagnose group process behaviors that either help or hinder group effectiveness
E.   Describe and recognize task and maintenance behaviors

Sample Design

6:00–6:15   Lecturette on self-managed work teams and group dynamics
6:15–7:30   Inner-Outer Exercise and subgroup analysis
7:30–8:00   Subgroup presentations and debriefing

Setting the Stage—Lecturette

Although we are fans of the Desert Survival and Lost at Sea type exercises, we have found that many students have already been exposed to them. Therefore, we chose a different group exercise that we hope you will like as well as or better than Lost at Sea. It sounds complex but works extremely well. This is an excellent way to begin a Saturday session in the beginning of the course. With undergraduates, we do this exercise sitting on the floor of a lounge.

We remind students at this point that OB has three levels of analysis—individual, group, and organizational—and we are focusing for the first time on the group level with this chapter. Our purpose here is to sensitize students to group process issues so they can learn to pay attention to both process and content dynamics in groups.

We try to keep the lecturette in this session as brief as possible to reserve more time for the exercise. We cover the growth of self-managed work teams, their benefits, and what they need to be successful. We present the two theories of group development presented in the workbook (T9.0, T9.1). We explain the difference between task and process (T9.2) and quickly run through the process issues that should be observed in groups—communication, decision making, task, and maintenance behavior. If time is short, we wait to talk about self-oriented behavior and norms during the exercise. Some instructors introduce the exercise by saying that students will finish this exercise with a whole new perspective on group functioning.

Issues to Consider in Leading the Experiential Exercise

A. Beforehand, instructors need to decide how many groups they wish to run in this session. You can simply join two learning groups together to make a subgroup or paired groups; that has the advantage of showing how an established group functions. If you have an odd number of learning groups and a small class, you can have people number off and form new groups. This will result in stranger groups, as they will not have the shared history of the learning groups. There are pros and cons to both methods; just make sure the paired groups are as equal as possible in size. The ideal size for each group is 6–10 (maximum of 15).

B. The first time you try this exercise you may want to stick to the instructions—four rounds of four minutes' duration, which adds up to 36 minutes. In the future, you can modify it slightly according to your particular situation. Reducing the rounds to three minutes doesn't seem to make much difference in the outcome, although it may make the groups feel more stressed if they have trouble coming to agreements. Larger groups need more time than smaller groups. Don't shortchange the subgroup analysis afterwards; if you're rushed for time, make the rounds shorter or eliminate a round. The consultation period, however, is crucial and should not be jettisoned, because it's a chance for organizational learning.

C. Put a schedule, like the following example, on the board or a transparency that explains the rounds and the times:

Introduction
Round One
        Group A   four minutes
        Group B   four minutes
Round Two
        Group A   four minutes
        Group B   four minutes
Round Three
        Group A   four minutes
        Group B   four minutes
Consultation   four minutes of mutual feedback
Round Four
        Group A   four minutes
        Group B   four minutes

If the chairs are not already in place, you may want to draw an inner and outer circle of chairs on the board so they can visualize it more readily.

D. Also write this on the board beforehand:

The two tasks are:
1.   Be the most effective group you can
2.   Create a list of the 10 characteristics of effective groups and rank order it.

E. Ask if anyone has ever done this exercise before. If so, are they willing to be observers? Ask for other volunteer observers so you have two for each pair of groups. If you have the option, select students who are perceptive. Tell them to read the observer instructions on page 203.

F. The timing of the rounds is important. It works best with a watch that can be set to beep when time is up. I usually delegate that job to a student in one of the groups who has a fancier watch than mine. Just make sure the timekeeper is immediately resetting the alarm and keeping time fairly for both groups. As soon as the alarm goes off, the groups quickly change places and the inner group begins work without waiting for the instructor to give them the go-ahead. This works better than waiting till they are all seated and ready to begin timing (although it looks a little like musical chairs).

G. **Don't tell them they can use the flip chart or blackboard**, but you can have a flip chart in the room and see if using it occurs to them. If they ask for permission, say something low key like "It's up to you." How they decide to keep track of their ideas will affect their group process. Some groups use the flip chart or blackboard, which allows everyone to see what's happening; other groups have one person who records the list and may assume ownership of it. It is more difficult to keep people involved with the latter method. In other groups, everyone keeps a copy of the list, but that is not very efficient. In the debriefing section, ask what effect their record keeping had on group dynamics. They may also mention that they mistakenly assumed they could not use the flip chart or blackboard, rather than testing how proactive they could be. Occasionally a student will suggest using the flip chart, only to be told by another student that it's against the rules! Groups and teams often accept boundaries without testing them, which hampers their creativity and effectiveness.

H. Make sure the observers understand how to use the Observer Chart. Each observer is responsible for only one subgroup. It's a good idea for them to switch locations occasionally so they can observe from a different perspective. Their job is extremely important. Most groups profit a great deal from this feedback. For example, in one group the observer noticed that a male student only made eye contact with the other U.S. males, ignoring the women and the international students unless they spoke. He was grateful for the feedback and subsequently worked hard to be more inclusive. In many groups, this feedback allows them to discuss who's talking too much and too little and to identify the consequences of these behaviors.

I. Although the rules prohibit talking among members of the outer circle, some people will want to continue working on their list. Politely remind them that their job is to observe silently.

J. When it comes time for the consultation round, reiterate that the person in the inner circle should turn around and consult with the person directly behind. This pair has four minutes that they should divide so both of them have an opportunity to give and receive feedback.

K. Note how much time each group devotes towards talking about or trying to be the best group they can be. Pay attention to whether the groups utilize the feedback they received during the consultation phase. If they don't, ask them why in the debriefing section.

L. When you reach Step 6, briefly go over the four tasks, either before or after you have divided the students into four heterogeneous groups. It's important that each subgroup has members from all the inner-outer groups. You can flesh out these concepts. For example, self-oriented behavior is an example of an individual goal that may be operating in a group. We use the analogy with "membership" of the person who joins a country club but is still not accepted. You can remind students of the "norms" they set in the first class about what was effective behavior in this course. Encourage them to provide specific examples in their presentations ("When so-and-so did such-and-such. . .")

M. Observe the discussion in each subgroup to see if they need help. If there was an autocratic leader who steamrollered his or her group, this person could come in for direct personal criticism by the leadership subgroup. This exercise usually provides a vivid comparison in leadership styles. Sit with this subgroup and ask how they are planning to present their findings ("How will you say that? How can you couch it so that person doesn't go home feeling like dogmeat but will consider changing his or her style?"). Encourage them to focus on the pros and cons of different leadership styles. They will have to name names but it can be done respectfully. When this group presents their findings, be prepared to support leaders who caused resentment. Make sure their side of it is heard as well as their frustration at being criticized. One of the best lessons that comes out of this exercise is the vulnerability of autocratic leaders and how to avoid this situation. Ask group members why they did not speak up at the time if they were unhappy with the way things were going and make the point that everyone shares the responsibility for effective group process, not just the leaders. This also demonstrates that silence does not always signify satisfaction or support. Sometimes we ask students how to transform an autocratic style into a more participative style. Simply turning statements into questions is a good beginning (What if we ___? Do you all agree?)

N. When the subgroup on goals has finished presenting, ask the groups how much time they devoted to the two assigned tasks. Usually a tiny percentage or no time at all is dedicated to the process goal (be the best group you can) and the task (ranking a list) receives all the attention (T9.2). Why is that? They often answer that due to time constraints, the list was more important. Or they simply assumed they were already doing the other task or else they just ignored it. Make the point that we always have time constraints of one sort or another, but a failure to discuss group process can also lead to wasted time. The failure to discuss the consultation feedback is another example of ignoring process issues. What could the groups have done to address the first assigned goal?

O. After the subgroup presentations, the groups revert to their original group configuration so that the observers can present their feedback.

Transparency Masters

T9.0   PUNCTUATED EQUILIBRIUM MODEL OF GROUP DEVELOPMENT
T9.1   FIVE-STAGE MODEL OF GROUP DEVELOPMENT
T9.2   CONTENT AND PROCESS

Workbook Exam and Review Questions

1.   The impetus for incorporating teams into organizational structures is
      a.   speed.
      b.   competitive advantage.
      c.   flexibility.
      d.*   All of the above.

2.   Self-managed work teams have all of the following characteristics *except*
      a.   they determine how they will accomplish their goals.
      b.   they are usually responsible for an entire process or product.
      c.*   they are leaderless.
      d.   they often select their own members.

3.   In order to succeed, teams require all of the following *except*
      a.*   a common purpose and general goals.
      b.   a supportive environment.
      c.   policies that promote teamwork.
      d.   team members with teamwork skills.

4.   Briefly describe the five stages in the most well known model of group development.

      Answer: See pg. 194 for further description
      ❑ Forming—meet, learn more about the group and each other, period of uncertainty
      ❑ Storming—issues of control surface, tension is typical, group can polarize
      ❑ Norming—members develop shared expectation about group roles and norms, members identify with the group
      ❑ Performing—energy is focused on achieving goals, increased cohesion is developed
      ❑ Adjourning—focus is on closure, often celebrate achievements

5.   When a group is focusing on work that must be done, this is an example of group
      a.   process.
      b.   communication.
      c.*   content.
      d.   Maintenance.

6.   There are two types of group process. Identify and describe both.

      Answer: *Task* process focuses on how groups accomplish their work, including setting agendas, figuring out time frames, generating ideas, choosing techniques for making decisions and solving problems, and testing agreement. *Maintenance* process concerns how groups function with regard to meeting group members' psychological and relationship needs, including issues such as leadership, membership, norms, communication, influence, conflict management, and dealing with difficult members and dysfunctional behaviors.

7. When a group member asks, "Does anyone object?" this is an example of which decision-making method?
   a. Handclasp
   b. Polling
   c. Self-authorized agenda
   d.* Minority decision

8. Types of behavior relevant to the group's fulfillment of its task include all of the following *except*
   a. initiating and seeking or giving information or opinions.
   b. clarifying, elaborating, and summarizing.
   c.* encouraging, harmonizing, and compromising.
   d. consensus testing, reality testing, and orienting.

9. A statement such as "It's time we moved on to the next item," is an example of which task behavior?
   a. Seeking or giving information or opinions
   b. Orienting
   c.* Initiating
   d. Clarifying or elaborating

10. A statement such as "Let's give Amy a chance to voice her opinion" is an example of which maintenance behavior?
    a.* Gatekeeping
    b. Standard setting
    c. Seeking or giving information or opinions
    d. Reality testing

11. There are four basic emotional causes of self-oriented behavior in groups. Identify the four causes.

    Answer:
    ❑ The problem of identity
    ❑ The problem of power and control
    ❑ The problem of goals
    ❑ The problem of acceptance and intimacy

12. Self-oriented behavior tends to be more prevalent
    a. towards the end of the group.
    b. when the group is focusing on task.
    c. midway into the life of the group.
    d.* when a new member joins an established group.

13. (Norms) are unwritten, often implicit, rules that define the attitudes and behaviors that characterize good and bad group members.

14. Which is *not* one of the "pure types" that represent the three different styles of reducing tension and expressing emotion?
    a. The friendly helper
    b.* The devil's advocate
    c. The logical thinker
    d. The tough battler

Reader Exam and Review Questions

Critical Success Factors for Creating Superb Self-managing Teams by Wageman

15. According to Wageman, what are the benefits of self-managed work teams?

     Answer:
     - ❑ Enhanced company performance
     - ❑ Enhanced organizational learning and adaptability
     - ❑ Enhanced employee commitment

16. Which of the following is *not* a critical success factor for a team as outlined by Wageman?
     - a.   Team rewards
     - b.   Material resources
     - c.* Experienced leaders
     - d.   Clear, engaging direction

Virtual Teams: The New Way to Work by Lipnack and Stamps

17. List at least three things a virtual team should do to overcome the challenges inherent in computer-mediated teamwork as discussed by Lipnack and Stamps.

     Answer:
     - ❑ Identify team sponsors, stakeholders, and champions
     - ❑ Develop a team charter
     - ❑ Establish the group's computer interface
     - ❑ Carefully select team members
     - ❑ Start with a face-to-face meeting
     - ❑ Establish team norms about how you will work and communicate
     - ❑ Determine how work will be managed and reviewed
     - ❑ Allow for multiple leadership, avoid a controlling style

Reader Articles

1.   CRITICAL SUCCESS FACTORS FOR CREATING SUPERB SELF-MANAGING TEAMS by *Ruth Wageman*
2.   VIRTUAL TEAMS: THE NEW WAY TO WORK by *Jessica Lipnack and Jeffrey Stamps*

Chapter 10
PROBLEM SOLVING AND CREATIVITY

Materials Needed: Three tennis balls per each group of 15 students if you want to do the creativity exercise.

Objectives: By the end of this chapter, students should be able to:

A. Explain the four stages of problem solving
B. Describe the red/green modes of problem solving
C. Explain the different roles a manager plays during problem solving
D. Identify what problem-solving stage a group is in and how to facilitate a group's progress
E. Describe the creative process
F. Explain the organizational conditions that promote creativity

Sample Design

6:00–6:15	Lecturette on problem management
6:15–6:45	Cardiotronics Case
6:45–7:00	Group Review
7:00–7:10	Summary Reports
7:10–7:30	Debriefing
7:30–8:00	Creativity

Setting the Stage—Lecturette

The purpose of this chapter is to teach students a problem-solving model that is more complete than the usual models. We emphasize the importance of a shared problem-solving model for team members (regardless of what model is used) so that everyone is "on the same page" at the same time. The Total Quality movement has given a major boost to team problem solving.

We ask students to identify counterproductive steps in problem-solving that they have observed (denying the problem, ignoring problems, blaming others or blaming oneself, getting too many or not enough people involved in the solution, etc.) so that they ground themselves in their past experiences and we can start compiling a list of characteristics of effective problem-solving efforts.

Next we carefully run through Kolb's problem-solving model, using the transparency (T10.0), and try to make it as simple as possible for them, using examples at each stage. We suggest they think of the green mode as diverging to gather information and ideas and the red mode as converging on a decision that allows the group to proceed to the next stage. Whenever possible, we take a problem that all students are familiar with and apply the model to it. Xerox's Problem-Solving Model incorporates the expansion/contraction idea, which may reassure students that this stuff is actually useful.

Issues to Consider in Leading the Experiential Exercise

A. Your greatest potential problem with this chapter is students who have not done their homework and prepared the case (i.e., come up with a list of questions that Marion could ask at each stage of the problem-solving process). Our purpose in the premeeting assignment is to give students practice in facilitating problem solving. To make sure students are prepared, you could ask them to type up the premeeting preparation to hand in, and collect it at the end of class.

The following are examples of the type of questions that can be asked in each stage of the process.

1. **Situation Analysis**
    Valuing/Exploration
    a.   What do you think about the situation?
    b.   How do you feel about it?
    c.   What's the real problem?
    d.   Is there something else we should be looking at first?
    e.   What do you hope is the outcome?
    f.   What's really important in this situation?
    g.   What other problems does this one relate to?
    h.   Let's see if we can draw a problem tree.
    i.   What values are involved in this situation?

    Priority Setting
    a.   What's the most important problem that, if resolved, would cause other things to
            fall into place? Why?
    b.   What do others in the organization think about this?
    c.   What would other parts of the organization say is the most important problem?
    d.   Do we all agree that this is the key problem that needs to be solved?

2. **Causal Analysis**
    Information Gathering
    a.   Let's try to put our biases aside and take an objective look at the situation. What
            do we know about it?
    b.   What do we need to know before we can really define the problem?
    c.   Who else should we talk to?

    Problem Definition
    a.   Do we have enough information to put together a model of the problem or to
            define the problem?
    b.   What's our model of what's causing this problem or situation? Can we draw it?
    c.   What factors caused it?
    d.   What else contributes to it?
    e.   What factors affect how we go about solving it?

3. **Solution Analysis**
    Idea Getting
    a.   Let's brainstorm possible solutions to the problem, but let's not evaluate them
            until the ideas are all out.

    Decision Making
    a.   Are we ready to evaluate these suggestions?
    b.   What criteria should our solution meet?
    c.   Which of these solutions meets all the criteria?
    d.   Are there any unintended consequences of this solution?

4. **Implementation Analysis**
    Participation
    a.   Who would be affected by the implementation of this solution?
    b.   How can we involve them?
    c.   Who else should be involved in implementing this?
    c.   Who has the most at stake or the most energy to get this accomplished?

    Planning
    a.   In the actual planning process, who does what and when?
    b.   What tasks need to be done? In what order?

c.   What deadlines are we facing?

d.   Who will do what?

e.   How shall we evaluate the implementation and the solution?

f.   Is everybody satisfied with our decision and our plan?

B. Read the instructions to the students for the group meeting exercise and the tips on role playing on page 225. All the names in the case are more or less unisex. Caution students <u>not</u> to read the role play instructions for others. The role play is very realistic. Emphasize that role players should be themselves as much as possible while being faithful to their role instructions; students should not view this as an opportunity to be the "employee from hell." Whenever we do role plays of managers, we mention that we don't expect people to perform perfectly as a manager—but we do expect everyone to learn from the role play.

C. If there are more than six members in your groups, ask for volunteers who can observe the groups using the Cardiotronics Case Review form on page 227. Observers can contribute a great deal to this exercise.

D. The instructor should also observe what is occurring in the groups so he or she can better facilitate the **debriefing**.

E. Marion's role is a difficult one because the person playing this role makes himself or herself vulnerable to criticism and even blame. We note the difficulty of this role and try to support the "Marion's" while still letting them hear the feedback on their performance. One of the authors adds in another step to this exercise before the general debriefing session; she asks each group to list what Marion did that helped the group and what he or she could improve upon. This is usually very valuable feedback for the person playing Marion, and it also sets a positive tone for the general debriefing.

If it looks as if a group is excessively blaming Marion in the debriefing, the instructor can shift the focus of the discussion. You can always ask why group members did not speak up, reinforcing the lesson that everyone in a group is responsible for how the group functions and not just the leader. The instructor can also note the positive things students did during the debriefing session. We seldom see this type of blaming problem because the groups usually develop a strong sense of liking and loyalty among their members.

F. These are five frequent solutions listed in order of effectiveness:

     1. **Transfer the problem to someone else**—"ask management to build another assembly unit or ask for pay bonuses or automated equipment." However, solutions that cost money are often unacceptable to management. Considering resource constraints is a part of good problem solving (one which is often less obvious to undergrads).

     2. **Fire Pat**—a weak solution that offers only marginal value, as Terry is almost as slow as Pat. Can you continue firing the slowest members?

     3. **Help Pat**—a moderate solution as some labor agreements don't allow management to order workers to help each other keep up.

     4. **Rotate workers at regular intervals through all jobs**—this way the line moves at the average speed of all workers rather than the speed of the slowest workers. This is an ideal solution that takes account of all information given in the case (desire of some to work faster, boredom, etc.)

     5. **Let each worker make the entire board**—a good solution that would allow for greater motivation and less boredom, **but** it depends upon the feasibility of reorganizing the assembly line equipment into individual stations.

Solutions #4 and #5 relate to the Job Characteristics Enrichment Model in Chapter 4, pg. 88.

G. When you go over the Cardiotronics Case Review, page 227, you can help students think of examples of behavior, like those shown below, that reflect each state of the problem-solving model. We always go over the first four items below, emphasizing the importance of getting off to the right start in problem solving.

> **Valuing:** *What issues did you discuss here?*
> Values = (a) age discrimination "How do we treat older employees?"; (b) work ethic values such as "Is it okay for employees to be working under capacity?"
> Opportunities = could we better utilize all workers and make the job more satisfying to those who are underutilized?
>
> **Priority Setting**: *What was the most important problem for your group?* Getting from 36 to 40 units is the correct problem.
>
> **Information Gathering**: *What type of information were you looking for?* "What is keeping the team from making 40 units a day?" is the best focus here.
>
> **Problem Definition**: *How did your group define the problem?* It's an employee utilization problem and a work flow imbalance.
>
> **Idea Getting**: *What possible solutions did you come up with?*
>
> **Decision making**: *What solution did you choose?*
>
> **Participation**: *Who needed to be involved to implement this?*
>
> **Planning**: *What plan did you come up with?*

H. In the debriefing, this case usually demonstrates the need for "green mode" information gathering to correctly define the problem and arrive at creative solutions. Younger students often see Pat as the problem and focus their energies on getting rid of him. They can be very insulting to Pat, which raises the issue of age discrimination and how we treat loyal employees who might be slowing down. If the students who play Pat are treated badly in some groups, the instructor can ask them how they felt during the role play. Thus, this case also demonstrates that individuals are often blamed for problems that are better viewed as system problems. We tell students that it is important to find "what, not who, is the problem?" (a basic tenet of OD consulting). In the rare instance when an individual, rather than a systemic problem, appears to be the sole cause, there is nothing to be gained by identifying him or her as "the problem." Doing so only provokes bad feelings and resistance and generates no energy to improve the situation. Even if you were planning to fire such a person immediately, face-saving is an important consideration.

I. The instructor may wish to go over the common obstacles to effective group problem solving, presented in Tips for Managers, pages 237–38.

J. After the debriefing is complete, the instructor can review the relationship between learning styles and the problem-solving model, which is covered in the Follow-Up section and presented on the transparency (T10–01), "The Learning Model and the Problem-Solving Process."

K. To tackle **creativity**, we go over their scores on a self-assessment instrument (like the one in the Robbins Self-Assessment Library or others) measuring creativity. Then we present the characteristics of creative people. Next we do an exercise called juggling. Divide the class into at least two groups with no more than 15 people per group and separate the groups as much as possible while keeping them in the same room. Give one tennis ball to a person in each group.

Have the students throw the ball randomly to everyone in the circle, raising their hand to indicate they have already received it. Tell them to remember the pattern—who threw to them and who they threw to. "Your task is to send the ball around this pattern as quickly as possible; your only rule is to "respect the sequence." After they have practiced a bit, have someone in each group time how long it takes to do the complete sequence. Announce the times of the different groups. Next, give the starting person another tennis ball, saying, "How fast can you do it with two balls?" Let them practice that a few rounds, then time them, and announce their times. Next, give a third ball to the person who starts the sequence and tell them to do the sequence with three balls. After a few practice rounds, time them, announcing their times. Then tell each group that you have confidence that they can greatly reduce their times if they are creative. Keep encouraging them to lower their times, "That's great, but I think you can do better if you put your minds together." There will probably be a spirit of competition in the room. Eventually someone will figure out that since the only rule is to "respect the sequence" they can move people around. Later, they come up with the idea of keeping the balls still and having students touch them in order. Some groups simply pile their hands on top of each other. I've never seen a group who couldn't get their time down to less than a minute by the end of the exercise.

We debrief this exercise around the conditions necessary for creativity. "What allowed you to be progressively more creative as the exercise went on?" "What hindered your creativity if anything?" They often note that they limited themselves by assuming they could not move, etc.," which relates to the importance of questioning assumptions and thinking outside the box. We note that there were incremental improvements and ask what happened to force a greater leap in creativity. One answer is the instructor's championship and confidence that they could do better. This leads into a discussion of creativity killers and the organizational conditions that promote creativity.

Transparency Masters

T10.0   Problem Solving as a Dialectic Process
T10.1   The Learning Model and the Problem-Solving Process

Workbook Exam and Review Questions

1.   In the view of many managers, the core task of management is (problem solving).

2.   What are the three premises of the problem-solving model in the text.

    Answer:
    ❑   It's a process of learning from experience.
    ❑   It's mind over matter.
    ❑   It's a social process.

3.   What are the four stages of the problem-solving model?

    Answer:
    ❑   Situation analysis
    ❑   Problem analysis
    ❑   Solution analysis
    ❑   Implementation analysis

4.   Solution analysis corresponds to which stage in the experiential learning cycle?
    a.   Active experimentation
    b.*   Abstract conceptualization
    c.   Reflective observation
    d.   Concrete experience

5. Problem (finding) is equally as important as problem solving.

6. According to the text, problem solving proceeds
   a.* in wavelike expansions and contractions.
   b. like a pendulum swings.
   c. in a top-down fashion.
   d. in a logical, linear fashion.

7. The dialectics of problem solving have been conceptualized in all of these ways *except*
   a. green light/red light.
   b. doubting/believing.
   c.* analyzing/implementing.
   d. divergence/convergence.

8. Identify the different management roles for the different stages of the problem-solving process.

   Answer:
   Situation analysis = *leader*
   Problem analysis = *detective*
   Solution analysis = *inventor*
   Implementation analysis = *coordinator*

9. The dialectically related processes involved in the situation analysis phase of problem solving are
   a. information gathering and problem solving.
   b. action and doing.
   c.* valuing and priority setting.
   d. participation and planning.

10. What is the potential drawback of the American orientation toward action and fixing problems as identified in the text?
    a. Solutions are too expensive.
    b. Solutions are technologically driven.
    c. Solutions are not transferrable to other situations.
    d.* Solutions are not thoroughly analyzed.

11. (Creativity) is the process by which individuals or small groups produce novel and useful ideas.

12. Which of the following is *not* a characteristic of creative people?
    a. Persistent
    b. Concerned with achievement
    c.* Attracted to simplicity
    d. High energy

13. Which of the following is *not* a stage in the creative process?
    a. Illumination
    b.* Implementation
    c. Preparation
    d. Incubation

14. Name three ways organizations can foster creativity.

    Answer:
    ❑ Set innovation goals

- ❑   Recognize and reward creativity
- ❑   Encourage autonomy
- ❑   Encourage risk taking
- ❑   Encourage participative decision making
- ❑   Encourage supportiveness by both peers and supervisors
- ❑   Promote internal diversity and interaction
- ❑   Establish flexible structures

15.   There is a parking problem on your campus—too many cars and not enough spaces. Students have decided to be proactive and analyze the problem and suggest solutions to the administration. What are three possible problems with this problem-solving approach? Explain. (essay)

Reader Exam and Review Questions

Putting Your Company's Whole Brain to Work by Leonard and Straus

16.   Preferences are either inherently good or inherently bad according to Leonard and Straus.
_____True or __X__False
Why or why not?

      Answer: Preferences are assets or liabilities depending on the situation.

17.   All of the following are tips by Leonard and Straus for managing the creative process *except*
    a.   create creative abrasion.
    b.   clarify why you are working together by keeping the common goal in front of you.
    c.*   make your operating guidelines implicit.
    d.   set up an agenda ahead of time that explicity provides time for both divergent and convergent discussion.

Of Boxes, Bubbles, and Effective Management by Hurst

18.   According to Hurst, under the soft bubble process of management rewards are
    a.   direct.
    b.   objective.
    c.   profit oriented.
    d.*   fun.

19.   Which is an element of the hard box leadership model in Hurst's view?
    a.   Roles
    b.*   Information systems
    c.   Groups
    d.   Networks

20.   As presented by Hurst, soft bubble leadership relies on
    a.   precise policies and rules.
    b.*   wisdom.
    c.   rationality.
    d.   a sense of humor.

Creativity as Investment by Sternberg et al.

21.   Which of the following is *not* a factor in developing creativity according to Sternberg et al.?
    a.   Motivation
    b.   Intellectual abilities

        c.   Personality
        d.*   Age

Reader Articles
1.   PUTTING YOUR COMPANY'S WHOLE BRAIN TO WORK by *Dorothy Leonard and Susaan Straus*
2.   OF BOXES, BUBBLES, AND EFFECTIVE MANAGEMENT by *David K. Hurst*
3.   CREATIVITY AS INVESTMENT by *Robert J. Sternberg, Linda A. O'Hara, and Todd I. Lubart*

Chapter 11
CONFLICT AND NEGOTIATION

Materials Needed: If using the Red/Green Game, either write the Scoring Chart on the blackboard or project it as an overhead..

Objectives: By the end of this chapter, students should be able to:

A. Describe behaviors that characterize group conflict
B. Identify common sources of conflict
C. Explain the five conflict-handling modes
D. Understand the functional and dysfunctional nature of conflict
E. Differentiate between distributive and integrative bargaining
F. Explain principled negotiation
G. Describe how culture influences conflict

Sample Design

6:00–6:15	Lecturette on Thomas-Kilman model
6:15–6:40	Red/Green game
6:40–7:00	Debriefing
7:00–7:05	Lecturette on principled negotiation
7:05–7:25	Introduction and preparation for the Film Equipment Negotiation
7:25–7:45	Negotiation
7:45–8:00	Debriefing

Setting the Stage—Lecturette

The purpose of this chapter is to provide students with an opportunity to simulate a conflict situation and practice negotiation skills. The sample design above is very tight; you can do the Thomas-Kilman model, discuss self-assessment scores, and do the Red/Green game in 80 minutes. Ideally, the negotiation exercise also takes 80 minutes. If you have short sessions, you can do one class on conflict and another on negotiation.

In the lecturette we present the Thomas-Kilman model, using transparency T11.0. Warn students not to confuse the accommodation style in this model with the accommodator Learning Style. We give examples of each style, advantages and disadvantages, and the situations for which they are appropriate. To apply this model, we ask students to think back on a recent conflict situation and identify what style they used.

If you are not using the Robbins Self-Assessment Library, which has a version of the Thomas-Kilman Conflict Mode Instrument, you can buy it from Xiocom, Inc. of Tuxedo, New York. The Strength Deployment instrument measures how people react both to "normal" conflict and when they are under the pressure of heavy conflict. If you obtain a self-assessment instrument, and we suggest you do, you can assign it as homework and go over their scores after explaining the theory.

If there is a major conflict in your environment (university, political, city), you can ask students to analyze the source of the conflict and identify what common characteristics are present.

Before doing the negotiation exercise, we present the concepts of distributive and integration bargaining and principled negotiation (T11.2). We give real-life examples of each of the principles and point out that this model is heavily based on things previously studied in the course, such as communication and perception as well as conflict management techniques.

Issues to Consider in Leading the Experiential Exercise

The Red/Green Game

A.   Ask the students to form a human continuum from Very Comfortable with Conflict at one end of the room to Very Uncomfortable with Conflict at the other end of the room. They'll need to talk to each other to find their relative position in the continuum. Have them count off by fours for the Red/Green exercise. This gives you heterogenous groups likely to have more intergroup conflict as they play the game.

B.   Ask if any students have previously done the Red/Green game. In our experience, it usually makes no difference if they play again, because other students only listen to their advice if they are informal leaders. If there are just a few repeaters, you can let them choose between observing and playing again. Observers watch without talking and write down interesting and outrageous comments they hear on a transparency, which they can present during the debriefing.

C.   This game is based on The Prisoner's Dilemma, which you may wish to discuss during the debriefing.

D.   After reading them the instructions, your job is to collect their votes every two minutes, record their votes, and make sure your math is right on the cumulative scoring. You'll probably have to remind the representatives to speak loudly enough so everyone can hear and hush everyone else. Otherwise, observe carefully so you know where to guide the debriefing.

E.   Once in a while, a class decides to be collaborative and votes green throughout the entire game. Usually, however, a group welches on what other groups perceive as an agreement, and conflict emerges. If a particular student or group comes across as arrogant or untrustworthy, tempers may run hot. Therefore, you'll need to handle the debriefing carefully. We try to bring out the different approaches or viewpoints on the simulation. Sometimes "betrayers" did not think an agreement had been reached. Or they say it's just a game and fail to understand why others are furious with them. "What exactly made you so angry?" Try to get them to identify the behaviors that bothered them, but don't let "betrayers" become the villains. Sometimes we ask, "Which groups would you want to do business with in the future and why?" This gets at the role of trust and long-term relationships in business and reemphasizes that you can win the battle and lose the war if you are too competitive. Some groups take the moral high road, in their opinion, and become quite self-righteous about always voting consistently or never lying, even though they ended up in the hole. Being self-righteous, however, can be another form of one-upsmanship and usually doesn't lead to a win-win solution.

F.   Make sure you demonstrate that the totals could be calculated in two different manners. Add them up for each team and then add them across the bottom to yield an "organizational" total. The instructions create ambiguity; in the face of ambiguity people resort to their natural styles. Competitive people perceive the situation as competitive; collaborative people perceive it as an opportunity to collaborate. Neither approach is wrong—but having different approaches in the room generates conflict. The lesson is that ambiguity is a source of conflict. Other lessons are that trust is easily broken but difficult to repair. It only takes one competitive person or group to change the nature of an interaction from collaborative to competitive. It's easier to prevent conflict than to resolve it. We ask them if they've observed companies where the departments behave like the teams in the simulation and then request examples.

G.   Direct the class's attention to the Follow-Up section on page 256 and check whether the behaviors Schein described were present in the class.

H.   Students are usually interested in how to resolve conflict once it begins. There are several suggestions in the Tips for Managers section that cover both preventing and resolving conflict.

THE FILM EQUIPMENT NEGOTIATION

I.   As the students negotiate, walk around and unobtrusively eavesdrop on them. There are usually some groups that cannot come to an agreement. Give them a 10-minute and 5-minute warning and then a "sudden death" threat if they can't reach an agreement (which some groups can't do).

J.   Write the outcomes of the different groups on the board. If you're lucky, they'll be very different. Don't forget to ask observers what they saw. After question a. in the debriefing is often a good point to turn to the observers. Let the groups describe what happened first.

The interests in this case are:

Ivy League U.
Get rid of equipment quickly (4 wk. deadline)
Sell for a good price

Intelligentsia U.
Obtain needed equipment
Pay as little as possible
Establish relationship with
      Ivy League U. to set up exchange program

The objective criteria are:
- ❑ the cost of new equipment
- ❑ the cost of used equipment
- ❑ the price offered by the secondhand store

The BATNA for each side is shown below:

Ivy League U.'s BATNA
Sell to secondhand store for $35,000

Intelligentsia U.'s BATNA
Buy used equipment for $40,000
Buy new equipment for $90,000.

Transparency Masters

T11.0   FIVE CONFLICT-HANDLING ORIENTATIONS
T11.1   PRINCIPLED NEGOTIATION

Workbook Exam and Review Questions

1.   (Conflict) is a form of interaction among parties that differ in interests, perceptions, and preferences.

2.   When the Sherifs used equal status contact and superordinate goals as techniques for reducing intergroup tensions in their experiment at Robbers Cave,
     a.   both techniques were successful.
     b.*   superordinate goals worked; equal status contact didn't work.
     c.   equal status contact worked; superordinate goals didn't work.
     d.   neither technique worked.

3.   Which of the following is *not* typical of conflict situations involving groups?
     a.*   Devaluation of one's own group
     b.   Stereotyping of the opposing or competing group
     c.   Distortion of perceptions
     d.   Polarization on the issues

4.   Escalation of group conflict is characterized by all of the following *except*
     a.*   focusing intensely on the core issue under dispute.
     b.   pursuing increasingly extreme demands or objectives.
     c.   using increasingly coercive tactics.
     d.   enlisting other parties to take sides in the conflict.

5.   What are the advantages and disadvantages of organizational reference groups?

Answer:
❑ Advantages—they provide individuals with a sense of belonging and identity
❑ Disadvantages—they can cause we-they attitudes to develop that can foster competition and a lack of collaboration that hinders productivity and achievement of the overall goals of the organization

6.   Competition between groups is always dysfunctional.
___X___True or _____False
Why or why not?

Answer: Competition is both functional and the essence of the marketplace when it results in greater team spirit and effort. It is dysfunctional when it siphons energy away from the overall mission of the organization.

7.   Name three potential sources of conflict that could create problems between a manufacturing and a marketing department.

Answer:
❑ We-they attitudes
❑ Competition for scarce resources
❑ Ambiguous authority
❑ Interdependence
❑ Deficient information
❑ Differences in values, goals, interests, personalities, education, culture, perceptions, and expectations

8.   Which of the following is *not* a result of dysfunctional conflict?
a.   Reduced job satisfaction
b.   Increased absenteeism
c.   Lower morale
d.*   All of the above are a result of dysfunctional conflict.

9.   Functional conflict does all of the following *except*
a.   forces us to articulate our views and positions.
b.   makes the values and belief systems of the organization more visible.
c.   serves as a safety valve to blow off steam.
d.*   makes it unnecessary to clarify organizational priorities.

10.   The two axes of the Thomas conflicting handling modes are
a.   cooperativeness and competitiveness.
b.*   cooperativeness and assertiveness.
c.   assertiveness and competitiveness.
d.   functional and dysfunctional.

11.   The conflict-handling mode characterized by an I lose—you win orientation is known as
a.   competition.
b.   compromise.
c.   avoidance.
d.*   accommodation.

12.   The phrase "winning the battle but losing the war" most accurately describes the gains and losses of which conflict-handling style?
a.   Accommodation

b.   Avoidance
c.*   Competition
d.   Compromise

13.   Describe two gains and two losses associated with the collaborative conflict style.

     Answer:
-   Gains
-   Both sides win
-   Better chance for long-term solutions
-   Creativity in problem solving
-   Maintains relationship
-   New level of understanding of situation
-   Improves quality of solution and commitment
-   Losses
-   Requires more time in short run
-   Loss of sense of autonomy

14.   When an issue is trivial, or more important issues are pressing, an appropriate conflict handling style would be
a.   accommodating.
b.   compromising.
c.*   avoiding.
d.   collaborating.

15.   Distributive bargaining is most closely related to
a.   compromise.
b.   accomodation.
c.   collaboration.
d.*   competition.

16.   List the four steps in Fisher and Ury's principled negotiation.

     Answer:
-   Separate the people from the problem.
-   Focus on interest, not positions.
-   Invent options for mutual gain.
-   Insist on objective criteria.

17.   Fisher and Ury recommend that negotiators arm themselves with an alternative in case the negotiation does not go as expected. What do they call this?

     Answer: BATNA—Best Alternative to a Negotiated Agreement

18.   Which of the following statements about conflict are *not* true?
a.   It is easier to create conflict than to resolve it.
b.*   Cultural differences in conflict handling are hard to discern.
c.   Too much conflict is dysfunctional.
d.   Too little conflict is dysfunctional.

Reader Exam and Review Questions

How Management Teams Can Have a Good Fight by Eisenhardt et al.

19.   Which of the following is *not* suggested by Eisenhardt et al. as guideline for positive conflict?

a.* Rally around processes
b. Use humor
c. Develop multiple alternatives
d. Don't force consensus

20. According to Eisenhardt et al., management teams in conflict should focus on (issues), not personalities.

World Class Negotiating Strategies by Acuff

21. Which of the following is *not* one of Acuff's 10 negotiating strategies that will work anywhere?
a. Ask lots of questions
b.* Have modest aspirations
c. Make patience an obsession
d. Maintain personal integrity

Reader Articles
1. HOW MANAGEMENT TEAMS CAN HAVE A GOOD FIGHT by *Kathleen M. Eisenhardt, Jean L. Kahwajy, and L. J. Bourgeois III*
2. WORLD CLASS NEGOTIATING STRATEGIES by *Frank L. Acuff*

Chapter 12
MANAGING DIVERSITY

Materials Needed: If you use the Embassy Reception exercise, you will need two rooms large enough for half the class to meet privately.

Objectives: By the end of this chapter, students should be able to:

A.   Explain the advantages and disadvantages of culture
B.   Define ethnocentrism and stereotyping
C.   Describe six dimensions of cultural differences
D.   List the positive aspects of managing diversity well
E.   Explain what happens to tokens in organizations
F.   Explain why diversity is a business issue
G.   Understand how to manage diversity in organizations

Sample Designs

6:00–6:15	Lecturette on culture
6:15–7:00	Groups plan strategy or skits
7:00–7:30	The Embassy Reception or Cross-Cultural Competency Skits
7:30–8:00	Debriefing and summary

Setting the Stage—Lecturette

This chapter focuses on both domestic and international diversity. With shorter class sessions, the instructor may wish to do domestic diversity one day and international diversity in the next session.

In a class devoted to domestic diversity, Kanter's "Tale of O" video (Goodmeasure Co.), based on the findings from her *Men and Women of the Corporation*, is effective, as is the simulation Star Power. We sometimes have students bring in internet articles on diversity and report on what they've learned. Some instructors use the premeeting preparation as the basis for an Individual Differentness Exercise that appeared in a previous edition of the workbook. The instructions for that exercise are included in this chapter of the manual. You can also use the Bestfoods Case, the last integrative course in the workbook, in a domestic diversity session.

For the international session, we begin the lecture by reiterating the need for managing diversity both domestically and internationally. We briefly present the material in the Topic Introduction—the pros and cons of culture, ethnocentrism and stereotyping, task versus relationship, individualism versus collectivism, and Hofstede's dimensions. We mention that Hofstede's theory has its critics and, while we don't necessarily agree with all the characteristics in his dimensions, the four dimensions do help us understand cultural differences when we contrast cultures. At this point, we show students the transparency (T12.0), "Hofstede's Value Dimensions."

As a way to segue into the exercise and profit from the resources in the classroom, we ask who has had (or is having) a cross-cultural experience. Next we ask these students what cultural differences they noted and why these differences exist. This helps students understand how cultures do things differently so they are more prepared to come up with ideas for the exercise.

Issues to Consider in Leading the Experiential Exercise

CROSS-CULTURAL COMPETENCY SKITS
A. If you wish, you can assign these skits ahead of time so the groups prepare them outside of class. These skits are generally hilarious as well as enlightening. Sometimes I turn this into a game-show contest with the rest of the class; learning groups or teams sit together and compete to get the right answers most quickly. Each team has a bell to hit, and winners are thrown some kind of intercultural treat (usually edible).

THE EMBASSY RECEPTION
B. This exercise is usually very entertaining and a wonderful opportunity for students to be creative. However, there is a danger that some students may clown around too much. It's good to have fun with the exercise as long as students are learning from it. Instructors can avoid problems here by taking a businesslike approach, conveying that students should take the exercise seriously, and ensuring in the beginning of the strategy section that groups are working well.

C. The purpose of this simulation is to have students create a culture from scratch by applying Hofstede's value dimensions. Make sure that students understand the task; some will be confused or even annoyed when told to create their own culture. State the instructions in your own words and remind them of all the different things they notice in another culture and encourage them to be creative. It is normal for groups to struggle with this task in the beginning moments.

D. Emphasize that groups should not read each other's instructions. Encourage students to try to be loyal to the description of their culture to gain maximum learning.

E. During the **debriefing**, we often find that the words used to describe the other group (question #a) are negative. If this occurs, we ask students why. They usually respond that we usually perceive differences in other cultures in a negative rather than a positive fashion.

In response to question #b, look for similarities and differences concerning interacting with the other culture. There are many common feelings (uncertainty, awkward, suspicious, scared, etc.) that are good to point out, especially if there are international students in your class who are not completely integrated.

The questions on norms and values may highlight that other cultures make perfect sense to their members, but outsiders make attributions that are often incorrect.

F. Instructors can take advantage of this chapter to help the class manage its own diversity better. Be careful not to put minority students on the hot seat without their permission. You can do this by directing questions to everyone, "What do you think it's like to be a minority or international student on this campus?" "What could we do to make minorities and international students feel more comfortable in this class or on campus?"

Instructions for the Individual Differentness Exercise

The purpose of this exercise is to explore group members' experiences of being different, to appreciate and learn from these experiences, and to use this learning to generate practical principles for the constructive management of differences among people—principles that would have helped you in the situation you described in the prework.

Step 1. Find the person in the group who is most similar to you on the "intensity of differentness" scale (20 minutes). Members of the total group should circulate to find the person with a similar score. Start with similar total scores and then try to find someone you agree with on each question. If there is an odd number of people, form one trio of individuals who are similar. Try not to pair up too quickly. Take your time to find the person most like you.

Step 2. Pair off with this person and share your experience of "differentness" with them (20 minutes). Listen carefully to your partner's description, asking questions of clarification only. In the next step you will need to be able to describe your partner's experience to someone else.

Step 3. Each pair should now find the pair of persons in the room who were most different from them on the intensity of differentness scale (10 minutes).

Step 4. In the resulting quartets, each individual's experience of difference should be reported by his or her partner (30 minutes).
— Discuss and ask questions about these experiences so that all four individual experiences are understood by everyone.
— Prepare a report for the total group listing ways in which the situations described in your group could have been managed more effectively—things the individual who felt different could have done and things that other people in the situation could have done.

Step 5. Reports and discussion in the total group (40 minutes). Each quartet should report its findings to the larger group. Discuss the following questions that relate the conclusions reached in the quartets to your here-and-now experiences in the exercise.

a.   During today's exercise, did I at any time feel different from others in the group?
b.   In what ways?
c.   Did others in the group experience my differences? How did they show it? Do they share this perception now?
d.   In what ways did I feel similar to others in the group?
e.   Are these differences and similarities the same as or different from the one(s) I listed in my preparation?
f.   How did the group(s) I was part of today manage difference?
g.   How did we use our differences to enrich our work? Or hinder it?
h.   How did we suppress our differences?

Leading the Exercise
A.   The aim in creating this exercise is to legitimize discussion of racial and sexual differences that often exist in groups. By beginning with a focus on each individual's experience of being treated as different, some empathy for others' feelings is stimulated.

B.   Encourage members to explore the group thoroughly to find the person whose score is most like theirs. There is a tendency to quickly pair up with the first person individuals talk to, which should be avoided. This is a chance for students to see the range of experiences in their class.

C.   Students are in a sensitive place when they return for the class discussion and somewhat hesitant to discuss any further their experiences, which were unpleasant for many of them. At this point, one instructor talks about a situation that all or most members of the class share, for example, living in a particular region of the country and being made to feel different because of that. This helps students rejoin the class.

Transparency Masters

T12.0   HOFSTEDE'S VALUE DIMENSIONS

Exam and Review Questions

1.   Those parts of you or your actions that do not fit into your organization's image of the "ideal" person are called
      a.   perceived competence.
      b.   perceived eccentricity.
      c.   perceived performance.

      d.   perceived image.

2.   Give an example, either real or hypothetical, of perceived competence = perceived eccentricity. Explain its importance in organizational life. (essay)

3.   The exaggerated tendency to think that one's own group or race is superior to another group or race is known as
      a.   cultural bias.
      b.   attribution error.
      c.   superiority complex.
      d.*   ethnocentrism.

4.   Identify and define each of Hofstede's five value dimensions.

Answer:
- *Power distance*—the extent to which a society accepts the fact that power in institutions and organizations is distributed unequally
- *Uncertainty avoidance*—the extent to which a society accepts or avoids uncertain and ambiguous situations
- *Individualism*—the extent to which people are responsible for taking care of themselves and give priority to their own interests. Its opposite is collectivism
- *Masculinity*—the extent to which the dominant cultural values are assertiveness, the acquisition of money and things—as opposed to its opposite, femininity, which refers to the dominant values of caring for others, quality of life, and people
- *Long-term vs. short-term orientation*—Long-term orientation show a greater concern for the future and values thrift and perserverance; short-term orientation is more concerned with the past and present and values tradition and fulfilling social obligations

5.   The notion that older workers are less productive is a
      a.   prejudice.
      b.*   stereotype.
      c.   myth.
      d.   projection.

6.   Which of the following is *not* a true statement?
      a.   Stereotyping blocks learning in organizations.
      b.   Stereotyping is partly responsible for the glass ceiling facing female executives.
      c.   Stereotyping denies individual uniqueness.
      d.*   Stereotyping is uncommon in non-American cultures.

7.   Which does Kanter identify as a typical experience of tokens in large organizations?
      a.   They are virtually ignored.
      b.*   Their behavior is closely scrutinized.
      c.   Performance pressures are low.
      d.   Differences are minimized.

8.   Which of these is *not* a common stereotype for tokens?
      a.   Militant
      b.*   Martyr
      c.   Mascot
      d.   Sex object

9.   What four reasons should prompt organizations to see diversity as a business issue?

Answer:

❑ There are clear benefits to having diverse viewpoints.
❑ You can better understand the needs of diverse customers.
❑ There are turnover costs to losing women and minorities to the competition.
❑ You will have a competitive advantage in attracting and retaining well-qualified employees.

10. Diversity training should emphasize all of the following *except*
   a. an appreciation of differences.
   b. a focus on similarities.
   c.* an understanding of the legalities.
   d. diversity as a competitive advantage.

Reader Exam and Review Questions

Gender Gap in the Executive Suite: CEOs and Female Executives Report on Breaking the Glass Ceiling by Ragins et al.

11. According to Ragins et al., the top career advancement strategy employed by successful women is
   a. have an influential mentor.
   b. network with influential colleagues.
   c. seek difficult or high visibility assignments.
   d.* consistently exceed performance.

Cultural Constraints in Management Theories by Hofstede

12. According to Hofstede, uncertainty avoidance refers to a country's
   a. social framework.
   b.* need for rules and regulations.
   c. power distribution.
   d. sense of history.

13. Hofstede found that Americans value equality, which means that they are
   a.* low in power distance.
   b. high in power distance.
   c. high in masculinity.
   d. high in individualism.

14. Americans value achievement and striving more than nurturance and support according to Hofstede. This makes them
   a. above average in power distance.
   b. low in uncertainty avoidance.
   c. average in power distance.
   d.* above average in masculinity.

15. Provide cultural examples for each of Hofstede's cultural dimensions.

Beyond Sophisticated Stereotyping: Cultural Sensemaking in Context by Osland and Bird

16. How do Osland and Bird define sophisticated stereotyping?

Answer: Sophisticated stereotyping expects all people from the same culture to display the same cultural value dimensions.

17.   Draw Osland and Bird's cultural sensemaking model.

       Answer: See Fig. 1 in Reader article

Reader Articles

1.   MYTHS ABOUT DIVERSITY by *Judith T. Friedman and Nancy DiTomaso*
2.   GENDER GAP IN THE EXECUTIVE SUITE: CEOS AND FEMALE EXECUTIVES REPORT ON BREAKING THE GLASS CEILING by *Belle Rose Ragins, Bickley Townsend, and Mary Mattis*
3.   CULTURAL CONSTRAINTS IN MANAGEMENT THEORIES by *Geert Hofstede*
4.   BEYOND SOPHISTICATED STEREOTYPING: CULTURAL SENSEMAKING IN CONTEXT by *Joyce S. Osland and Allan Bird*

Chapter 13
LEADERSHIP

Materials Needed: Blindfolds for everyone but the observers. (You can cut up old sheets if you have no budget for materials.) A length of rope or clothesline for each group of no more than 18 people. For the length of the rope, figure a yard for each person and then add at least 4 yards more. It does not hurt if the rope is much longer than that is permitted by the space you are using; the exercise will be compromised, however, if the rope is too short. Please note that the facilitator instructions for the exercise are found on page 301 of the workbook.

Objectives: By the end of this chapter, students should be able to:

A. Define leadership
B. Describe what followers expect of leaders
C. Differentiate between leadership and management
D. Identify the traits related to leader success
E. Define initiating structure and consideration behavior
F. Explain what we mean by a contingency theory of leadership
G. Distinguish among transformational, transactional, and charismatic leaders
H. Explain servant leadership

Sample Design

6:00–6:30	Lecturette on leadership
6:30–7:00	Group exercise
7:00–7:10	Individual reflection
7:10–7:30	Group discussion
7:30–8:00	Debriefing

Setting the Stage—Lecturette

This is the first chapter in the third part of the book. The focus in this part of the course is on leadership in relation to organizational culture, decision making, power and influence, empowerment and coaching, and performance appraisal.

In the opening lecturette, we briefly explain the evolution of leadership theory. There are transparencies of the leadership continuum (T13.0) and the "Path Goal Theory" (T13.1). We try to make sure that students have a thorough understanding of the contingency aspect of leadership, especially because the exercise provides an opportunity to see what type of leadership emerges in a unique situation.

Issues to Consider in Leading the Experiential Exercise

A. This is a very effective exercise. However, the larger the groups, the more difficult and frustrating the exercise becomes. If your class is large, divide it into smaller groups of no more than 18 people and make at least three people per group into observers. The ideal group size is 8–14. This is an exercise in which students may learn more by not being in their normal learning groups with established leadership patterns. It is not difficult to run several groups at a time if you have a large area so that you can keep your eye on all of them at once. Another way to work with a very large class is to assign a facilitator for each group and give them responsibility for managing the exercise, a bag with the blindfolds and rope they will need, and the **Facilitator Instructions for the Perfect Square** found on page 301 of the workbook. Tell them when they need to return to the classroom. The only warning here is to make sure they read and assimilate the instructions. You may want to give them a copy before the class with the understanding that they will not tell other students what will happen in the exercise.

Variation: You can ask each group to identify the informal leaders and then mute them for the exercise, either publicly or after the exercise has already started. This forces other leaders to step forward and teaches some lessons to those who feel compelled to lead all the time.

B. The instructor should ask if anyone has done the Perfect Square exercise in the past and would therefore like to be an observer. (Even if a person has done the exercise before, that is no guarantee that the rest of the group will listen to his or her instructions.)

C. Keep your eye on the person who has the excess rope. What did that person do about it? How long did it take for the group to become aware of this? This is an analogy for people in organizations who have information that leaders lack.

D. Some groups will come up with the idea of having a member go inside the square and walk around it to measure off the sides. As long as both hands are kept on the rope at all times, this is permissible. Some instructors suggest this to the groups near the end of their time period if the group appears to be failing. If you don't suggest it and one group does it on their own, this can be a lesson in taking initiative and pushing against perceived constraints.

E. In the **debriefing**, do not let the group focus too much on strategies for making the square. There are a variety of ways to form the square successfully; there is no one best strategy. The factor that determines whether a particular strategy works is how effectively the group functions. For the sake of their learning, keep the focus on the process issues. ("We could continue talking about strategies for making perfect squares, but we can probably learn more useful, generalizable lessons from how you worked together as a group.")

F. The major issues that usually surface in debriefing this exercise are leadership, communication, and decision making. Many students have trouble hearing or being heard in this exercise and therefore become angry or frustrated. It is not uncommon to see students whose body language indicates that they have "given up" and are simply waiting for the exercise to end. Students often remark that groups need basic communication ground rules—listening to everyone, active listening, and two-way communication.

G. Because the students are blindfolded, an autocratic leader often emerges (he or she who talks the loudest). If the group is not successful, they may blame the leader. This points up the dangers of autocratic leadership—heaven help you if you're wrong. If this occurs, support the leader by acknowledging there's a price to be paid for taking on leadership and help the leader see the effect of his or her leadership style.

H. You may want to write on the board the answers to questions Step 5. b. and c. (things that helped and hindered).

I. Sometimes leaders push the group to follow a strategy without gaining their approval or commitment. In the debriefing, students often mention that they should have followed the problem-solving cycle—asked for solutions from everyone, chosen the best solution, and then moved ahead. Most groups who have not worked together have no vehicle for making decisions.

J. One of the best leadership analogies that usually comes out in this exercise is the importance of communicating the leader's vision. Because people are blindfolded, someone has to transmit a vision (the strategy for making the square) to all the members. If a leader just gives instructions without communicating the overall plan and its logic, group members unwittingly make mistakes during the exercise (e.g., letting go of the halfway point of the rope that a leader has painstakingly measured).

K. At some point, students will probably talk about the effect of being blindfolded. In response to Step 7. d., students define good followers as good listeners, being disciplined and not taking up air time for frivolous reasons, asking for clarification when they are not sure about what's been communicated, voicing reservations, and having a positive attitude.

L.   We bring in Kouzes and Posner's five practices and ask students to identify examples of these practices during the exercise. After a brief summary of the findings on charismatic leaders, we bring up the concept of servants as leaders and ask if they've ever seen one in action.

M.   General procedure for the exercise (for facilitators only). The group should form a moderately tight circle away from a wall or sidewalk that would make it too easy for them to determine their location. (Once you've passed out the blindfolds and they can't see, some facilitators like to lead the group around in a twisting fashion so they really have no idea where they are.) Pass out the blindfolds. Ask for a predetermined number of volunteers to be observers. When the others are blindfolded and cannot see, give them the instructions below and pass out the rope. Don't let them see the rope ahead of time because they should not know its length. When you pass out the rope, make sure there is a lot of rope left over at one end. Leave this slack behind the last group member to receive the rope. This should be a quiet person so we can see whether the group listens to people who aren't leaders. Don't tell the group that there is leftover rope. Note what time they start and when 15 minutes have passed, tell them they have 5 minutes left. Call time and have them answer the questions in Step 5 indiviuidally. Then discuss these as a group during the next 20 minutes and choose a representative to report back to the class as a whole.

FACILITATOR INSTRUCTIONS FOR THE PERFECT SQUARE
1.   *Read the participants these instructions:*
        Please form a circle. Who would like to observe this exercise? The observers can stand outside the circle and read their instructions on page 294. Everyone else should put on a blindfold so you cannot see. I'll give you the rest of the instructions once everyone is blindfolded.

        Your task is to form a perfect square utilizing all the rope that I am passing out. Here are the rules:
        1.   Use all the rope so that your square is taut, with no slack.
        2.   You must keep both your hands on the rope at all times.
        3.   You have 20 minutes to form a perfect square.
        I can repeat these rules if you like, but after that I cannot answer any questions. Shall I repeat the rules?

2.   Notification of 5-minute warning (after 15 minutes have passed).

3.   Call time when 20 minutes are up and refer them to Step 5 on page 293.

Transparency Masters

T13.0   CONTINUUM OF LEADERSHIP BEHAVIOR
T13.1   THE PATH GOAL THEORY

Workbook Exam and Review Questions

1.   In the vignette, "Arrogance: The Executive Achille's Heel" in addition to arrogance, what were the other two reasons for manager failure?
        a.   Lack of honesty and people skills
        b.   Lack of communication and organizational skills
        c.   Lack of creativity and tact
        d.*   Lack of commitment and loyalty

2.   Which of the following is *not* part of the definition of leadership?
        a.*   Establish procedures for a group

b. Motivate group members to achieve goals
c. Establish direction for a group
d. Gain group members' commitment

3. According to U.S. research, followers expect four characteristics of their leaders. What are they?

Answer:
- ❑ Integrity
- ❑ Competence
- ❑ Forward-looking
- ❑ Inspiring

4. When employees perceive leaders to have high credibility and a strong philosophy, employees are more likely to do all of the following *except*
a. be proud to tell others they are part of the organization.
b. talk up the organization with friends.
c.* feel affirmed in their independence.
d. feel a sense of ownership.

5. Schemas of what constitutes good leadership vary from one culture to another. In the United States, people value
a. authoritarian leaders.
b. energetic leaders.
c. independent leaders.
d.* charismatic leaders.

6. When working with people from different cultures or ethnic groups, it is very important to understand their accustomed leadership style and
a. conform.
b.* adapt.
c. retrain them.
d. enlighten them.

7. What's the key difference between managers and leaders?

Answer: Leaders tend to produce change whereas managers tend to produce order and predictability, the key results expected by stakeholders.

8. Good leadership makes it easier for employees to adapt to (change).

9. Leader are born, not made.
_____True or __X__False
Why or why not?

Answer: Although some leadership traits, such as intelligence and high energy, are inherited, many more are learned, such as drive, honesty and integrity, leadership, motivation, self-confidence, knowledge of the business, creativity, and flexibility. Therefore, it *is* possible to develop and train people to be leaders.

10. Leader behavior that organizes and defines what group members should be doing to maximize output is called
a. consideration.
b. supportive.
c. achievement-oriented.
d.* initiating structure.

11. There is no "one best way" to lead; it depends on the (situation).

12. According to path-goal theory, leaders motivate employees when they do all of the following *except*
    a. clarify the path that will result in employee achievement.
    b.* link satisfaction to the problem-solving cycle.
    c. provide the necessary guidance and support to get the job done.
    d. remove the obstacles that block the path to goal achievement.

13. Why is House's path-goal theory called a contingency theory? Provide an example by applying this example to an organizational situation.

    Answer: In path-goal theory, the leadership style is contingent on the situation. The leader analyzes both employee and environmental factors and then decides which of the four leadership styles (supportive, directive, achievement-oriented, or participative) is most appropriate.

14. The way women and men lead
    a.* are more similar than different.
    b. are more different than similar.
    c. are the same.
    d. is inherited.

15. (Transformational) leaders are value-driven change agents who make followers more conscious of the importance and value of task outcomes.

16. Kouzes and Posner identified all of the following leadership practices *except*
    a. challenging the process.
    b. inspiring a shared vision.
    c.* empowering the mind.
    d. encouraging the heart.

17. (Transactional) leaders exchange rewards for performance.

18. Charismatic leaders develop a special relationship with their followers that includes high levels of
    a. performance, empowerment, and loyalty.
    b.* loyalty, enthusiasm, and sacrifice.
    c. commitment, empowerment, and social interaction.
    d. communication, compromise, and sacrifice.

19. Hitler was a charismatic leader.
    __X__ True or _____ False
    Why or why not?

    Answer: It's true that Hitler was charismatic and engendered loyalty, commitment, enthusiasm, and sacrifice in his followers. However, he was also unethical and motivated by personalized power, pursued his own vision and goals, censured critical or opposing views, and encouraged blind obedience, dependency, and submission.

20. Servant leadership is rooted in
    a.* spirituality.
    b. environmentalism.
    c. empowerment.
    d. philosophy.

Reader Exam and Review Questions

What Makes a Leader? by Goleman

21. According to Goleman, emotional intelligence is comprised of all of the following *except*
    a. self-awareness.
    b. motivation.
    c.* sympathy.
    d. social skill.

Why Does Vision Matter? by Nanus

22. In the article by Nanus, he asserts that the power of vision includes all of the following *except*
    a. creates meaning.
    b. provides a worthwhile challenge.
    c.* focuses on the present.
    d. creates a common identity.

SuperLeadership: Beyond the Myth of Heroic Leadership by Manz and Sims

23. Define and describe the four types of leaders mentioned by Manz and Sims. What are the pros and cons of each type of leader? (essay)

24. (Self-leadership) is the influence we exert on ourselves to achieve the self-motivation and self-direction we need to perform, according to Manz and Sims.

25. Which of the following is *not* one of Manz and Sims' seven-step processes of SuperLeadership?
    a. encourage self-set goals.
    b. create positive thought patterns.
    c. promote self-leadership through teamwork.
    d.* develop self-leadership through transactions.

Reader Articles:

1. WHAT MAKES A LEADER? by *Daniel Goleman*
2. WHY DOES VISION MATTER? by *Bert Nanus*
3. SUPERLEADERSHIP: BEYOND THE MYTH OF HEROIC LEADERSHIP *by Charles C. Manz and Henry P. Sims, Jr.*

Chapter 14
LEADERSHIP AND ORGANIZATIONAL CULTURE

Materials Needed: You may want to bring a nonpermanent marker for each learning group and make a transparency of the Ecoquest Case Summary on page 315. You can also use flip chart paper for the group summaries if you want the results to be posted for comparison purposes.

Objectives: By the end of this chapter, students should be able to:

A.   Define organizational culture and explain its function
B.   Explain how it evolves and is transmitted
C.   Describe the characteristics of a strong culture
D.   Explain the relationship between strong cultures and high performance
E.   Describe how leaders can manage culture
F.   Identify the four stages in the organizational life cycle

Sample Design

6:00–6:15	Lecturette on organizational culture
6:15–6:45	Ecoquest Case
6:45–7:05	Group Reports
7:05–7:25	Ecoquest Case Part II and debriefing
7:30–8:00	Assessing the class culture (students come with Step 1 prepared ahead of time)

Setting the Stage—Lecturette

Assign students to write up the premeeting preparation if you have doubts that all students will come to class having prepared the case. Valuable class time will be lost if they have not read Part I. **Warn students ahead of time _not_ to read Part II of the case.**

Some instructors do only the case in this session and combine the class culture assessment with the following chapter so there is more time to debrief the case. If you are going by the sample design, students should prepare their statements for Step 1 to decrease the time needed in class.

The purpose of this chapter is to help students discover the relationship between leadership and organizational culture. We highlight the fact that organizational culture is another tool that managers can use to influence motivation and performance.

In the lecturette, we briefly question students about key points in the Topic Introduction: definition of organizational culture, challenges of external adaptation and internal integration, and definition and characteristics of strong cultures. We ask students to name the most popular employer in town and figure out what makes them so popular. They usually identify a company with a strong culture. Then we ask them to analyze that organizational culture and make the point that strong cultures attract employees. We ask students what they see as the pros and cons of strong cultures. We point out the link between high performance and strong cultures that focus on key constituencies (customers, stockholders, and employees) and have good leadership at all levels. We ask MBAs for (and give undergraduates) examples of organizational culture and "fit" issues in local companies.

When we have time, we have learning groups diagnose the University's culture and bring in artifacts that relate to the University's basic values and beliefs. A spokesperson from each group explains their conclusions.

Sometimes students ask us to distinguish between climate and culture. Many large organizations periodically undertake climate surveys to "take the temperature" of their organizations. Climate measures the extent to which individuals' expectations about what it should be like in an organization are being met. Culture, on the other hand, is a pattern of beliefs and expectations. Culture is more concerned with the nature of the expectations themselves than with measuring them.

We touch on the growth stages and Greiner's model of evolution and revolution during the debriefing. Afterwards, we talk about subcultures and Schein's article on three cultures in the reader.

Issues to Consider in Leading the Experiential Exercise

A. If you are using transparencies or flip charts, pass those out in the beginning of the exercise.

B. The purpose of the case is to determine the person with the optimal managerial style and job fit to take the company through a coming period of transition in which there will be more of a premium on rational management and less on entrepreneurial activity.

C. As with most case discussions, there will be much disagreement about who the appointee should be and what should be done to provide continuity. This may even be a little exaggerated by the procedure, which asks the students to do the original analysis first as individuals and then as a small group before sharing their recommendations. As a result, their positions sometimes harden.

D. You may want to remind students to use their group skills to come to a consensus. Usually by this time in the course, the groups do not experience too much difficulty making a decision. If there is a group that cannot compromise and their time is running out, remind them of lessons learned in previous classes (problem solving, conflict, group dynamics) and ask them what process skills they could use to arrive at a decision. Agreeing on criteria first helps some groups. Usually all the instructor has to do is remind them of the time deadline and their upcoming presentation.

E. In Step 3. a., ask the group representatives to give their report from the front of the room when it's their turn. You may want to announce that it is not necessary to repeat points (characteristics of each manager) that other groups have already made. This prevents boredom from hearing the same thing numerous times and encourages students to listen to other groups, think on their feet, and consider their audience. We clap for presenters and sometimes provide public speaking tips.

F. Have the students read Part II to themselves and answer the Class Discussion Questions that follow. In the **debriefing**, you should avoid getting caught up in a right-wrong decision. This case underscores the complexity of succession decisions and the difficulty of predicting human behavior.

We ask if anyone has experience working with small businesses run by principals. "Did you notice any similarities or differences with the Ecoquest case?"

G. When discussing question #2, you can show them transparency T14.1, "The Five Phases of Growth," and ask students to determine which stage best describes Ecoquest (collectivity with some need for more formalization). This is further justification for choosing Mike. He is a good example of a person whose strengths threaten to become weaknesses. He is not a master manager in Quinn's terms because he is overly focused on rational goal and internal process to the exclusion of human relations.

H. One of the most significant lessons of the case is the importance of fit with regards to leadership and organizational culture. Sometimes students ask if Mike's failure means that an organization is doomed to always have the same type of leader. The lesson of Greiner's "Evolution and Revolution" article is that organizations do need different types of leaders to pilot companies through different stages of growth. The answer to the students' question, then, is that organizations can and should hire different types of leaders. However, the success of doing so will depend on several factors: an understanding of the organizational culture and its strength and resistance to change, the new leader's capacity to modify the culture and make the necessary organizational changes, and, if necessary, the leader's ability to adapt his or her own leadership style so there is a closer fit with the culture. This leads into Schein's primary mechanisms for creating or modifying culture.

I.   By utilizing Assesing the Organizational Culture of the Classroom in the last portion of the class (or a second session in the case of shorter class sessions), instructors can check on how students feel about both the classroom and their learning group. This is an excellent time to trot out the transparency (T1.2) of Sherwood and Glidewell's Pinch Model of planned renegotiation from Chapter 1. If the data seem to indicate dissatisfaction with the way the class is going, it is useful to renegotiate the original understanding in light of what has happened since then. There should be no blaming, just an acknowledgment of changing needs and the necessity of taking corrective action.

If you have used a midcourse evaluation form like the one in Appendix E before this session, this is a good time to make some of that feedback known to students. In addition to suggestions for the instructor, there is often feedback for students, elicited by the question, "Is anything hindering your learning?" We strongly recommend midcourse evaluations.

NOTE: If you are using Chapter 15 next, it helps to take a few minutes at the end of this class to explain what they must do in the premeeting preparation for Chapter 15.

Transparency Masters

T14.0   UNCOVERING LEVELS OF CULTURE
T14.1   FIVE PHASES OF GROWTH

Workbook Exam and Review Questions

1.   What is the definition of organizational culture?

Answer: The pattern of shared values and beliefs which produces certain norms of behavior; "the way we do things around here."

2.   Which of the following factors has the *least* influence on determining an organizational culture?
a.*   Attitudes about your competitors
b.   Values of the founder(s)
c.   The external environment
d.   Solutions to problems over time

3.   Which of the following is *not* a characteristic of a strong culture?
a.   Employees can easily identify the dominant values.
b.*   To add diversity, the selection processes target people who will challenge the culture and enrich it.
c.   Managers measure and control what is important to the culture.
d.   By their behavior, leaders and managers send clear, consistent signals about desired values and norms.

4.   What is the main difference between weak and strong cultures? Give an example of an organization with a strong culture.

Answer: Strong cultures have core values and beliefs that are intensely held, more widely shared, and more ordered. Employees know which values are most important.

5. According to the text, there should be a "fit" between the organizational culture and all of the following *except*
    a.   people.
    b.*   structure.
    c.   strategy.
    d.   organizational task.

6. Lack of external (adaptation or fit) was the impetus for some of the widespread restructuring that U.S. industry has undergone in recent years.

7. What are the advantages and disadvantages of strong cultures?

    Answer:
    Advantages:
    ❑   High performance under certain conditions
    ❑   Clear sense of purpose
    ❑   More value-driven decision making
    ❑   Employee commitment, loyalty, and pride
    Disadvantages:
    ❑   Pressure for conformity
    ❑   Resistance to change

8. Name three ways in which culture is transmitted. Give an example of one way in which Southwest Airlines transmits culture according to the opening vignette.

    Answer: Culture is transmitted through socialization, stories, symbols, jargon, rituals and ceremonies, and statements of principles.

9. (Socialization) is the systematic process by which organizations bring new members into their cultures.

10. The pink Cadillacs awarded to successful salespeople by Mary Kay Cosmetics is a (symbol) of the company's cultural values.

11. The primary mechanisms a leader can use to create, transmit, or change culture include all of the following *except*
    a.*   the reactions of leaders to the day-to-day business of the organization.
    b.   deliberate role modeling, teaching, and coaching.
    c.   criteria for recruitment, selection, promotion, retirement, and excommunication.
    d.   criteria for allocating rewards and status.

12. All of the following are organizational stages of growth according to the text *except*
    a.   entrepreneurial.
    b.   elaboration.
    c.*   embryonic.
    d.   formalization.

13. What managers do to reinforce culture is stronger than what they (say).

14. Cultures that promote ethical behavior were found to be high in both
    a.   rules and socialization.
    b.   rules and conflict avoidance.
    c.   nonconformity and risk taking.
    d.*   risk taking and conflict tolerance.

Reader Exam and Review Questions

Uncovering the Levels of Culture by Schein

15. Which level of culture is the easiest to decipher, according to Schein?
    a.   Values
    b.   Basic assumptions
    c.*   Artifacts & creations
    d.   Theories in action

Three Cultures of Management: The Key to Organizational Learning by Schein

16. List the three cultures of management according to Schein.

    Answer:
    ❑ Operator culture
    ❑ Engineering culture
    ❑ Executive culture

17. Which of the following is *not* an assumption of the executive culture as defined by Schein?
    a.*   Cultural focus
    b.   Hierarchical and individual focus
    c.   Task and control focus
    d.   Financial focus

Evolution and Revolution as Organizations Grow by Greiner

18. According to Greiner, which of the following statements concerning organizational growth is true?
    a.   Most growing organizations expand for two years and then retreat for one year.
    b.*   Evolutionary periods tend to be relatively short in fast-growing organizations.
    c.   Revolutions are easier to resolve when the market environment is poor.
    d.   Periods of evolution have little effect on periods of revolution.

19. The coordinated phase of organizational growth is caused by demand for
    a.   a strong business manager.
    b.   greater autonomy on the part of lower-level managers.
    c.   decreased red tape.
    d.*   control over the total company.

20. Greiner writes that organizational solutions cause problems for the future.
    __X__ True or _____False
    Why or why not?

    Answer: The solution to a growth problem is often carried to extremes or becomes unwieldy as the organization grows. Therefore, the solution becomes a problem as the organization becomes larger. Each of Greiner's revolutions has its seeds in the solution to the previous phase.

Reader Articles

1. UNCOVERING THE LEVELS OF CULTURE by *Edgar H. Schein*
2. THREE CULTURES OF MANAGEMENT: THE KEY TO ORGANIZATIONAL LEARNING by *Edgar H. Schein*
3. EVOLUTION AND REVOLUTION AS ORGANIZATIONS GROW by *Larry Greiner*

Chapter 15
DECISION MAKING

Materials Needed: None.

Objectives: By the end of this chapter, students should be able to:

A.   Explain why decision making is a social process
B.   Describe four models of decision making
C.   Explain groupthink
D.   Identify your personal approach to organizational decision making
E.   Apply the leader-participation model of decision making

Sample Design

6:00–6:30	Lecturette on decision making
6:30–7:00	Teams reach consensus
7:00–7:20	Debriefing
7:20–8:00	Groupthink and intuitive decision making

Setting the Stage—Lecturette

You can do the classroom exercise in 80–90 minutes. With a longer class session, you may want to use a video like "Groupthink Revisited." Bear in mind, however, that subsequent research does not support Janis's findings in full (see the research cited in the workbook, endnote #12). Nevertheless, it doesn't hurt for students to be aware of group pressures for conformity and to learn ways to minimize them.

It is essential that students come to class with the cases prepared.

We do a desert-survival type exercise in the Saturday Special where we cover the rational decision-making process. However, you can briefly review that model as well as bounded rationality and the garbage can in your lecturette if you wish.

It is not feasible to teach the highly complex version of Vroom and Jago's work without their computer software. But the workbook does include the latest, simplified version of their model. **Please note there are several differences from the previous edition with regard to the model**: fewer leadership styles to choose from, no distinction between group and individual problems, four decision criteria, a simpler decision tree, and slightly different answers to the cases.

Previous work on the issue of leadership and decision making consistently identifies three factors that need to be taken into account in determining appropriate decision making styles (e.g., Tannebaum and Schmidt leadership continuum):
1.   Leaders' personal preferences and predispositions
2.   Subordinates' personal preferences and predispositions
3.   The nature of the situation or decision

Earlier units in this text have as their primary focus the first two of these factors—the motives, needs, and interpersonal styles of individuals. Vroom's work (with others) allows for examination of how decisions ought to be made from a rational analysis of the nature of the situation or decision. Vroom's theory seems complex to some students, so make sure they have a good understanding of the theory before you begin the exercise.

In the lecturette we state that, as we saw in the Perfect Square exercise, the leader does not have to come up with the solution or decision. He or she is responsible, however, for determining how the decision should be made. When should managers make decisions on their own and when should they involve others? To determine this, managers have to know who has the necessary information and what are the attitudes and likely reactions of people affected by the decision. We introduce the idea of compliance and commitment here (which comes up again in the power and influence chapter) in relation to the implementation of decisions. Thus, decision making is a social process rather than a logical choice. The difference between Vroom's model and decision trees that students may come across in other business courses is that it includes contingencies that reflect our knowledge of human behavior.

We acknowledge a few intellectual debts that help us understand Vroom's model: (1) Follett's contribution that the natural reaction of people being bossed is to become less and less proactive. This is a built-in danger to an autocratic style. Her suggestion that we look at the "situation as the boss" helps set students up for a contingency approach to decision making. (2) Barnard's "zone of indifference" helps us zero in on the idea of the acceptance of the decision made by a boss. At any point in time, there's usually at least one juicy example on a university campus in which the administration has made a decision that was outside the students' zone of indifference. It's also easy to come up with examples of administrators asking faculty to participate in decisions that fall within their zone of indifference, provoking another round of complaints about time-wasting committee meetings. The lesson here is that managers have to know their employees or stakeholders well enough to know what falls within and without their zone of indifference. (3) Schmidt and Tannenbaum's "Continuum of Leadership Behavior" (T13.0) to give students a visual image of the leadership continuum. We note that we are building on the contingency theory groundwork laid in the preceding chapter on leadership.

We show the students Vroom's leadership styles continuum (T15.0) and explain the letters and numbers (II = involves more people/group). We explain the four criteria of decision effectiveness and the difference between structured and unstructured problems. Some students have difficulty with "the quality or rationality" of the decision, so you may have to explain this in greater depth.

We try to convey the logic of the model, which is captured in Table 15.2. Then we put up the transparency (T15.1) of the decision tree and ask them to answer each question and trace our route through the example on page 339.

Issues to Consider in Leading the Experiential Exercise

A. Make it clear when reading the Procedure for Group Meeting that learning groups should trace through the tree for each case, just as we just did for the example. If the group traces the cases in different workbooks and labels them, it is much easier for the group to know where their analyses differed from Vroom's when we get to the debriefing.

B. We tell groups to quickly record their answers on the Case Analysis Record Form so they have enough time to trace through the decision tree with every case.

C. It saves time if the instructor makes a chart on the blackboard, similar to the Case Analysis Record Form, where groups can write the style they chose for each case.

D. As the groups are working, we circulate and answer occasional questions about the definition of quality requirements and structured problems.

E. Sometimes groups have trouble figuring out how they came up with such a different set of answers from Vroom's. If you suggest that they follow their trail for a particular case as you read the answers, you can avoid this problem.

F. Before reviewing Vroom's choices on page 348 to debrief, we remind students that the major opportunity for learning is to see how and where they differ from Vroom's analysis. Sometimes they depart from Vroom's trail because they are not clear on a definition; other times it's due to their own predispositions and experiences. When they've missed the definition, we point that out. However, there are instances when people can make a good case for disagreeing with Vroom. Therefore, we don't set ourselves up as the defenders of his choices or state that his are the only right answers; we merely explain why we think he made that decision. ("You have a good point there, but it looks like Vroom interpreted it like this. . .and that's why you came out differently on the tree.") Make sure you can explain to them why he made each decision.

G. The focus in the debriefing should be on factors that led people to interpret the situation as they did and how personal preferences may have intervened. For example, students often disagree with the GII decision on Case Three. If you ask them why, they say things like, "What if nobody wants to go and they start fighting about it?" or "The employees should accept the assignment whether or not they want to go." If you follow up with the question, "What assumption underlies your opinion?" they begin to understand their personal predispositions. Incidentally, Osland's research on expatriate managers found that people who had a strong desire to go abroad were more effective and more satisfied overseas. Therefore, acceptance of this particular decision is very important.

H. With the last case, the discussion often centers on how much participation to allow. Students may mention the zone of indifference here. We ask why a manager would ever use a style that is more time consuming. Among other answers, we highlight the idea of developing employees and teaching them to make good decisions (which lays some groundwork for Chapter 17, Empowerment and Coaching). We mention that it's unrealistic to expect employees who have never made any decisions to be proficient when they are first promoted to a supervisory or managerial job.

I. Step 5 #b refers to the underlying assumptions of the model that are noted in the Follow-Up section:
1.   Managers are equally skilled in using the different styles.
2.   Groups are equally skilled in their adaptation to these styles.
3.   Organizational history and culture have no impact on a single decision.
Therefore, we have to understand decision making within the broader context, which a normative model like this cannot do.

J. We summarize the findings regarding the effectiveness of the model—managers who follow the model have more productive operations and satisfied subordinates.

K. Students often ask, "Do managers actually use this model?" In our experience, many good managers use some or most of it intuitively—often because they have been burned in the past by handling decisions poorly. Former students have written to say they still refer to the model when they are faced with an especially tough decision. This question is a good lead-in to the considerations listed in the Follow-Up.

L. We cover the remaining key points in the Follow-Up: the new Vroom model, cultural differences regarding decision making, and intuitive decision making. There's a lot of practical information in the Tips for Managers that we include at this time.

Transparency Masters

15.0   LEADERSHIP STYLES
15.1   THE REVISED LEADERSHIP-PARTICIPATION MODEL
15.2   THE RECOGNITION-PRIMED DECISION MODEL

Workbook Exam and Review Questions

1. It's important for leaders to understand that decision making is not an individual process but a (social) process.

2. The manager's job is to manage the decision process by
   a. not letting other decisions influence the process.
   b. guiding decision makers to the "best" solution.
   c.* assessing which information and which employees need to be involved.
   d. streamlining the process.

3. Research has found two commonly used managerial tactics that are less likely to result in successful decisions. They are
   a. intervention and subversion.
   b. rationalization and persuasion.
   c. edicts and intervention.
   d.* persuasion and edicts.

4. Name two managerial tactics that have a higher success rate than the two in the question above.

   Answer:
   ❑ Setting realistic objectives for the decision before moving on to consider options
   ❑ Intervention—pointing out performance gaps and the need for the decision, networking, calling attention to ideas that might work, and identifying and justifying new performance norms
   ❑ Participation—task forces with key individuals
   ❑ Integrated benchmarking—studying several organizations to learn from their best practices

5. Bounded rationality is based on the following assumptions *except*
   a. managers select the first alternative that is satisfactory.
   b. managers use judgment shortcuts.
   c.* managers prefer to look at all the alternatives before making a decision.
   d. both the available information and the definition of the situation are incomplete and inadequate to some degree.

6. (Heuristics) are rules of thumb based on past experience that managers use to simplify decision making.

7. In the garbage can model of decision making, the factors floating randomly inside the organization include all the following *except*
   a.* data.
   b. solutions.
   c. problems.
   d. participants.

8. In groups, people are sometimes more cautious or more risky decision makers than they would be individually. According to the text, the determining factor about which way groups shift is
   a. the persuasive abilities of group members.
   b. the environmental factors.
   c. the financial factors.
   d.* the premeeting position of the members.

9. (Groupthink) is the tendency for members of a highly cohesive group to seek consensus so strongly that they fail to do a realistic appraisal of other alternatives.

10. To avoid decisions such as Ford's decision to produce the Edsel, what should groups do about their decision-making process?
   a. Assign a devil's advocate to challenge assumptions and arguments.
   b. Adopt the perspectives of other constituencies with a stake in the decision.
   c. "Sleep on it" before a tentative decision becomes finalized.
   d.* All of the above.

11. The leader-participation model is based on evidence that the choice of leadership styles can affect these four outcomes:
   a. cost, effectiveness, time, and quality.
   b.* quality, commitment, time, and development.
   c. commitment, cost, conflict, and affect on culture.
   d. effectiveness, conflict, time, and development.

12. One of the situational contingencies that determines the appropriate leadership style concerns whether or not the problem is
   a. controversial or noncontroversial.
   b. expensive or inexpensive.
   c. structured or unstructured.
   d. product oriented or process-oriented.

13. According to Vroom, under what circumstances would an autocratic decision be justified?

   Answer: When the leader has all the necessary information and the problem is structured, subordinates are likely to accept an autocratic decision.

14. What are the pros and cons of group decisions?

   Answer:
   Pros:
   ❑ More complete information and knowledge
   ❑ Diverse views
   ❑ Increased commitment to the decision
   ❑ Increased legitimacy of the decision
   Cons:
   ❑ Time consuming
   ❑ Influenced by conformity pressures
   ❑ Influenced by a dominant person or subgroup

15. You are designing a completely new spaceship. In terms of Vroom's model, what kind of problem is this and what kind of leadership style would be most effective?
   a. Structured—autocratic
   b. Structured—participative
   c. Unstructured—autocratic
   d.* Unstructured—participative

16. The "zone of indifference" refers to the area within which employees
   a. will carry out directives without commitment.
   b. will passively resist decisions.
   c.* willingly accept decisions made by their boss.
   d. don't care whether they are consulted on decisions or not.

17.   (Intuition) is a cognitive conclusion based on a decision maker's previous experiences and emotional inputs.

18.   In Sweden, as in America, rationality is highly valued.
        _____ True or __X___False

        Answer: It's false. Swedes are more comfortable with intuitive decision making.

Reader Exam and Review Questions

Two Decades of Research on Participation: Beyond Buzz Words and Management Fads by Vroom

19.   Managers tend to use nonparticipatory decision processes when
        a.*   they possess all the necessary information.
        b.   the problem they face is unstructured.
        c.   their subordinates' acceptance of the decision is critical.
        d.   subordinates' personal goals are incongruent with the goals of the organization as manifested in the problem.

How People Really Make Decisions by Klein

20.   According to Klein, the following is true about how experienced people makes decisions *except*
        a.   they look for the first workable option, not the best option.
        b.*   they wait until all evaluations have been completed to act.
        c.   by imagining the option being carried out, they spot weaknesses and improve it.
        d.   they don't generate a large set of options.

Reader Articles

1.   TWO DECADES OF RESEARCH ON PARTICIPATION: BEYOND BUZZ WORDS AND MANAGEMENT FADS by *Victor H. Vroom*
2.   HOW PEOPLE REALLY MAKE DECISIONS by *Gary Klein*

Chapter 16
POWER AND INFLUENCE

Materials Needed: None.

Objectives: By the end of this chapter, students should be able to:

A.   Identify the three possible outcomes of an influence attempt
B.   Describe the various sources of power
C.   Identify the influence tactics people use at work
D.   Describe and utilize the four influence styles

Sample Design

6:00–6:20	Lecturette on power and influence
6:20–6:40	Share self-diagnosis prework
	Prepare for role plays
6:40–7:40	Role plays
7:40–8:00	Debriefing

Setting the Stage —Lecturette

We begin the lecturette with a demonstration of power (ordering them to do something and then asking why they did so—if you're lucky they'll say you have expert power rather than just position power), which leads into identifying powerful people and the source of their power. We ask students why it's a good thing to have power in organizations.

After defining power and influence, we present the three potential outcomes of influence attempts (commitment, compliance, or resistance) and link this back to the need for acceptance in Vroom's decision-making model. We ask students how they see people exerting influence at work and then review the "Influence Tactics" transparency, T16.0. After noting that people usually exert power in organizations by either pushing or pulling, we explain more carefully each of the four influence styles, using the "Influence Styles" transparency (T16.1) and examples (analyzing the style of well-known politicians in their countries is something students can easily relate to). We ask students what happens when someone uses a "push" style of influence; the result is often pushing back. Push styles are more likely to generate resistance, compliance when the person really wanted commitment, and "winning the battle but losing the war." This brings up the importance of understanding our own level of competitiveness; people who are both excessively competitive and noncompetitive have difficulty exerting influence. We relate this back to the competitive and accommodative conflict handling styles.

We mention once again that we need to take a contingency approach with these styles and ask students under what circumstances they would use each style.

When people seek a win-win outcome, they usually demonstrate the following behaviors.
   a.   Attending—giving others undivided attention, which is conveyed by direct eye contact and verbal and nonverbal signs that we are paying close attention.
   b.   Asking—Asking questions in a nonjudgmental manner that allows us to gain greater insight into the other party's thoughts and feelings.
   c.   Understanding—Understanding indicates to the other party that we comprehend their meaning.
   d.   Empathizing—Acknoweldges the other party's feelings.
Not harming the relationship is important in influence attempts, just as it was in negotiation.

Issues to Consider in Leading the Experiential Exercise

A. The purpose of the exercise is to give students practice in both spotting and using influence styles and seeing the results of their influence attempts.

B. You may wish to have them form their four-person groups with people outside their own learning groups. At this point in the course, they are usually ready for variety.

C. If you have a class that seems to benefit by seeing examples, you can ask for two volunteers to act out one of the role plays in front of the entire class and then critique it together. This takes more class time, but clarifies the task and models good critiqueing behavior. Before doing a role play like this, we mention that we are not expecting perfection from the person in the influencing role —they are simply providing a live example from which we can learn. When it is over, we ask that person to evaluate his or her performance first, before asking the class members to voice their opinions.

D. Make sure students do the planning questions before the role plays to emphasize that this should be a conscious, carefully thought-out process.

E. If students do not like any of the cases, they can use an example of their own—someone they want to influence in their life. The only problem with this is they sometimes get so involved in explaining the details to the person playing opposite them that they have little time left for the role play.

F. When you ask what they learned in the general **debriefing** from doing the role plays, students often mention how difficult it was to deviate from their natural style. We suggest they try to recognize and diagnose influence styles (both their own and others) in the next week since recognition is the first step towards expanding their behavioral repertoire.

We point out how managers establish influence, which is located in the Follow-Up section. We mention cultural and gender differences and ask if they observed any differences of this type in the role play exercise. Finally, we end with Drucker's advice in the vignette on managing the boss. It is natural in this type of course for students to focus on what their boss and organization does wrong. Drucker adds another perspective on the employee-boss relationship and emphasizes the employee's responsibility for working well with the boss.

Transparency Masters

T16-0   INFLUENCE TACTICS
T16-1   INFLUENCE STYLES

Workbook Exam and Review Questions

1.   Drucker (in the opening vignette) states that the subordinate's duty to the boss is to
        a.   protect the boss from unpleasant information.
        b.*   make the boss as effective as possible.
        c.   be responsible for his or her own performance.
        d.   always be available to assist the boss.

2.   Which of the following is *not* part of Drucker's advice on managing the boss?
        a.   Never expose the boss to surprises.
        b.*   Never overrate the boss.
        c.   Accept the boss as a fallible person.
        d.   Create a relationship of trust.

3. What is the difference between power and influence?

Answer: *Power* is defined as the <u>capacity</u> to influence the behavior of others; *influence* is the <u>process</u> by which people successfully persuade others to follow their advice, suggestions, or orders. A manager cannot "make a difference" without exerting power and influence over employees.

4. Briefly explain the three possible outcomes of an influence attempt.

Answer:
- Commitment—implies internal agreement
- Compliance—going along with a request or demand but not believing in it
- Resistance—rejection of influence attempt; refusal or passive-agressive behavior or seeking out a third party or superior to overrule the request

5. In the lateral relationships found in staff positions, self-managed work teams and network organizations, power does *not* come from
   a. expertise.
   b.* position.
   c. effort.
   d. charisma.

6. Which of these influence styles is *least* preferred by managers?
   a. Consultation
   b.* Pressure tactics
   c. Inspirational appeals
   d. Rational persuasion

7. The two "pull" influence styles as identified by Berlew and Harrison are
   a. common vision and assertive persuasion.
   b. assertive persuasion, participation, and trust.
   c. assertive persuasion, reward, and punishment.
   d. common vision, participation, and trust.

8. Which influence style is least likely to result in commitment?
   a.* Reward and punishment
   b. Common vision
   c. Assertive persuasion
   d. Participation and trust

9. Active listening is associated with the <u>(participation and trust)</u> influence style.

10. Individuals who are high in socialized power
    a. are unconcerned about group goals.
    b.* use a win-win approach.
    c. use a win-lose approach.
    d. desire personal dominance.

11. It is important to remember that influence attempts have both of these outcomes:
    a. win-win.
    b. win-lose.
    c. reward and punishment.
    d.* content and relationship.

12. Which of the following is *not* a characteristic of people who obtain and exercise a great deal of power?

a.*   Ambitious and political
b.   Energy and endurance
c.   Personal toughness
d.   Flexibility

Reader Exam and Review Questions

The Necessary Art of Persuasion by Conger

13.   As described in the article by Conger, which of these are *not* ways to persuade?
      a.   Resist compromise
      b.   Use a hard sell up-front
      c.   Give it an energetic one-shot effort
      d.*   All of the above

14.   Describe the four essential steps in persuasion according to Conger.
      Answer:
      ❑   Establish credibility
      ❑   Frame for common ground
      ❑   Provide evidence
      ❑   Connect emotionally

Influence with Authority: The Use of Alliances, Reciprocity, and Exchange to Accomplish Work by Cohen and Bradford

15.   Define the law of reciprocity as discussed in the Cohen and Bradford article and provide an example.

      Answer: Reciprocity is the almost universal belief that people should be paid back for what they do.

16.   Name three things influencers should do to make the exchange process effective according to Cohen and Bradford

      Answer:
      ❑   Think about the person to be influenced as a potential ally, not an adversary.
      ❑   Know the world of the potential ally, including the pressures as well as the person's need and goals.
      ❑   Be aware of key goals and available resources that may be valued by the potential ally.
      ❑   Understand the exchange transaction itself so that win-win outcomes are achieved.

17.   Think of a person at work or school that you need to influence. Apply the lessons from Cohen and Bradford's article to your situation. Analyze the situation and devise an action plan for yourself. (essay)

Reader Articles

1.   THE NECESSARY ART OF PERSUASION by *Jay A. Conger*
2.   INFLUENCE WITH AUTHORITY: THE USE OF ALLIANCES, RECIPROCITY, AND EXCHANGE TO ACCOMPLISH WORK by *Allan R. Cohen and David L. Bradford*

Chapter 17
EMPOWERMENT AND COACHING

Materials Needed: None.

Objectives: By the end of this chapter, students should be able to:

A. Describe the characteristics of high-performance organizations
B. Distinguish between command-and-control and involvement-oriented approaches of management
C. Define empowerment
D. Explain the four aspects of empowerment
E. Describe how managers can empower employees
F. Identify four different types of coaching
G. Distinguish between effective and ineffective feedback

Sample Design

6:00–6:20	Lecturette on empowerment and intro to exercise
6:20–6:40	Enterprise prepares for production
	Merger plans and observe
6:40–6:50	Production Period I and purchase
6:50–7:10	Merger teams help Enterprise teams
7:10–7:20	Production Period II and purchase
7:20–7:40	Group Analysis of consultation process
7:40–8:00	Group reports and debriefing

Setting the Stage—Lecturette

We do a very brief lecturette, as this exercise requires a good deal of time. We explain the difference between the command-and-control mentality and the involvement-oriented approach (T17.0). We define empowerment and ask them for examples of the four components (T17.1) from their own work. Students sometimes confuse meaning and impact. We introduce the exercise, pointing to the frequency of mergers and acquisitions.

Issues to Consider in Leading the Experiential Exercise

A. This is a paper-folding exercise that fabricates the Space Ship Enterprise, an aerodynamically unsound aircraft with nice lines. In actuality, the lines on the materials may be off-center. We have tried repeatedly to remedy this problem, but apparently the thickness of the workbook makes it impossible to print the lines correctly. Here's hoping they will be perfect in the 7th edition. One meticulous prof prints out his own supply. Once students understand they should guide themselves by the corner fold rather than the lines, this doesn't present a problem. You also need to ignore defective lines when you are buying planes and go by the corners.

B. We usually have pairs of learning groups work together—one becomes the Enterprise Team and the other the Merger team. If you have an uneven number of learning groups, you can have the class count off to form the appropriate number of groups. The ideal production group size is approximately 5–6 people. Facilitator teams can have fewer members (3–4) if necessary.

C. The instructions to this game sound complex, so you may want to put the schedule on the board so they can refer to it during the exercise. We usually bring an assembled spacecraft to class to serve as a prototype (even though this may involve a loss of face with your colleagues). If you make a prototype, be sure to observe the quality requirements found at the end of the instructions. Students always manage to figure out the assembly instructions, so there is no need to do more than read them the procedure instructions on page 388.

D. We usually serve as the game coordinator and also evaluate and buy the spacecraft. If you take on this role, you will need to be familiar with the time schedule and stick to it pretty rigidly so there is enough debriefing time. You also have to master the quality control points for the spacecraft. When you are buying the spacecraft, students will usually try to influence your decisions. Be strict on quality control and consistent in your judgments so you don't become a target of frustration in the exercise. Have students throw away the practice spacecraft before the first production round begins. We throw rejects directly into the wastebasket to avoid confusion. Actually we put the wastepaper basket in the center of the room and have at it.

E. Put a chart like the Enterprise Team Accounting Form on the blackboard so teams can compare their scores. Ask the students to figure out and post their own statistics.

F. It is very common to see intergroup dynamics and even conflict in this exercise. Many pairs of teams will have amicable, positive relationships, but Merger teams sometimes act in an autocratic, arrogant fashion that provokes strikes, slowdowns, or barely concealed impatience on the part of the Enterprise teams. Occasionally, the Enterprise teams want nothing to do with the Merger teams. Other than calling out warnings about time deadlines, we don't intervene.

G. Try to observe carefully how the Merger teams approach the Enterprise teams to offer help. The Merger teams often focus more on task issues—technical improvements and finances -- rather than the process issue of how the two groups will work together.

H. Have individuals on the separate teams fill out the Analysis of the Consultation Process in Step 5, page 390, and average their Enterprise or Merger team score. Put these scores on the board so students can compare the scores for each pair of teams. There is usually at least one pair in which the Merger team evaluated themselves more highly than their Enterprise team. Sometimes this results in disbelief, hurt feelings, or a sense of betrayal—in other words, a reflection of the difficulty of helping relationships. During the **debriefing**, we acknowledge these negative feelings and push the class to figure out why they occurred. That is the purpose of the helped and hindered question. It allows the class to approach it more generally and takes the heat off groups that were unsuccessful. However, sometimes it becomes obvious that a team or individual is very frustrated with what occurred and wants to focus specifically on their group experience. To use this as a learning opportunity, we first ask them to briefly list what their feelings are (so they can get beyond them) and move to analysis. ("Let's figure this out. What behaviors on the part of each team contributed to this result and why are the scores so different?") If possible, we diagram their behaviors on the board as you would an escalating conflict situation—team A did this, Team B responded with this, so team A did that, and so forth. Help them see what both teams contributed to the situation.

I. Frustrated Merger teams sometimes ask, "What can you do if the other team doesn't want you there at all?" We answer that this is not uncommon in real-life situations, in both mergers and when consultants are brought in. You can acknowledge that they don't want you and try to negotiate a psychological contract that you can both live with. ("We know you'd rather not work with us, but our boss wants us to do this. Frankly, this isn't easy for us either, but how can we make the best of it?")

J. The way the Merger teams begin their relationship with the Enterprise teams receives a lot of attention in the debriefing section. Because the latter groups have just seen the results of their efforts and how much money they won or lost (most groups lose money in the first round), their first reaction is to discuss how they can make improvements. Merger groups often unwittingly interrupt this process and disempower the Enterprise team. This is what makes this exercise such a good way to learn about empowerment and coaching. Students usually learn that they should first gauge what's happening in the Enterprise team and ask what they have come up with on their own before telling Enterprise what to do. Students often find that the teams have misconceptions about each other. Another issue that surfaces here is Theory Y and the learning curve of the

Enterprise team. For example, does the Merger team assume that Enterprise people will improve from one production round to another or do they immediately opt to replace less-productive members with their own people?

K. This is a jam-packed class session. If pressed for time, you can give the Merger Team only 15 minutes to consult. Or you can have the class as a whole talk through the chart in Step 6 after they average their subteam scores and put them on the board. If you have shorter class sessions, you can run the simulation one day and assign Steps 5 and 7, plus the chart in Step 6 after class as homework for the next session. It's not ideal to separate the debriefing from the exercise, but written reactions are better than nothing.

L. After the debriefing, we discuss coaching and turning around marginal performers. We emphasize that you need to know where marginal employees fall in the willing/unwilling and able/unable categories before you can determine what to do with them. Switching to the organizational level, we refer to the people-related best practices found in the Pfeffer & Veiga and Ulrich articles in the *Reader*. We present the characteristics of effective and ineffective feedback (T17.2) in the beginning of the Performance Appraisal class, which follows.

Transparency Masters

T17.0   COMMAND-AND-CONTROL VS. INVOLVEMENT
T17.1   FOUR ASPECTS OF EMPOWERMENT
T17.2   EFFECTIVE AND INEFFECTIVE FEEDBACK

Workbook Exam and Review Questions

1.   What are the four characteristics of today's high performance companies?

        Answer:
        ❑   Cost competitiveness
        ❑   High-quality products and services
        ❑   Innovation
        ❑   Speed

2.   In which management approach do managers make decisions, give orders, and make sure they are obeyed?
        a.   Involvement-oriented
        b   Empowerment
        c.*   Command and control
        d.   Coaching

3.   (Empowerment) is granting employees the autonomy to assume more responsibility within an organization and strengthening their sense of effectiveness.

4.   Organizations can encourage and foster empowerment by doing all of the following *except*
        a.   reducing bureaucracy.
        b   increasing access to power sources in the organization.
        c.*   training all employees to enjoy empowerment.
        d.   encouraging an organizational culture that values empowerment.

5.   Which of the following is *not* an aspect of empowerment?
        a.*   Coaching
        b.   Meaning
        c.   Impact

d.   Competence

6.   (Coaching) is a conversation that follows a predictable process and leads to superior performance, commitment to sustained improvement, and positive relationships.

7.   What are the four types of coaching?

Answer: Tutoring, counseling, mentoring, and confronting

8.   Which type of coaching would you use with an employee selected for a team who does not know how to run a meeting?

Answer: Tutoring

9.   Which type of coaching would you use with an employee who is consistently late to work?

Answer: Confronting

10.   *Fill in the blanks for these statements about feedback.*
Effective feedback is:

(descriptive)	rather than	evaluative
solicited	rather than	(imposed)
(immediate)	rather than	delayed
(suggests)	rather than	prescribes
intended to help rather than		(punish)

11.   Which of the following is *not* one of the "seven R's" used by AT&T to create a high performance culture?
a.   Respect
b.   Risk taking
c.*   Rightsizing
d.   Role modeling

Reader Exam and Review Questions

Putting People First for Organizational Success by Pfeffer and Veiga

12.   Name five of the seven practices of successful organizations according to Pfeffer and Veiga

Answer:
- ❑ Employment security
- ❑ Selective hiring
- ❑ Self-managed teams and decentralization as basic org. design elements
- ❑ Comparatively high compensation contingent on organizational performance
- ❑ Extensive training
- ❑ Reduction of status differences
- ❑ Sharing information

13.   When a private company shares its financial results with employees, would Pfeffer and Veiga view this as a positive or negative practice? Why?

Answer: This would be viewed as a positive practice because it is a means of sharing information.

Intellectual Capital = Competence X Commitment by Ulrich

14. Which of the following is *not* a tool for increasing intellectual capital according to Ulrich?
    a. Buy talent
    b.* Bundle the best people together
    c. Build talent
    d. Borrow from customers to find new ideas

Management Dialogues: Turning on the Marginal Performer by Schermerhorn, Gardner, and Martin

15. According to Schmerhorn et al., what are the three factors that comprise the individual performance equation?

    Answer: Performance = Ability X Support X Effort

16. Which of the following are *not* suggested by Schermerhorn et al., as steps to use in turning on marginal performers?
    a. Ask in a nonthreatening manner for an explanation of performance.
    b.* Address the problem in the annual performance appraisal.
    c. Express confidence that the individual will improve his or her performance.
    d. Describe the implications of their substandard work.

17. Identify a marginal performer in your organization. Apply the lessons from "Turning on the Marginal Performer" to this person. Analyze the situation and devise an action plan for improving his or her performance. (essay)

18. (Learned helplessness) refers to the tendency for people who are exposed to repeated punishment or failure to believe they do not possess the skills needed to succeed at their job.

19. When people feel competent in their work they can be expected to work harder at it.
    __X__True or _____False
    Why?

    Answer: The effectance motive comes into play. This is a natural motivation that occurs from feelings of self-efficacy.

Reader Articles

1. PUTTING PEOPLE FIRST FOR ORGANIZATIONAL SUCCESS by *Jeffrey Pfeffer and John F. Veiga*
2. INTELLECTUAL CAPITAL = COMPETENCE X COMMITMENT by *Dave Ulrich*
3. MANAGEMENT DIALOGUES: TURNING ON THE MARGINAL PERFORMER by *John R. Schermerhorn, Jr., William L. Gardner, and Thomas N. Martin*

Chapter 18
PERFORMANCE APPRAISAL

Materials Needed: None.

Objectives: By the end of this chapter, students should be able to:

A.   Explain the importance of performance feedback
B.   Describe the process of performance appraisal
C.   Identify the components of effective appraisals
D.   Demonstrate the skills required for a good appraisal
E.   Describe 360-degree feedback
F.   Explain the opposition to appraisal systems

Sample Design

6:00–6:20	Lecturette on performance appraisal
6:20–6:40	Role play demonstration
6:40–7:40	Performance Appraisal Role Plays
7:40–8:00	Debriefing

Setting the Stage—Lecturette

We begin the lecturette by asking how many students receive performance appraisals at work. Next we ask students to identify the characteristics of effective and ineffective appraisals. The class creates a list on the board.

We cover the purpose and importance of appraisals, what they symbolize to employees, and emphasize that it's a process, not an event. We ask students about the link between perception and appraisal to cover the dangers of bias. If we haven't already done so, we go over the characteristics of effective and ineffective feedback (T17.2). We also remind students about I-statements in Chapter 7 and Gibb's defensive and nondefensive climates (T7.2) asdefensiveness is one of the major difficulties in the appraisal interview. Finally, we very carefully go over the steps in the **Performance Appraisal Interview Guidelines,** which are found on page 430.

Issues to Consider in Leading the Experiential Exercise

A.   The purpose of this exercise is to give students an opportunity to practice performance appraisal skills and to consider their own performance in the course. For this reason, some instructors use this chapter near the middle of the course because that gives students time to modify their performance.

B.   It is very helpful to model for the students an appraisal interview before they evaluate one another. We ask students if they would like to see a demonstration, but if so, we need a volunteer willing to be evaluated. The other students observe and analyze the role play using the Observer Worksheet. The role play becomes a real evaluation and coaching session. This can be very helpful, for example, when the volunteer brings up a problem, such as a difficulty with speaking up in class, that other students may share. When the interview is done, we go over the Observer Worksheet questions. If the instructor is open and nondefensive about shortcomings, this creates a good learning climate for the class. Obviously, if instructors make glaring errors and come nowhere close to the guidelines, they will lose credibility.

C.   Occasionally students will complain that they do not know how another student is performing in class. It's true they may be unaware of grades, but members of one's learning group will know whether students come to class prepared and if they devote energy to the class exercises. By this time in the course, they have also had an opportunity to observe the student in a variety of situations. This is why it is important that students evaluate members of their own learning group. They have worked together on a major group project by this time, which constitutes another data point.

D. If your learning groups have more than six members, time considerations may determine whether you use trios or some other formation. Try to have groups of the same number, as smaller groups will finish earlier than larger groups. You may wish to diagram on the board how the exercise will work so that everyone in the groups has a chance to both evaluate and be evaluated (Person A evaluates Person B; Person B evaluates Person C; and Person C evaluates Person A).

E. In the debriefing, students usually mention that they found the exercise very helpful and that it is difficult to give negative feedback to a peer. Many students report that it is difficult not to give gratuitous advice when they are playing the manager.

F. Our classes have usually done a group project by this point so they also evaluate team members, using a form like that found in Appendixes C and M. We often ask students to set the evaluation criteria for team projects in class when the assignment is made. This is part of our Saturday Special. This makes the Thompson article in the *Reader* on team evaluation more relevant.

G. Carolyn Jensen, an MBA student of Dr. Jay Liebowitz at Duquesne University, designed the excellent role play exercise found in Appendix L. This exercise can be used in place of the workbook exercise.

Transparency Masters

T18.0   APPRAISAL PROCESS

Workbook Exam and Review Questions

1.   Performance appraisals are intended to improve performance and (motivate) employees.

2.   Performance appraisal should be viewed as
      a.*   an ongoing process.
      b.   a chance to rank and compare employees.
      c.   a once-a-year management task.
      d.   a chance to weed out underachievers.

3.   Performance appraisal requires that managers take on the role of
      a.   interviewer.
      b.   therapist.
      c.*   coach.
      d.   friend.

4.   The ideal performance appraisal system is designed to achieve five objectives. What are they?

      Answer:
      ❑ Provide feedback to employees to facilitate their ability to achieve organizational and personal goals.
      ❑ Provide management with data to make salary and promotional decisions.
      ❑ Identify areas for improvement to facilitate employee career development.
      ❑ Motivate employees to be more effective workers.
      ❑ Comply with equal opportunity regulations and ensure fairness.

5. One way organizations can stimulate attention from managers to the performance appraisal process is to
   a. reward managers with the least staff turnover.
   b. evaluate managers on the number of subordinates who receive high appraisals.
   c.* evaluate managers on how well they develop their subordinates.
   d. All of the above

6. Saving up negative feedback and "dumping" on an employee in an appraisal can cause a (defensive) reaction.

7. When doing performance appraisals, managers tend to rate those who are similar to them
   a. lower than those who are different from them.
   b.* higher than those who are different from them.
   c. about the same as those who are different from them.
   d. on a different scale.

8. Effective appraisal systems measure
   a. results.
   b. behaviors.
   c. personality traits.
   d.* Either a or b

8. When employees receive feedback from supervisors, peers, subordinates, and customers as well as themselves, this is known as
   a. MBO feedback.
   b. BARS feedback.
   c.* 360-degree feedback.
   d. None of the above.

10. What do total quality management proponents suggest instead of formal performance appraisals?

   Answer: Continuous feedback and coaching

Reader Exam and Review Questions

On the Folly of Rewarding A, While Hoping for B by Kerr

11. Kerr argues that behaviors that are rewarded are often those
    a. that most resemble the behaviors of the evaluator.
    b. that demonstrate emotional behaviors.
    c. that demonstrate nonemotional behaviors.
    d.* that the rewarder is trying to discourage.

12. Define goal displacement and provide an example that did not appear in the article by Kerr.

   Answer: Goal displacement occurs when the means become the ends, displacing the original goal.

13. Explain Kerr's principal argument and provide an example that did not appear in the article, which proves his thesis. Analyze your own organization—are there instances of rewarding A while hoping for B? What are they? (essay)

Team Performance Appraisals **by Thompson**

14.   Which pay system does Thompson recommend for use in a team-based organization?
       a.   Skill-based
       b.   Job-based
       c.   Education-based
       d.*   Competency-based

Reader Articles

1.   ON THE FOLLY OF REWARDING A, WHILE HOPING FOR B by *Steven Kerr*
2.   TEAM PERFORMANCE APPRAISALS by *Leigh Thompson*

Chapter 19
ORGANIZATION DESIGN

Materials Needed: Students may want to use PowerPoint.

Objectives: By the end of this chapter, students should be able to:

A. Distinguish between mechanistic and organic structures
B. Describe the three traditional types of organizational structures and their advantages and disadvantages
C. Describe horizontal and network organizations and their advantages and disadvantages
D. Distinguish between formal and informal organizational structure
E. Describe the boundaryless organization
F. Explain the differentiation-integration issue in organization design

Sample Design

6:00–6:05	Introduction to the exercise
6:05–7:05	Group Presentations
7:05–7:30	Debriefing
7:30–8:00	Lecturette and consultation on 7-S analyses

Setting the Stage—Lecturette

This is the first chapter in the last module, which is concerned with organizational effectiveness and design.

We assign the group presentations several weeks in advance. This means they can bring a handout for the class on their structure. There is no need for us to present on the functional, horizontal, and network forms in the lecture. We talk very briefly in the beginning of class, as they are focused on giving their presentations. We mention the challenges of finding the right design and provide current examples of companies struggling with this.

Issues to Consider in Leading the Experiential Exercise

A. Set whatever ground rules you wish for the presentations in terms of time, etc. If you want to focus on presentation skills, you can give them an evaluation form in advance and let students evaluate each other. This allows for more input to the grading process if you have decided to make the presentations a graded assignment.

B. Watch carefully for any differences in their presentations that might relate to working within different structures. In the **debriefing**, the success of this comparison (Step 3 b. and c.) depends on how strictly they adhered to the instruction in Step 1 b. We write the names of the three structures on the board and write down the differences they note in the appropriate column.

C. After the debriefing, we talk briefly about the contingencies and imperatives (T19.1) that drive organization design. We also talk about e-business at this point (T19.2).

D. We show the 7S model (T19.0), state the importance (and danger) of fit, and note that structure is only one aspect of design. In pairs, we have them compare the Premeeting Preparation Assignments they did analyzing their own organization using the 7-S model. We ask students to function as consultants with one another—listening actively and asking perceptive questions—as they hear their analyses and recommendations.

E. Alternative option: Sometimes we assign groups to prepare creative skits on either mechanistic or organic structures. We do this for two reasons: to give them an opportunity to practice being creative and to really think about these structures. The skits are always excellent.

Transparency Masters

T19.0 THE 7-S MODEL
T19.1 STRATEGIC IMPERATIVES AND ORGANIZATIONAL CHALLENGES
T19.2 E. ORG DIMENSIONS

Workbook Exam and Review Questions

1. A central characteristic of the open systems view of organizations is
    a. impermeable organizational boundaries.
    b. positive entropy.
    c.* environmental influence.
    d. independence of structural components.

2. When applying concepts of open systems theory, the knowledge that students gain from colleges and universities would be identified as
    a. input.
    b.* output.
    c. feedback.
    d. creative transformation.

3. What are the categories of the 7-S model? List *all* and explain *three* as they apply to your college or university.

    Answer:
    ❑ Strategy—the goals and objectives to be achieved as well as the values and missions to be pursued, the basic direction of the organization
    ❑ Structure—the anatomy of the organization that shows the formal reporting relationships and how job tasks are formally divided, grouped, and coordinated
    ❑ Systems—the formal and informal procedures that make the organization work: compensation system, training systems, accounting procedures, etc.
    ❑ Style—the way managers behave to achieve the organizations goals; how they generally interact with employees
    ❑ Staff—a demographic description of important personnel categories
    ❑ Skills—the distinctive capabilities of key personnel or the competencies for which the firm is noted
    ❑ Superordinate goals/shared vision—the guiding concepts of the organization, the values and aspirations that are taught to members

4. In the 7-S Model for organizational analysis, staff is
    a. distinctive capabilities of key personnel.
    b. line staff.
    c. administrative personnel.
    d.* demographic description of personnel categories.

5. Which is *not* a hard S in the 7-S model?
    a. Strategy
    b.* Skills
    c. Systems
    d. Structure

6. Contrast mechanistic and organic organizations and provide examples of each.

Mechanistic		Organic	
1.	Tasks broken down into specialized, separate parts	1.	Employees contribute to the common task of the unit
2.	Rigidly defined tasks	2.	Broadly defined task
3.	Centralized authority and control	3.	Decentralized authority and control
4.	Vertical communication	4.	Horizontal communication
5.	Rigid departmentalization	5.	Cross-functional teams
6.	Clear chain of command	6.	Cross-hierarchical teams
7.	Narrow span of control	7.	Wide span of control
8.	High formalization	8.	Low formalization

7. Organization (structure) is the pattern of roles, authority, and communication that determines the coordination of the technology and people within an organization.

8. The text describes three traditional organizational structures. Which of the following is *not* one of them?
   a.   Matrix
   b.*   Process
   c.   Functional
   d.   Divisional

9. The (functional) structure is becoming less popular because it does not facilitate responsiveness to variety and speed.

10. What structure is differentiated by both product and function?
   a.   Horizontal
   b.   Parallel
   c.*   Matrix
   d.   Process

11. New organizational forms such as horizontal and network organizations increase this capability according to Galbraith.
   a.   Marketing capabillity
   b.   Communication capability
   c.   Training capability
   d.*   Lateral capability

12. (Horizontal) structures focus on a complete flow of work.

13. Another name for a network organization is
   a.   modular.
   b.   hollow.
   c.   virtual.
   d.*   All of the above.

14. Describe the network organization structure and give an example of one.

   Answer: Network organizations consist of brokers who subcontract needed services to designers, suppliers, producers, and distributors linked by full-disclosure information systems and coordinated by market mechanisms. Examples are Nike, Apple Computer, Reebok, Emerson Radio, Benetton, etc.

15. When the legal department develops a particular mind-set toward their work that is quite different than people in the sales department, this is known as
    a.   formality vs. informality.
    b.*   differentiation.
    c.   interpersonal orientation.
    d.   goal horizon.

16. Champy suggests that the design principle "form follows function" be modified to
    a.   form follows environment.
    b.*   form follows customers.
    c.   form follows boundaries.
    d.   form follows resources.

17. In terms of environmental complexity, a high-moderate uncertainty environment indicates that the organization's environment is
    a.   stable and simple.
    b.   unstable and complex.
    c.*   unstable and simple.
    d.   stable and complex.

18. What are three of the strategic alliances companies may choose to minimize the risk of uncertainty in global markets?

    Answer: Joint ventures, licensing, and consortia

19. (Family businesses) are the most common form of business organization throughout the world.

Reader Exam and Review Questions

The Organization of the Future: Strategic Imperatives and Core Competencies for the 21st Century by Nadler and Tushman

20. According to Nadler and Tushman, what traditionally drives strategy?
    a.   Product
    b.   Process
    c.*   Environment
    d.   Superordinate goals

21. Which of the following is *not* a new strategic imperative as seen by Nadler and Tushman?
    a.*   Cutting edge technology
    b.   "Go-to-Market" flexibility
    c.   The management of intraenterprise cannibalism
    d.   Increased strategic clock speed

Organizing in the Knowledge Age: Anticipating the Cellular Form by Miles et al.

22. Miles, et al., discuss the organizational eras of Standardization, Customization, and Innovation in their article. Contrast the three eras in terms of their defining characteristic in the chart below:

Era	Standardization	Customization	Innovation
Org. Form	(Hierarchy)	(Network)	(Cell)
Key Asset	(Capital goods)	(Information)	(Knowledge)
Influential Mgr.	(Chief Operating Officer)	(Chief Info. Officer)	(Chief Knowledge Officer)
Key Capability	(Specialization and Segmentation)	(Flexibility and Responsiveness)	(Design Creativity)

23.   Which of the following is *not* a building block of the cellular form as theorized by Miles et al.?
      a.   Member ownership
      b.*   Symbiotic relationships
      c.   Self-organization
      d.   Entrepreneurial, adaptive cells

Up the (E)Organization!: A Seven-Dimension Model for the Centerless Enterprise by Neilson et al.

24.   In the e. org, which of the following in no longer relevant according to Neilson et al.?
      a.   Cascading leadership
      b.*   Organizational chart
      c.   Distributed governance
      d.   All of the above

Reader Articles

1.   THE ORGANIZATION OF THE FUTURE: STRATEGIC IMPERATIVES AND CORE COMPETENCIES FOR THE 21ST CENTURY by *David A. Nadler and Michael L. Tushman*
2.   ORGANIZING IN THE KNOWLEDGE AGE: ANTICIPATING THE CELLULAR FORM by *Raymond E. Miles, Charles C. Snow, John A. Mathews, Grant Miles, and Henry J. Coleman, Jr.*
3.   UP THE (E)ORGANIZATION!: A SEVEN-DIMENSION MODEL FOR THE CENTERLESS ENTERPRISE by *Gary L. Neilson, Bruce A. Pasternack, and Albert J. Viscio*

Chapter 20
MANAGING CHANGE

Materials Needed: Most instructors prefer to use **puzzle pieces** made of cardboard (ranging from cut-up folders to stronger cardboard) or some type of plastic. The audio visual departments in many universities can prepare these materials. You (or the planning teams) can cut out the pieces at the end of the book, but pieces made of stronger material are easier to manipulate. You need one set of **four envelopes** containing a total of 16 pieces for each group of 8–9 students; each envelope should be labeled A, B, C, or D. The implementation teams will need **another classroom** or area in which they can wait. **It's preferable that you provide the pieces.** If you are using the puzzle pieces in the workbook, however, students will need scissors to cut them out. However, students should not look at and work with the pieces until the group exercise begins.

Objectives: By the end of this chapter, students should be able to:

A.   Describe the nature of change
B.   Explain the essential components of the change process
C.   Understand the leader's role in the change process
D.   Define resistance to change and its function
E.   List tactics for dealing with resistance to change

Sample Design

6:00–6:20	Lecturette on managing change
6:20–6:30	Introduction to the Hollow Square exercise
6:30–7:00	Planning period
7:00–7:15	Assembly period
7:15–7:30	Group discussion
7:30–8:00	Debriefing and summary

Setting the Stage—Lecturette

We begin the lecturette by noting the need for managers to understand the change process. Many organizational decisions could be more readily implemented if they were perceived as a change process. We ask students to list what they already know about change and put their responses on the board. If necessary, we add key aspects that are missing. We acknowledge the common roadblocks to change and then present the process of planned change, using the transparency (T20.0).

The simulation relates to the stage of the process entitled "Communicating the Change." Our purpose is to allow students to experience what it's like to plan for others and communicate a change.

Issues to Consider in Leading the Experiential Exercise

A.   The instructor's first consideration is group formation. There is some advantage to having the entire class number off so that students do not work in their regular learning groups. More of the dynamics that occur in organizations will appear in these "stranger" groups than in the learning groups. As the workbook notes, each group of eight students further subdivides into a team of four implementers and four planners (3–5 planners in case of odd numbers of students). Always have four people on the implementation teams.

If you have extra students, they can be observers and assist you with the simulation. Their instructions are to note, without commenting, how the teams behave and react. Observers can also ensure that the teams observe the rules.

B. Have the groups of eight quickly decide who will be planners and who will be implementers. Tell the implementers to tear out the page containing their instructions or, if they are opposed to textbook desecration, to take their workbooks with them and a pencil and paper. However, warn them not to read anything in the workbook until the instructor arrives to give them their instructions. If the instructor is doing this, do so after you have instructed the planning teams, which need more time. Another alternative is to have a student instruct the planning team, which involves reading their instructions aloud to them. Make sure the implementers do not read ahead in the workbook and find the instructions with the puzzle key.

C. Read the planning team's instructions to them. Students can call in the implementation team whenever they wish during the 30-minute planning period. If the planners do not call them in, the implementation team will show up automatically five minutes before assembly. Write the time of the assembly and the latest time at which the implementers can enter on the board (e.g., 6:55 and 7:00). Tell the planners not to let the implementers see their instructions and, in particular, the puzzle key on the bottom of the page. Ask them to hide it or turn it over whenever implementers are in the room. Make sure you understand the rules and the logic behind them.

D. There are always students who do not really hear the instructions, which becomes obvious later on in the exercise. The most common rule transgressions are assembling the puzzle before the assembly time, mixing up the pieces (a major headache), writing down instructions for the implementers, marking the puzzle pieces, and coaching the implementers when they should only be observing. As you observe the planning teams at work, make sure they follow the rules but do so without coming off like "the enforcer." Otherwise, you may find your behavior a topic of discussion in the debriefing section. Calmly remind them of the rules ("I'm sorry, but if you check back on the rules, you'll find that the planning team is not allowed to assemble the puzzle or switch pieces because this would be an unfair advantage.")

E. It is tempting for instructors to give the teams hints. For example, students invariably ask if they can write down instructions for the implementation team. The answer, which appears in rule 3, is "no." But there is no need for you to tell them that the implementation team can take notes or make all the drawings they wish; let them figure everything out on their own.

F. Students can learn a great deal from the comparison between planning groups that call their implementation teams in early and those that do not. Therefore, if no planners think of this on their own, some instructors go to the implementers after 15 minutes have passed and "agitate." We tell each implementation team, "You're going to have to do a complex task and if they don't call you in soon, it'll be tricky to get all the instructions." Usually someone will go in and ask the planners when they will be called. **You may need to casually remind the planners at this point to cover up their puzzle keys**. Watch how the planners react. Some immediately call in the implementers while others become downright hostile at being interrupted. Note at what time each planning team calls in their implementers because this could be important in the debriefing section. If the planners never call them in, send in the implementation teams five minutes before assembly.

G. The planners should put the puzzle pieces back into the envelopes in which they came right before the assembly period begins. Make sure the teams are ready and call out a one-minute warning. At the beginning of the assembly period, remind planners <u>not</u> to talk or distract the implementers; there are always students who find this difficult.

H. You can intervene and change the exercise rules to give the implementers greater chance of success if you decide that would be best for the class. We change the rules <u>after</u> the implementation teams that have a good chance of success have already completed the puzzle and <u>if</u> it looks as if the remaining implementation teams have no chance of success (i.e., they were called in late and given confusing instructions, they have zero spatial aptitude, and they appear wildly frustrated). Our rationale is that unsuccessful groups may focus so much on losing that they overlook the other lessons of the exercise. By changing the rules about 9–10 minutes into the assembly period, groups can experience and contrast both frustration and, hopefully, some degree of success.

We announce that there will be a rule change, "For the next minute, everyone should refrain from touching the puzzle pieces; the planners can talk but the implementers may not." Some students will have trouble not touching the pieces at this point.

If there are only 2–3 minutes remaining in the assembly period and some teams are still lost, you can add another rule change. "For the next minute, no one should touch the puzzle pieces, but both planners and implementers may talk." The differences in these rule changes allow the issue of one-way and two-way communication to surface in the debriefing.

I.   When teams complete the puzzle, tell them they can silently observe the other teams at work but not distract them.

J.   The purpose of the evaluation forms on both teams, which are filled out by everyone, is to see if there are different perceptions between the two teams. Some teams may be angry with each other, especially if they were unable to complete the puzzle due to inadequate instructions.

K.   The lessons that commonly surface during the **debriefing** concern the importance of a common language (shape descriptions), an overall vision of what the team is supposed to construct (hollow square), two-way communication (which necessitates more than a 5-minute instruction period), making sure that the implementers really understand, and thinking about how to transmit the message so implementers can easily understand it (empathy).

The debriefing question about what point the planners called in the implementers is significant because the first team to do so usually wins. Implementers have enough time to digest the instructions, ask questions, and feel like part of the team rather than a "pair of hands." Planners can include implementers from the very beginning if they wish, as long as they do not show them their key to the puzzle. (A team did this once and their implementers completed the puzzle in less then a minute.) Planners too often get hung up on coming up with the perfect plan and forget all about what is occurring with the implementers. We emphasize (1) the necessity for both a high-quality solution and acceptance of the change and (2) the importance of cohesive teams for successful change.

Once the students have exhausted their own lessons, you can direct their attention to Figure 20.3.

L.   After the exercise, we talk about the manager's role in the change process, the role of resistance and how to deal with it. If the implementer teams exhibited resistance in the exercise, we ask students how this could have been avoided or handled.

Transparency Masters

T20.0   STEPS IN THE CHANGE PROCESS

Workbook Exam and Review Questions

1.   According to the text, what makes or breaks any change initiative?
      a.   People and technology
      b.   Processes and systems
      c.*   People and culture
      d.   Structure and culture

2.   (Incremental) change is linear, continuous, and targeted at fixing or modifying problems or procedures.

3. (Transformational) change is radical, discontinuous, multidimensional, and multilevel, and modifies the fundamental structure, systems, orientation, and strategies of the organization.

4. The smallest number of people and/or groups who must be committed to a change for it to occur is called
   a. sponsorship size.
   b. sponsorship mass.
   c.* critical mass.
   d. change mass.

5. Describe the three-step process of change as defined by Lewin.

   Answer: *Unfreezing* is a stage accompanied by stress, tension, and a strong felt need for change. *Moving* is a stage when old ways of behavior are relinquished and new behaviors, values, and attitudes are tested. *Refreezing* is the stage when new behavior is either reinforced, internalized, and institutionalized or rejected and abandoned.

6. What is the first step in the change process?
   a. Developing a shared vision
   b. Forming a guiding coalition
   c. Analyzing potential resistance to change
   d.* Determining the need for change

7. $C = (D \times S \times P) > X$ is a formula for determining the readiness for change where P stands for
   a. number of people to change.
   b. number of processes to change.
   c.* a practical plan for achieving the desired end state.
   d. None of the above

8. (Change agents) are people who act as catalysts and assume the responsibility for managing change activities.

9. Which of the following is *not* part of the manager's role in the change process, according to Beer et al.?
   a. Mobilize commitment to change through joint diagnosis of business problems.
   b.* Announce your personal vision for the change along with a clear plan.
   c. Institutionalize revitalization through formal policies, systems, and structures.
   d. Monitor and adjust strategies in response to problems in the change process.

10. According to Tichy, what are the three roles of transformational leaders?

    Answer: Envisioning, energizing, and enabling

11. What is the positive contribution of resistance to change?

    Answer: Resistance helps us perceive the potential problems of a planned change and ensures that plans for change and their ultimate consequences are thought through carefully.

12. List three tactics for dealing with resistance to change that are most likely to result in commitment to change rather than compliance.

Answer: Education and communication, participation and involvement, and facilitation and support.

13. A systemwide process of data collection, diagnosis, action, planning, intervention, and evaluation aimed at enhancing organizational fit, problem solving, effectiveness, health, and self-renewal is known as
     a.   organizational change.
     b.   organizational behavior.
     c.*   organizational development.
     d.   organizational transformation.

14. (TQM–Total Quality Management) is a good example of a program that was treated like a fad in some companies and later dropped, while it produced—and is still producing—impressive results at other organizations.

15. Which of the following statements about change is *not* true?
     a.*   Change requires personal vision and symbolic gestures by managers.
     b.   Trust is an important aspect of any change effort.
     c.   Changes often upset the political system in organizations.
     d.   Cultures vary in terms of their comfort with change.

Reader Exam and Review Questions

Managing the Extended Enterprise in a Globally Connected World by Kanter

16. Which of the following is *not* a global connectivity trend as identified by Kanter?
     a.   Multi-localism
     b.*   Regional standards
     c.   Collaborative advantage
     d.   Community embeddedness

Surfing the Edge of Chaos by Pascale

17. Which of the following is *not* a characteristic of a complex adaptive system, according to Pascale?
     a.*   Prevents entropy
     b.   Capacity for pattern recognition used to anticipate the future
     c.   Comprised of many agents acting in parallel
     d.   Continuously shifting multiple levels of organization and structure

18. According to Pascale, complex adaptive systems are at risk when
     a.   in chaos.
     b.   complexity is increased.
     c.*   in equilibrium.
     d.   None of the above

Rules of Thumb for Change Agents by Shepard

19. Shepard's rule of thumb for change agents that is known as the Empathy Rule is
     a.   keep an optimistic outlook.
     b.   engage in active listening.
     c.   listen to employee's change complaints.
     d.*   start where the system is.

20. Shepard appeals for an organic rather than a mechanistic approach to change when he advises change agents to
   a. stay alive.
   b.* never work uphill.
   c. load experiments for success.
   d. follow guidelines.

Reader Articles

1. MANAGING THE EXTENDED ENTERPRISE IN A GLOBALLY CONNECTED WORLD by *Rosabeth Moss Kanter*
2. SURFING THE EDGE OF CHAOS by *Richard T. Pascale*
3. RULES OF THUMB FOR CHANGE AGENTS by *Herbert A. Shepard*

UNDERGRADUATE ORGANIZATIONAL BEHAVIOR COURSE
FALL SEMESTER MWF 13:35–14:30 P.M.

	DATE	TOPIC	ASSIGNMENTS (TO BE COMPLETED PRIOR TO CLASS)
1.	(F)	MANAGING THE PSYCHOLOGICAL CONTRACT	**Reader**: Rousseau, Dessler **Workbook**: Introduction, p. xix and Ch. 1, premeeting preparation, p. 4. **Homework**: reaction piece on reader article
2.	(M)	THE ROLE OF THE MANAGER THEORY X AND Y	**Reader**: Mintzberg, Teal **Workbook**: Ch. 2, premeeting preparation, p. 23. Don't read Topic Intro yet.
3.	(W)	THEORIES OF MANAGEMENT	**Reader**: Quinn **Workbook**: Topic Intro
4.	(F)	LEARNING STYLES	**Reader**: Daudelin **Workbook**: Ch. 3, Premeeting preparation, p. 40. COMPLETE AND SCORE INVENTORY BEFORE CLASS
5.	(F)	LEARNING STYLES (cont.) Formation of Learning Groups	**Reader:** Senge **Homework:** HAND IN PERSONAL THEORY OF MANAGEMENT
6.	(M)	VALUES	**Reader:** Conger (ch. 1) **Workbook**: Ch. 5, premeeting preparation, p.97.
7.	(W)	ETHICS	**Reader:** Neilsen, Dundee & Donaldson Roger Worsham Case
8.	(F)	MOTIVATION PERSONAL DIAGNOSIS	**Reader**: McClelland **Workbook**: Ch. 4, premeeting preparation, p. 63. **DO THIS FIRST—WRITE LONG STORIES.**
9.	(W)	MOTIVATION THEORY	**Reader**: Nadler **Workbook**: Topic Intro p. 77.
10.	(M)	CAREER DEVELOPMENT	**Reader**: Shepard, Hall **Workbook**: Premeeting Preparation, p. 119.

11.	(M)	COMMUNICATION	**Reader**: Tannen **Workbook**: Ch. 7, premeeting preparation, p. 149.
12.	(W)	ACTIVE LISTENING	**Reader**: Rogers, Gibb **Workbook**:
13.	(F)	PERCEPTION AND ATTRIBUTION	**Reader**: Adler, Murphy **Workbook**: Ch. 8, premeeting preparation, p. 172. **Homework**: COMPLETE GROUP PROCEDURE—STEPS 1—3, p. 177.
14.	(M)	GROUP DYNAMICS EXERCISE	**Reader** :Lipnack **Workbook**: Ch. 9, premeeting preparation, p. 191.
15.	(W)	GROUP DYNAMICS TEAM BUILDING	**Reader**: Wageman, Thompson
16.	(F)	PROBLEM SOLVING	**Reader**: Straus, Hurst **Workbook**: Ch. 10, premeeting preparation, p. 214.
17.	(M)	MIDTERM AND MIDCOURSE EVALUATION	
18.	(W)	MANAGING CONFLICT SIMULATION	**Reader**: Eisenhardt **Workbook**: Ch. 11, premeeting preparation, p. 244.
19.	(F)	THE NATURE OF CONFLICT AND NEGOTIATION	**Reader**: Acuff **Workbook**:
20.	(M)	EMPOWERMENT AND COACHING	**Reader**: Schermerhorn **Workbook**: Ch. 17, premeeting preparation, p. 380.
21.	(W)	PERFORMANCE APPRAISAL THEORY	**Reader**: Kerr, Pfeffer **Workbook**: Ch. 18, premeeting preparation, A–E, p. 477, read Topic Introduction.
22.	(F)	PERFORMANCE APPRAISAL PRACTICE	**Reader**: Ulrich **Workbook**: Ch. 18, read group procedure. **Homework**: CAREFULLY FILL OUT SELF-EVALUATION (#F, p. 424) AND PEER EVALUATION (p. 428).

23.	(M)	MANAGING DIVERSITY GENDER ISSUES	**Reader**: Friedman, Ragins **Workbook**: Ch. 12, premeeting preparation, p. 266.
24.	(W)	CROSS-CULTURAL DIVERSITY	**Reader**: Hofstede, Osland **Workbook**:
25.	(F)	LEADERSHIP	**Reader**: Goleman, Nanus **Workbook**: Ch. 13, premeeting preparation, p. 287.
26.	(M)	ORGANIZATIONAL CULTURE	**Reader**: Scheins **Workbook**: Ch. 14, premeeting preparation, p. 303. AS A LEARNING GROUP COMPLETE UP TO STEP 2, p. 314. BRING COMPLETED CHART TO CLASS, BUT DON'T READ ANY FURTHER IN THE CHAPTER.
27.	(W)	POWER AND INFLUENCE	**Reader**: Greiner, Bradford **Workbook**: Ch. 16, premeeting preparation, p. 352.
28.	(F)	INFLUENCE ROLE PLAYS	**Reader**: Conger, Sims **Workbook**: p. 359.
29.	(M)	DECISION–MAKING THEORY	DO WORKBOOK TASK FIRST. **Reader**: Klein **Workbook**: Ch.15, premeeting preparation, p. 327.
30.	(W)	DECISION–MAKING PRACTICE—CASES	**Reader**: Vroom **Workbook**: p. 386-393.
31.	(F)	ORGANIZATIONAL CHANGE	**Reader**: Kanter, Shepard **Workbook**: Ch. 22, premeeting preparation, p. 619.
32.		FINAL EXAM (TO BE SCHEDULED)	

NOTE: This is a relatively heavy reading load. You may wish to use only one article per session or make half the class responsible for teaching one of the articles to the other half.

Course Prerequisite: None.

Course Description: In spite of their satisfactory technical skills, people often discover at some point in their career that they do not know how to work effectively with others or have the interpersonal skills to be a good manager. BUS503 presents the same type of content and training found in executive development programs (only cheaper). The course seeks to help you understand why you and others behave as you do in organizations and groups. By the end of the course, you should know yourself better and have better people skills. The focus of the course is the "micro" level in organizations—issues concerning individuals, interpersonal relations, and groups. The overall purpose of the course is to help you develop the people skills you need to be effective employees or managers in effective organizations. The topics to be covered are the practical skills all managers should possess; you can begin to apply them immediately at work and home.

Course Objectives:
- To increase your self-awareness
- To help you become more skilled at analyzing behavior in organizations
- To help you learn what actions are appropriate for different situations
- To help you acquire a larger repertoire of behaviors or skills

Text:
1. **Organizational Behavior: An Experiential Approach**
   by Osland, Kolb, and Rubin. Prentice Hall
2. **The Organizational Behavior Reader** by Osland, Kolb, and
   Rubin, Prentice Hall

The first text, the workbook, consists of content, exercises, and tips for managers. **Please bring the workbook to every class**. The reader is a compendium of the best articles in the field, in the authors' opinions. It consists of classic articles, recent developments in the field, and both theoretical and practical pieces. Some of the articles are not as easy to read as the workbook. They will, however, accustom you to the language and type of writing found in the field so that you can continue reading them on your own throughout your career. Always read the assigned articles in the reader before coming to class, but it is not necessary to bring the reader with you. **Always bring with you the key points from the reader articles**. Please master the material before you come to class so that we can use class time to clear up any questions you may have and to focus on the experiential part of the course.

Class Format

The most effective method for teaching interpersonal and managerial skills is experiential learning. This means that we will turn the classroom into a laboratory and create conditions for understanding concepts through experience as well as readings. We will use role plays, exercises, and simulations so that you can pull out your own learning points from these experiences. **This type of course requires students to take responsibility for their own learning**. In order for an experiential course to be successful, students must do all the reading and homework preparation **and** participate actively in the classroom. Therefore, attendance is mandatory because what goes on in class is not a repeat of the readings but the heart of the course. If you have an emergency and cannot attend class, please call me beforehand so we can make special arrangements if need be.

Please do not underestimate the importance of participation in this course. It is an important part of your final grade, not to mention that it gives you an opportunity to practice your communication skills. You have to learn to speak up sometime; you may as well do it here among friends. If you find it difficult to participate in class, please come see me in the beginning of the course so we have time to remedy the situation.

You will receive a packet of self-assessment instruments. The instruments are to help you understand yourself better and are usually filled out prior to class, as indicated on the syllabus (see Packet Homework). Please fill them out carefully and do the scoring before coming to class. The more honestly you answer these instruments, the more accurate a self-portrait you can construct.

One of the most important skills in today's business world is the ability to work effectively in groups. To give you more practice, you will usually work with the same learning group in class and will receive feedback from this group on your performance in the course.

The Saturday Special
The best way to develop teams is through team challenge courses in which people work in groups to solve physical problems. Therefore, we will spend one Saturday (8:00 A.M. to 5:00 P.M.) early in the course participating in a team development program. This session will take place either September 13 or 20th depending upon student availability. The Saturday Special is the equivalent of three class sessions; therefore, the course will end three weeks early. **Please wear old, comfortable clothes and sneakers; plan to get dirty. The assignments for that day are listed on the last page under "Saturday Special." Attendance is mandatory for this session**, as it is the equivalent of three classes and the highlight of the course. The class as a whole will decide which Saturday is most convenient.

Assignments:
• Current Issue Group Project
• One PAA (Personal application assignment)
• A Manager Profile or second PAA

Class contribution (attendance, preparation & participation) **(5%)**
Each student is expected to be an active participant in each class session and take part in the exercises and make meaningful comments on both the readings and the experiences in the classroom. I value quality rather than quantity—talking for the sake of talking does not improve your class contribution grade. I am looking for evidence of good critical thinking on your part: getting to the nub of an article, asking thought-provoking questions, coming up with learning points from our experiences in class, and sharing what you have learned about yourself and others during the exercises. Another aspect of participation is how well you help your learning group accomplish the tasks and exercises assigned both during and outside class. Merely coming to class is not sufficient; attendance is a first step, but you must also participate actively.

The best ways to prepare yourself to contribute in class are:
a. **Always fill out the Premeeting Preparation**, which is the first few pages of each chapter in the workbook.
b. **Come to class with the key points of the articles you had to read for the day written on a large index card or typed on one sheet of paper**. Be prepared to explain the highlights of the article in class because this is an important part of your participation grade.
c. Be ready to help pull together the learnings from the class.

Peer Evaluation (5%)
At the end of the semester, every student will turn in a peer evaluation plus a self-evaluation that assesses both class preparation and in-class contributions for every member of their learning group.

Course Calendar:

DATE	TOPIC	READER & WORKBOOK ASSIGNMENTS
	Psychological Contract	Ch. 1
	Theories of Management	Ch. 2
	Saturday Special	Ch. 9 & 10
	Learning	Ch 3
	Motivation	Ch. 4
	Ethics and Values	Ch. 5
	Career Development & Stress	Ch. 6
	Communication & Perception	Ch. 7 & 8
	Conflict and Negotiation	Ch. 11
	Empowerment & Performance Appraisal	Ch. 17 & 18
	Managing Diversity	Ch. 12
	Leadership	Ch. 13
	Organizational Culture	Ch. 14
	Decision Making	Ch. 15
	Power and Influence	Ch. 16
	Organization Design	Ch. 19
	Managing Change	Ch. 20

Name_____   BUS360A
                                                Fall 2000

As you know, your study group allots 5 percent of your final grade. Please take this grading responsibility seriously (it's a chance to think like a manager and evaluate performance), and do not give everyone the entire five points unless you can justify that everyone really earned it. As with any performance evaluation, your personal feelings about the person should not enter into your decision; be as objective as possible.

CLASS CONTRIBUTION. Assign **0 to 5** points in both column A and B. (These will be averaged later on.) This refers to participation **within your learning group rather than total class discussions**.

Name	Class Preparation (Reading & Homework)	In-Class Contribution (Group Participation)

NOTE TO PROFESSORS: Figuring out these grades is quicker if student names are typed in ahead of time. We use different colors for each learning group to keep them separate.

Name_____   BUS360A
                                         Fall 1999

As you know, 5 percent of your final grade is allotted by your study group. Please take this grading responsibility seriously (it's a chance to think like a manager and evaluate performance), and do not give everyone the entire five points unless you can justify that everyone really earned it. As with any performance evaluation, your personal feelings about the person should not enter into your decision; be as objective as possible.

CLASS CONTRIBUTION. Assign **0 to 5** points in both column A and B. (These will be averaged later on.) This refers to participation **within your learning group rather than total class discussions**.

Name	Class Preparation (Reading & Homework)	In-Class Contribution (Group Participation)
Travis Andrews		
Kyle Bebout		
Lisa Erickson		
Jack Nicholson		
Susan Rance		

Name_____   BUS360A
                                                        Fall 1999

As you know, 5 percent of your final grade is allotted by your study group. Please take this grading responsibility seriously (it's a chance to think like a manager and evaluate performance), and do not give everyone the entire five points unless you can justify that everyone really earned it. As with any performance evaluation, your personal feelings about the person should not enter into your decision; be as objective as possible.

CLASS CONTRIBUTION. Assign **0 to 5** points in both column A and B. (These will be averaged later on.) This refers to participation **within your learning group rather than total class discussions**.

Name	Class Preparation (Reading & Homework)	In-Class Contribution (Group Participation)
Phillip Dejworek		
Cathy Hernandez		
Jason Lesh		
Aaron Lindner		
Hans Rasmussen		
Anthony Reel		
Jennifer Swinton		

Name_____   BUS360A
                                              Fall 1999

As you know, 5 percent of your final grade is allotted by your study group. Please take this grading responsibility seriously (it's a chance to think like a manager and evaluate performance), and do not give everyone the entire five points unless you can justify that everyone really earned it. As with any performance evaluation, your personal feelings about the person should not enter into your decision; be as objective as possible.

CLASS CONTRIBUTION. Assign **0 to 5** points in both column A and B. (These will be averaged later on.) This refers to participation **within your learning group rather than total class discussions**.

Name	Class Preparation (Reading & Homework)	In-Class Contribution (Group Participation)
Gavin Hare		
Lee McDonald		
Christie Prasnikar		
Erin Rice		
Rayann Speakman		
Paula Messinger		

As you know, 5 percent of your final grade are allotted by your study group. Please take this grading responsibility seriously (it's a chance to think life a manager and evaluate performance), and do not give everyone the entire five points unless you can justify that everyone really earned it. As with any performance evaluation, your personal feelings about the person should not enter into your decision; be as objective as possible.

CLASS CONTRIBUTION. Assign **0 to 5** points in both column A and B. (These will be averaged later on.) This refers to participation within your learning group rather than total class discussions.

Name	Class Preparation (Reading & Homework)	In-Class Contribution (Group Participation)
Chastity Baro		
Marianne Hoonakker		
Brian Kohler		
Russell Maughan		
Scott Smith		

Name_____   BUS360B
Fall 1999

As you know, 5 percent of your final grade are allotted by your study group. Please take this grading responsibility seriously (it's a chance to think life a manager and evaluate performance), and do not give everyone the entire five points unless you can justify that everyone really earned it. As with any performance evaluation, your personal feelings about the person should not enter into your decision; be as objective as possible.

CLASS CONTRIBUTION. Assign **0 to 5** points in both column A and B. (These will be averaged later on.) This refers to participation within your learning group rather than total class discussions.

Name	Class Preparation (Reading & Homework)	In-Class Contribution (Group Participation)
Carol Chiu		
Morry Jones		
Linh Khan		
Quang Nguyen		
Joanna Wascisin		

As you know, 5 percent of your final grade are allotted by your study group. Please take this grading responsibility seriously (it's a chance to think life a manager and evaluate performance), and do not give everyone the entire five points unless you can justify that everyone really earned it. As with any performance evaluation, your personal feelings about the person should not enter into your decision; be as objective as possible.

CLASS CONTRIBUTION. Assign **0 to 5** points in both column A and B. (These will be averaged later on.) This refers to participation within your learning group rather than total class discussions.

Name	Class Preparation (Reading & Homework)	In-Class Contribution (Group Participation)
Josh Anderson		
Melissa Malone		
Kevin Newton		
Erin Sciaraffo		
Amy Yribar		

Name_____ BUS360B
Fall 1999

As you know, 5 percent of your final grade are allotted by your study group. Please take this grading responsibility seriously (it's a chance to think life a manager and evaluate performance), and do not give everyone the entire five points unless you can justify that everyone really earned it. As with any performance evaluation, your personal feelings about the person should not enter into your decision; be as objective as possible.

CLASS CONTRIBUTION. Assign **0 to 5** points in both column A and B. (These will be averaged later on.) This refers to participation within your learning group rather than total class discussions.

Name	Class Preparation (Reading & Homework)	In-Class Contribution (Group Participation)
Stephanie Beck		
Katrina Curtis		
Iris Kersting		
Jerry Lau		
Carl Lawson		
Scott Nelson		

As you know, 5 percent of your final grade are allotted by your study group. Please take this grading responsibility seriously (it's a chance to think life a manager and evaluate performance), and do not give everyone the entire five points unless you can justify that everyone really earned it. As with any performance evaluation, your personal feelings about the person should not enter into your decision; be as objective as possible.

CLASS CONTRIBUTION. Assign **0 to 5** points in both column A and B. (These will be averaged later on.) This refers to participation within your learning group rather than total class discussions.

Name	Class Preparation (Reading & Homework)	In-Class Contribution (Group Participation)
Steve Doepke		
Eric Goveia		
Lisa Guinn		
Sherine Iskander		
Jeremy Riss		
Hanh Ta		
Quang Nguyen		

Name_____   BUS360C
                                          Fall 1999

As you know, 5 percent of your final grade are allotted by your study group. Please take this grading responsibility seriously (it's a chance to think like a manager and evaluate performance), and do not give everyone the entire five points unless you can justify that everyone really earned it. As with any performance evaluation, your personal feelings about the person should not enter into your decision; be as objective as possible.

CLASS CONTRIBUTION. Assign **0 to 5** points in both column A and B. (These will be averaged later on.) This refers to participation within your learning group rather than total class discussions.

Name	Class Preparation (Reading & Homework)	In-Class Contribution (Group Participation)
Meghan Bair		
Matthew Brubaker		
Patrick Currall		
Jamin Martin		
Nori Trevarthen		
Orien Wilkinson-Huff		

As you know, 5 percent of your final grade are allotted by your study group. Please take this grading responsibility seriously (it's a chance to think life a manager and evaluate performance), and do not give everyone the entire five points unless you can justify that everyone really earned it. As with any performance evaluation, your personal feelings about the person should not enter into your decision; be as objective as possible.

CLASS CONTRIBUTION. Assign **0 to 5** points in both column A and B. (These will be averaged later on.) This refers to participation within your learning group rather than total class discussions.

Name	Class Preparation (Reading & Homework)	In-Class Contribution (Group Participation)
Paul Desilet		
Toby Flesher		
Jen Railsback		
BJ Rush		
Petra Voskes		

Group Project: If your group has rewritten your group PAA, please assign percentages that reflect what each person contributed to the entire project. In other words, what percentage of your group grade does each individual deserve (0–100%)?

Name	Group PAA	

APPENDIX D
GETTING ORGANIZED REPORT

If teams discuss and come to an agreement on the following questions, they have a much greater likelihood of avoiding common problems and achieving success. Please provide your professor with a copy of your team's answers to these questions.

1. What are your team goals?

2. What roles will each person assume (facilitator, leader, scribe, timekeeper, editor, compiler, researcher, etc.)? If you are planning on rotating roles, specify how and when you will do that.

3. What tasks must be assigned? Include due dates for each task using the following responsibility chart.

Tasks	Members	Due Dates

4. What processes and procedures will you use in your group? How will you get the work done e.g., organization of tasks, deadlines, revision and editing, use of email, I-drive, evaluation of meetings, etc.? How will you compile the final product to ensure its quality?

5. What norms and expectations has your group established to ensure that your team has positive interpersonal relationships?

6. What kind of leadership does your team think will be most effective? How will you make sure you get it?

7. What is your plan of action if a problem occurs?

7. TEAM MEETING REPORT

Team Name: Beginning Time:
Meeting Date: Ending Time:
Team Members Present:

Team Members Absent:
Reporting Secretary:
Timekeeper:

1. Purpose/Goal of the Meeting

2. Discussion Points (summarize major points of discussion including any specific contributions of team members).

3. Decisions made towards accomplishing goal(s).

4. Tasks/responsibilities assigned to members at the meeting (list each specific task along with the name of the responsible team member and the **due date** for each assigned task.

Tasks	Members	Due Dates

5. Time/location of next meeting:

6. Always end the meeting with an evaluation of how it went. What went well? What could be improved upon in future meetings—be specific.

7. Any constructive advice for the meeting facilitator? What did the facilitator do well? What could be improved upon?

MIDCOURSE EVALUATION: IN SEARCH OF PINCHES
BUS _____ SECTION _____
FALL 2000

Is the course meeting your expectations so far?

_____ yes   _____no   _____sometimes

Why?

What is occurring during the course that helps your learning?

Is anything occurring that hinders your learning?

If you could give the professor one suggestion about how to be a better instructor, what would it be?

Other comments/suggestions:

APPENDIX F
THE PERSONAL APPLICATION ASSIGNMENT (PAA)

A variety of texts and articles over the past few years have argued for the use of an alternative approach to teaching organizational behavior, one that emphasizes experiential learning. This approach "emphasizes an existential, emergent view for learning organizational behavior" (McMullen, 1979), where the role of the instructor is that of learning facilitator, responsible for designing experiences for students to base learning upon, rather than as teacher, responsible for lecturing on theory and concepts. Although gaining wide acceptance, this approach has nevertheless created problems in the assessment of students' performance. Significant learnings in this model of teaching occur not only from the development of concepts, but also from the experiences themselves. McMullen (as well as others) has proposed the use of a personal application assignment to help solve the problem of performance assessment. This assignment is based on the experiential learning model formulated by Kolb (1971).

Kolb's model argues that learning occurs through a process that might begin with a <u>concrete experience</u>, which leads to <u>reflective observation</u> about the experience. The next stage is <u>abstract conceptualization</u>, in which people apply models, paradigms, strategies, and metaphors to the results of the experience. <u>Active experimentation</u> concludes the cycle as the concepts are then put into practice, thus generating new concrete experience.

In one sense, persons able to learn using all modes of the model will be better able to take away learning from the variety of contexts in which they interact. We feel that the Personal Application Assignment is a useful tool for both evaluation of a student's work in courses taught using an experiential approach; and further, that the Personal Application Assignment can serve as a way to help students <u>learn to learn</u>. The PAA is both an evaluation <u>and</u> a teaching technique.

Our past history of teaching using this method has shown that the PAA, in order to be most useful, must include clear guidelines for the student. To that end we have undertaken to set forth the guidelines below to help students to understand the requirements for effective PAAs.

<u>General Comments</u>

First of all, we believe that a zero-based grading system is important. In this system, 20 points are given for the total PAA. Four points are awarded for each of the four elements in the learning style model, and four points are awarded for the integration and synthesis and general quality of the PAA. Students start with zero points and are given specific points for each area, depending on their having met the criteria listed in the following section. For the instructor's part, we believe that instructors need to provide specific feedback as quickly as possible to students on why they were awarded points in each area and, more importantly, what they need to do to achieve the maximum points in each area.

Choosing a good topic is essential. Select an experience that relates to the assigned course topics. It should be an experience that you would like to understand better (e.g., there was something about it that you do not totally understand, that intrigues you, that made you realize that you lacked certain managerial skills, or that was problematical or significant for you). When students are excited about learning more about the incident, their papers are lively and interesting. The topic must be meaty enough to take it through the entire learning cycle. The incident does not have to be work related; an incident in any setting (sports teams, school, family, club, church, etc.) that relates to the course topics is acceptable.

<u>Elements of the PAA</u>
<u>1. Concrete Experience (CE)</u>

In this part of the paper, students briefly describe what happens in the experience. A simple description of the events that occurred is <u>not</u> sufficient. The feelings experienced by the student as well as his or her thoughts and perceptions during the experience are relevant to this discussion.

Another way of looking at CE would be that it possesses an objective and a subjective component. The objective part presents the facts of the experience, like a newspaper account, without an attempt to analyze the content. The subjective part is the "here-and-now" personal experience of the event. This experience is composed of feelings, perceptions, and thoughts.

Helpful hints: (1) It often helps students to replay the experience in their mind. After reviewing the experience, students should write a report of what they saw, heard, felt, thought, and heard and saw others doing. (2) Students should avoid presenting the detailed mechanics of the experience unless these are critical to the remainder of the paper. This section of the paper should be no longer than 1–1.5 pages long. (3) Students should avoid reporting the feelings and thoughts experienced <u>after</u> the experience being described. This retrospection is more appropriate in the reflective observation section.

Example:

> *We all sat at the table together. Not a sound came from any of us. Finally, after what felt like an hour to me, I simply had to say something. "Why are all of you taking this course?" I asked. One person, a small foreign-looking man said, "I needed this course to complete my MBA." Others laughed. Another person, a nicely dressed woman, said, "I'd like to get an easy 'A.' " I thought to myself: What a bummer! I didn't want to be in a group with people who didn't take the subject matter seriously. When the meeting ended, my perceptions of the group had somehow changed. Maybe this was a good group to be in after all. Some of the members had similar interests to mine, and most of them were nice people that I could see getting along with. I felt somehow hopeful that this semester wouldn't be so bad after all.*

2. Reflective Observation (RO)

The student should ask him/herself: What did I observe in the experience and what possible meanings could these observations have? The key task here is to gather as many observations as possible by observing the experience from different points of view. The main skill to work on is <u>perspective taking,</u> or what some people call "re-framing." Try to look at this experience and describe it from different perspectives. For example, how did other participants view the situation and what did it mean to them? What would a neutral ("objective") observer have seen and heard? Now that you are older do you see the situation differently? What perspective did your parents have, if any? Look beneath the surface and try to explain why the people involved behaved the way they did. <u>Reflect</u> on these <u>observations</u> to discover the personal meaning that the situation had for you.

Helpful hints: (1) Discuss the experience with others to gain their views and clarify your perceptions. (2) "Unhook" yourself from the experience and meditate about it in a relaxed atmosphere. Mull over your observations until their personal meaning comes clear to you. Try to figure out <u>why</u> people, and <u>you in particular,</u> behaved as they did. What can you learn about yourself, looking back on the experience? If you write about a conflict or interaction, be sure to analyze both sides and put yourself in the shoes of the other people involved.

Examples:

> *In thinking back on the meeting, I began to see how the group might have taken my comments. They were, after all, somewhat aggressive. Some might even call them belligerent. Had I said these things before this class, or at work, I must confess that I would have surprised even myself.*

> *But it seemed there was more going on here than met my eye at the time. Sarah and Bob at first didn't seem to be the kind of people to combine forces on this job, so why was I arguing against them this time? Then it dawned on me: Their departments were about to be combined into the same division! Why hadn't I remembered that during the meeting?*

> *Many thoughts raced through my head. Was the cause of last night's "high" that we won the game? Was it the first time we had worked together as a group? Maybe the fact that member*

X wasn't there that night helped! But I still had a nagging hunch that my decreased involvement, in comparison to the dominant role I had played in previous meetings, helped.

3. Abstract Conceptualization (AC)

By relating assigned readings and lectures to what you experienced, you are demonstrating your ability to understand conceptually abstract material through your experiences. This process will help you refine your model of people and organizations. Although some assigned readings and lectures will have varying degrees of relevance to your experience, it is important that you make several references and not limit your conceptualizing to just one source. Use at least two concepts or theories from the course readings. Provide the source for each reference in the following manner: (workbook, p. 31) or (reader, p. 97). This is also the place to insert your own personally developed theories and/or models if they assist you in making sense of the experience.

By reviewing theoretical material, you should be able to identify several specific concepts or theories that relate to your experience. First, briefly define the concept or theory as you would for someone who was not familiar with it. Next, apply the concept <u>thoroughly</u> to your experience. The tie-in should include the specific details of how the theory relates to and provides insight into your experience. Does the experience support or refute the theory? Avoid merely providing a book report of what you have read—you should discuss in some detail how you see concepts and theories relating to your experiences.

Helpful hints: (1) It is sometimes useful to identify theoretical concepts first and then search out and elaborate on an experience that relates to these concepts. (2) A slightly more difficult approach is to reverse the above procedure and search out those concepts that apply to your "raw" experience.

Example:

There are several organizational behavior concepts that help me understand this experience. One is the Thomas-Kilman theory of conflict (workbook, pp. 284–285), which is based on two axes, either the concern for one's own interests or the concern for the interests of the other party. The five styles reflect a low or high position on these two axes and are labeled competition, compromise, avoidance, accommodation, and collaboration. In the incident I described, my coach began with a collaborative style, high concern for both his own interests and the interests of the other party. He tried to work out a solution that would satisfy both of us but I neither saw nor heard his point of view. I just wanted to get my own way and practice in the same way I had on my previous team. I see now that the conflict style I used was the competitive style, high concern for my own interests and low concern for the interests of the other party. Looking back, this is the style I have used most often throughout my life; I usually got away with it before because I was such a good athlete. However, my experience with the coach supports the workbook's description of the losses that may result from using this style. I lost everything when I was kicked off the team. I certainly alienated the coach and the other players and discouraged them from wanting to work with me.

4. Active Experimentation (AE)

This section of the paper should summarize the practical lessons you have learned and the action steps you will take to make you more effective in the future. How can you test out your concepts developed in the preceding phase? These ideas can be stated in the form of rules of thumb or action resolutions. (Future actions must be based on the experience reported in Concrete Experience.) You should elaborate <u>in detail</u> how you see your action ideas being carried out. Be <u>specific</u> and <u>thorough</u>. Don't just repeat tips from the workbook. Include at least one action resolution that is based on new knowledge that you have gained about yourself as a result of writing the paper. Depending on the complexity of your ideas, you should present at least four things that you learned and a well-thought-out description of how you will apply them in the future. If you were to relive your experience, what would you do differently? If you were the manager in the story, what would you do differently? Based on the insight you've gained about yourself and others, how would you handle a similar situation in the future? Label your action steps so the reader does not have to dig for them (e.g., "First,..." "Second,..." "Third,... and "Finally,...").

Helpful hints: (1) Project a future experience in which you envision the implementation of your ideas and then elaborate on that experience as a way of demonstrating how your actions will be carried out. (2) Where does this model exist in your life (home, work, school)? Do you need a support system to make it happen? Someone to "contract" with? (3) Try to imagine the final results of your experimentation. What will it be like if you accomplish what you want to do?

Example:

How then can I best utilize and improve my achievement motivation? First, I must arrange for some accomplishment feedback. This will be done by designing or perceiving tasks so that I succeed bit by bit, gaining a reward each time and thus strengthening my desire to achieve more. Also, I must look to "models of achievement." If people around me succeed, it will further stimulate me. Third, I should modify my self-image to include my desire for personal challenges and responsibilities and my requirement of continual feedback. (As a first step, I imagine myself as a person who requires or must have success, responsibility, challenge, and variety.) Fourth, I must learn to control my reveries. Just beyond the borderline of awareness, many of us are constantly talking to ourselves. Finally, although I would never admit so, I agree that salary is a potential "dissatisfier" for me. Therefore, I must insist on what I perceive as a "fair return" for my performance. Wish me luck!

5. Integration and Synthesis

The well-written PAA has a focal issue and a story line with themes that are carried throughout each of the four sections. The idea of synergy applies here: "The whole is greater than the sum of the parts." If integration is present, then the reader can attend to the content without distraction; if integration is absent, barriers prevent the reader from gaining a full appreciation of the content.

Other barriers that prevent the reader from fully appreciating the paper's content are spelling and grammatical errors. Because good writing skills are so important in the business world, there should be no errors in your paper. Use the spell and grammar check on your computer and have others read your paper before you hand it in.

Helpful hints: (1) See a writing guide like Strunk and Whites's *Elements of Style* or a grammar guide like *Woe Is I* if you feel in need of a refresher course. (2) Keep in mind the following points:

- Decide on the plot for your paper and outline what information is needed in each section to carry that plot throughout the entire paper.
- Label each section: Concrete Experience, Reflective Observation, etc.
- Transitions are important (between sentences, paragraphs, and sections) and make the paper flow.
- The four sections should be equally well developed and fairly similar in length.

APPENDIX G
PERSONAL APPLICATION ASSIGNMENT GRADING SHEET

Please bear these grading criteria in mind as you are writing your paper and doing your final revision.

CONCRETE EXPERIENCE—4 Points

_____ Does the paper contain a clear, <u>objective</u> description of facts in your personal experience? (2 points)

_____ Does it contain a <u>subjective</u> description of feelings, perceptions, and thoughts that occurred during (not after) the experience? (2 points)

_____ Does this section provide enough information so the reader will understand the rest of the paper, but not too much irrelevant detail? For an individual PAA, this section should not exceed 1–1.5 pages. (Delete 1 point)

REFLECTIVE OBSERVATION—4 Points

_____ Did you look at the experience from the different points of view of all the major actors? (2 points)

_____ Did you make an attempt to figure out why the people involved, and you in particular, behaved as they did? (1 point)

_____ Did the different perspectives and behavioral analyses add significant meaning to the situation? (1 point)

ABSTRACT CONCEPTUALIZATION—4 Points

_____ Did you briefly define and explain at least two different concepts or theories from the assigned readings that relate to your experience, and did you reference them properly? (2 points)

_____ Did you thoroughly apply the concepts/theories to your experience? (2 points)

ACTIVE EXPERIMENTATION—4 Points

_____ Did you summarize the practical lessons you derived from analyzing your experience? (1 point)

_____ Did you describe thoroughly at least four action steps you will take in the future so you can be more effective? (2 points)

_____ Did you identify and include at least one action step that is based on what you have learned about yourself as a result of this analysis? (1 point)

INTEGRATION AND WRITING—4 Points

_____ Does the PAA have major themes that are woven thoughout each section of the paper? Are the sections well integrated and fairly equally developed? (1 point)

_____ Is the paper clear and well written (few awkward phrases, etc.)? (1 point)

_____ Is the paper free of spelling errors? (1 point)

_____ Is the paper free of grammar errors? (1 point)

_____ TOTAL

APPENDIX H
SAMPLE PAA

<u>Concrete Experience</u>

I worked for one year in the marketing group in the Chicago office of a large public accounting firm. The internal service departments were organized into profit centers and operated like little fiefdoms. We worked very closely with the graphics department. We provided the majority of their work but that did not mean the two departments got along well. In fact, we spent more time battling each other than collaborating. A constant bone of contention for both groups was missed deadlines. Most of the time, a marketing person was the contact with the client, usually a partner in the firm. We set up a production schedule, to which the client would agree, and made every effort to stick to it. But 99 times out of 100, something would happen on the partner's end that would cause a delay. However, the original deadline was never modified to take these setbacks into account because we were not allowed to tell the partners their requests were unreasonable. This put terrific pressure on <u>both</u> departments, but graphics personnel continually accused us of purposely holding onto information or dragging our feet in order to make their jobs more difficult.

It was very frustrating for me to get my projects completed. From the very beginning, I felt they thought I was an incompetent jerk who was just trying to make their job more difficult. It wasn't long before I adopted the perception of the rest of my department—graphics was a bunch of uncooperative whiners. I never expected to get good service from them and I didn't. I dreaded going into their office with changes and kept my communications with them to a minimum. Occasionally, I'd have a confrontation with an artist, which would escalate into an argument with two or three other graphics people. Then I was angry for the rest of the day. I had no idea how to remedy the situation and I was under such pressure to get my work done that I had no time to repair the relationships, even if I had known how to do it.

<u>Reflective Observation</u>

Looking back, I think that if I had not been so caught up in the intergroup fighting, I would have recognized that the graphics personnel were under as much pressure as I was. At the time it always seemed like "once again graphics was being uncooperative." But I never stopped to ask myself why they were being so hostile to me and I never put myself in their shoes. One of the things this taught me was that I can be somewhat self-centered and ignore the problems of others when they are a barrier to getting my work done. When graphics stereotyped me, I let myself be influenced by my co-workers rather than making the effort to develop a positive relationship with graphics and get beyond the stereotypes. I felt like one of the gang when we all shared our horror stories about the latest thing graphics had done.

For their part, graphics was probably struggling to keep up with their work and deadlines. Just when they thought they had things under control, we would appear with new changes and requests. Perhaps a lot of their resentment stemmed from feeling that, because of us, they could not control their own workflow. We didn't want to lose the partners' business by asking for extended deadlines since they could have hired an outside firm, but graphics had no investment in our service to the partners. Instead, they were worried about satisfying their own clients. And our last-minute changes got in the way of serving their other clients.

There was another person in a different department who was very positive about the graphics department. At the time I remember thinking, "Oh, he must not deal with them on a regular basis like I do or they wouldn't be so cooperative with him." It never occurred to me that this person was doing something different than I was and, as a result, had a better relationship with the graphics personnel. And it certainly never occurred to me to ask him what he did to have such a great rapport with the group.

Since other people and groups managed to have good relations with graphics, we could hardly be justified in thinking that they were totally in the wrong. But both groups had stereotyped the other and were unwilling to change their opinions. Even though both our managers knew about the problem, they did not intervene, perhaps because the work always got done somehow. These managers were more focused upon tasks than people, so they never worried about the personal cost of the conflict, and probably did not know how to resolve the problem.

Abstract Conceptualization

Conflict, defined as "a form of interaction among parties that differ in interests, perceptions, and preferences" (reader, p. 305) is the concept that best helps me understand my experience. Our two departments had different interests in serving our customers and different perceptions about each other and our work demands.

The situation between marketing and graphics was an example of when too much conflict occurs. The following passage could have been written about us. "The <u>combination</u> of negative stereotypes, distrust, internal militance, and aggressive action creates a vicious cycle: 'defensive' aggression by one group validates suspicion and 'defensive' counter aggression by the other, and the conflict escalates (Deutsch, 1973) unless it is counteracted by external factors" (reader, p. 307). Graphics never believed that we weren't holding back information or dragging our feet on purpose. And we never trusted them to do our work well without giving us a hard time. We both complained bitterly about each other and never lost an opportunity to slander the "enemy" to others in the organization, which is a form of aggression. Brown (reader, p. 306) states that managers must intervene when conflict reaches a dysfunctional level but our managers never did. They probably did not want to "rock the boat" as long as things were getting done. But it makes me wonder how much more effective we could have been, had we been able to work through our differences. Someone should have helped the two groups diagnose the conflict and its underlying causes (competing for the scarce resource of time, struggling with uncontrollable last-minute demands and iron deadlines, and allegiance to our department rather than the company as a whole).

Another concept that applies to this incident is perception, the process by which we read meaning into stimuli (workbook, p. 204). Marketing and graphics personnel constructed barriers to communication between each group by using the techniques of selective exposure, selective attention, distrusted source and erroneous translation. We saw, heard, and paid attention to what we wanted to, not necessarily the behaviors that may have been actually occurring. Our stereotypes were consistently reinforced by the perceptions we chose to respond to.

Active Experimentation

If I were in situation like this again, I would first try to do a better job of managing myself. I would remember that it takes two sides to make a conflict and I need to be as objective as possible and not go along with the group in criticizing "them" so that I feel more a part of the group. Second, had I made the effort, I might have been able to establish at least one positive relationship with someone in graphics. I should have asked my positive colleague how he managed to develop such a good relationship with them. I suspect his advice would have been to spend more time with them, treat them with greater respect, refrain from blaming them when things go wrong, and be more empathetic.

Third, I would talk to my manager or supervisor about the problem. By making my feelings known and telling him or her that I wanted to do my part in conflict management maybe he or she would be more willing to take action. If not, at least I tried. Ultimately, my negative actions only made my job more difficult. I now realize that was not a very smart or effective way to conduct myself.

Finally, I will have a better chance of avoiding conflict if I refrain from distancing myself from difficult people. I will work harder at building and maintaining relationships in situations like this, even though my natural inclination is to "write them off."

The positive thing about having negative experiences is that hopefully I learn from them. I do not have control over other people but if I act appropriately, I will have a much better chance of getting the cooperation I desire. This experience taught me about the dangers of going along with the group. I know that the next time I am in this situation I will behave differently.

APPENDIX I
SPECIAL INSTRUCTIONS FOR GROUP PAA

1.   Begin by carefully reading the instructions for the individual PAA.

2.   Choose a portion of the Saturday Special to write about. Pick an exercise that strikes you as the most significant or most confusing—the one that is likely to yield the most learning. Decide on the "plot" of your paper and brainstorm what needs to go into each section so the paper is well integrated **before** you start writing.

3.   Make sure all your group members appear throughout the PAA. Talk about the different things they were thinking and feeling in the Concrete Experience; analyze why they behaved as they did in the Reflective Observation. Refer to their behavior when you are applying theory in the Abstract Conceptualization part. Make sure there is an individual action step for each member in the Active Experimentation section.

4.   In the Active Experimentation section, **include a paragraph of lessons you've learned as a group as well as three group action steps concerning action you will take to be more effective in the future. There should also be one individual action step for each group member concerning what they learned <u>about themselves</u> (not about groups) and the personal action plan that stems from that self-knowledge.**

5.   You can mention other class members who are not in your group in the PAA if it's crucial to your plot; otherwise it's not necessary.

6.   Unlike the individual PAA with its five-page limit, there is no page limit on this assignment, and you do not have to hand in a copy as you do with an individual PAA.

7.   Do not write about the Saturday Special for your individual PAA unless you have the instructor's permission.

8.   Hand in the first draft February 10 and the final copy February 17.

1. Approach another person in the class (preferably someone you don't know) and guess which category might fit him or her. If your guess is incorrect, you may make one and only one more guess about another category. If your second guess is also incorrect, let your partner make a guess about you and then move on to someone else.

2. If your guess is correct, write the person's name in the appropriate box.

3. The object of the exercise is to fill in names for as many boxes as possible. A person's name may not appear more than once.

Has never played a video game	Hates pizza	Wanted to be a rock star	Has 7 brothers & sisters	Speaks 3 languages fluently
Writes poetry	Plays 3 musical instruments	A rabid _____ fan	Ran cross country	Has 4 or more kids
Gourmet cook	Painted outside of a house	Dislikes beer	Vegetarian	Parachuted from an airplane
Never watched a soap opera	Played in a marching band	Poker demon	Flew over the Pacific	Worked in last presidential campaign
Born in another country	Owns a bowling ball	Reads philosophy in spare time	Does not own a credit card	Drives a car over 10 yrs. old

HOW TO SUCCEED IN ORGANIZATIONAL BEHAVIOR BY REALLY TRYING

PRIOR TO CLASS

- Think back on an experience related to the subject to be studied for the next class session. (For example, before the group dynamics session, think about a group to which you belonged. What made it effective or ineffective?) Do you have any theories or models about the subject and, if so, what are they?

- What do you want to learn about the subject? (Returning to the group dynamics example, when should managers use their staff to make decisions and when should they make them alone? How could I learn to conduct better staff meetings? Why do some people act so differently in groups than they do outside them? What are groups good for?)

- What are the significant learning points in the readings? Write them down; you'll have an opportunity to contribute them in class. Did you find some answers to what you want to learn about this subject in the readings?

- How can you apply what you've learned from the readings at work or in other areas of your life?

- Are there any particular behavioral skills you want to practice during the experiential exercise that will take place in class?

DURING CLASS

- Tell your learning group when there is a particular skill you want to practice during class so you can get feedback from them.

- Did you find some answers to what you wanted to learn about the subject during the class session? If not, raise your questions with your learning group or the instructor.

- Figure out how you can apply the learning from the class exercise to your work or other areas of life.

- Contribute your theories about the subject, your experiences, and what you've gleaned from the readings and the exercise to class discussions.

AFTER CLASS

- Take time to reflect on what happened in class and read the learning points at the end of the chapter. Review what you learned and try it out.

APPENDIX L
PROCEDURE FOR GROUP MEETING:
PERFORMANCE APPRAISAL ROLE PLAYS BY CAROLYN JENSEN

Time Allotted: One hour and 30 minutes for both role plays (45 minutes a piece)

This exercise provides students with the opportunity to participate in, as well as observe, an appraisal interview. The class should be divided into groups of three. This exercise consists of two role plays. One takes place in a manufacturing environment, while the other occurs in a white-collar setting. Each role play simulates a performance appraisal interview between two group members; one acts as employee or rater, while the other acts as the supervisor or rater. The third group member acts as observer. If time allows for both role plays to be conducted, roles should be rotated so each group member has the opportunity to perform two of the three roles. The performance to be evaluated in each role play is outlined in the "script" of each individual role play.

STEP 1.   Decide who will act as rater, employee, and observer.

STEP 2.   Take 10 to 15 minutes for each group member to read his or her section of the role play.

A.   The student acting as rater should read only the section of the exercise with RATER at the top.
B.   The student acting as employee should read only the section of the exercise with EMPLOYEE at the top.
C.   The student acting as observer should read both the RATER and EMPLOYEE section.

STEP 3.   During the interview, the rater should ask the employee for his or her self-appraisal on each of the five criteria. The employee should present his or her self-appraisal on each criterion individually, followed by his or her reasoning for such a rating. At this time the rater should present his or her rating of the employee on these criteria, as well as the reasoning behind it. The rater has the opportunity at this time to adjust his or her rating of the employee on the blank scale provided. If the ratings are adjusted, the rater should explain why they were changed. If they were not changed, the rater should also explain why he or she feels such ratings are justified.

STEP 4.   After each individual criterion is discussed the rater has the opportunity to improvise a bit, selecting one or several of the issues below for discussion.

The rater can guide the interview toward:

A.   The employee's opinions regarding their problems, performance, motivations, and career goals
B.   Problem solving with an individual or organization focus
C.   Training needs of the organization
D.   The employee's view of the organization's performance and related problems

STEP 5.   Discuss and determine the training and development need of the employee.

STEP 6.   The rater should properly conclude the interview. Included in this step the rater should share the final rating with the employee.

STEP 7.   After the performance appraisal interview is completed, the rater and employee should answer the questions at the end of their sections, and the observer should answer the observer questions at the very end of the role play.

In today's exercise....
You are Pat Cole, and Chris Smith is one of your employees on day shift.

Background...
You are a line supervisor at Sweetlane Candy, Pennsylvania's largest candy manufacturer. It is time for you to conduct your annual performance appraisals of the 55 employees you supervise on your shift. You are not looking forward to conducting the appraisals. A memo from management has stated that not only must you evaluate these employees, but you must also submit a list of employee training and development needs (something you have never done before). Due to an open-bid system that started this year, you have only supervised 18 of your employees for nine months. You are uncomfortable because you don't know them or their work as well as you'd like.

Next Appraisal to be Conducted....
You have already conducted 11 appraisals, all with employees you have worked with for three or more years. This next appraisal is with Chris Smith, who has been working for you only nine months. Adding to your apprehension over the appraisal are two factors: (1) Sweetlane's new policy of asking employees to conduct a self-appraisal prior to your meeting, and (2) the lack of knowledge you have about the machines in your department, as it has updated 11 of the 45 production lines. Although you rose to a management position from these same ranks, you have not been "one of them" in nine years.

How you see it....
You have evaluated Chris' performance below, knowing you can change it if you wish after your meeting.

Work Quantity -
Defined as the amount or volume of the work produced. Your line expects employees to move 20 units a minute, or 1,200 units an hour. With two 10-minute breaks, and a 40-minute lunch, 8,400 units should be produced a day by an employee. A counter appears at the end of each line that cannot be seen by the employee without moving approximately 12 feet from where he or she needs to stand on the line. Chris' production has averaged 8,259 units a day.

Work Quality -
Defined as the reliability and accuracy of the work produced. Employees are expected to produce 8,400 units a day with a 98% accuracy rate. Thus only 2%, or 168 units out of the 8,400 average daily production, should fail quality standards. Chris' average over the nine months of units failing the quality test is 1.9%.

Work Quantity and Quality schedule for Chris

Month	Average Units a Day	Average % Per Day Failing Quality Test
1	8290	1.8%
2	8300	1.9%
3	8390	1.9%
4	8400	1.9%
5	8400	1.9%
6	8500	1.8%
7	7900	2.0%
8	8000	2.0%
9	8150	1.9%
Average Over Nine Months	8259	1.9%

Rater

Absentee Rate -
Employees are allowed 5 days (or 40 hours paid absences a year for illness without a doctor's excuse, and an additional 4 days (or 32 hours) paid absences with a doctor's excuse. They are allowed 2 personal days (16 hours). Employees are docked for late time up to one hour, on 9 occasions. After that, disciplinary action is determined by the immediate supervisor. One option is to dock sick time on an hourly basis. Chris has been from 25 minutes to 40 minutes late four times. The fourth time Chris' sick time was docked 30 minutes. In addition, Chris has missed 2 days, or 16 hours sick time, in this 9-month period.

Cooperation -
Defined as the willingness of an employee to accept supervision and adapt to various situations. As the supervisor, you have noticed Chris has been unresponsive to your help lately. Chris seems to have changed in the last three months, rejecting the help of other employees as well.

Compatibility -
Defined as the ability of the employee to get along with others including supervisory personnel, peers, and subordinates. Chris seems to get along well with fellow employees on breaks and in any situation where advice is not being given. Chris seems to like doing his job without the input of others.

Here are the ratings you have come up with:

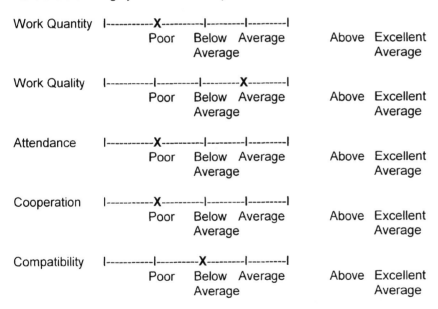

Note: Before deciding on Chris' ratings you just rated Sidney, one of your best employees. You and Sidney both bowl on Saturdays at the same alley.

Final ratings after your meeting with Chris...

Note: You do not have to change the previous ratings. Only do so if you feel your previous ratings were incorrect.

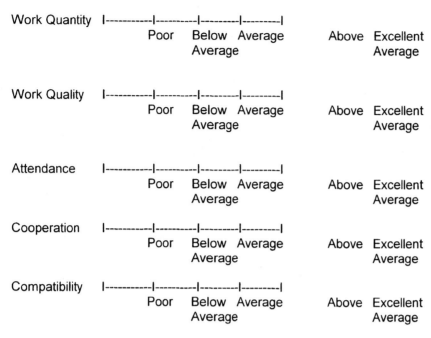

Work Quantity |----------|----------|---------|---------|
                    Poor   Below   Average   Above   Excellent
                             Average   Average

Work Quality |----------|----------|---------|---------|
                    Poor   Below   Average   Above   Excellent
                             Average   Average

Attendance |----------|----------|---------|---------|
                    Poor   Below   Average   Above   Excellent
                             Average   Average

Cooperation |----------|----------|---------|---------|
                    Poor   Below   Average   Above   Excellent
                             Average   Average

Compatibility |----------|----------|---------|---------|
                    Poor   Below   Average   Above   Excellent
                             Average   Average

After the meeting...

1)   Did your ratings of Chris change after the meeting? If so, how and why?

2)   What have you determined to be Chris' training and development needs (if any)?

3)   What form of bias did you exhibit?

4)   How could your company's performance appraisal system be improved?

5)   What active listening skills did you use?

6)   In retrospect, what would you do differently if you were to act as rater again?

In today's exercise...
You are Chris Smith, and your supervisor on day shift is Pat Cole.

Background...
You are an employee at Sweetlane Candy, Pennsylvania's largest candy manufacturer. It is time for your annual performance appraisal. You are not looking forward to this particular appraisal. You are uncomfortable with the fact that due to an open-bid system, you are one of 18 new employees on day shift whose performance appraisal will be conducted by a supervisor who has only known you for nine months. Most of the other employees on this shift have been in this department for at least three years.

Your performance appraisal...
Adding to your apprehension over the appraisal are two factors: (1) Sweetlane's new policy of asking employees to conduct a self-appraisal prior to their meeting with their supervisor, and (2) the lack of familiarity you feel in your department, as it has updated 11 of the 45 production lines. It updated these lines in the seventh month of your employment in this department.

How you see it...
You have evaluated your performance below, knowing it's probably not seen in the same light by your supervisor, Pat Cole.

Work Quantity -
Defined as the amount or volume of the work produced. Your line expects employees to move 20 units a minute, or 200 units an hour. With two 10-minute breaks, and a 40-minute lunch, 8,400 units should be produced a day by an employee. A counter appears at the end of each line which cannot be seen by the employee without moving approximately 12 feet from where he or she needs to stand on the line. Your production has averaged 8,259 units a day. When you first started here it took you two to three months to get up to speed. On your sixth month here you hit a high daily average of 8,500 units per day. After that they switched you to one of the new production lines without any hands-on training, and only a half hour verbal introduction to the line in a classroom environment. You know your production has dropped, but you only know just how slow you're going at break time and at lunch when you can check the counter at the end of the line. You feel you can't learn from others there. No one on the new lines, from what you can see, is doing well.

Work Quality -
Defined as the reliability and accuracy of the work produced. Employees are expected to produce 8,400 units daily with a 98% accuracy rate. Thus only 2%, or 168 units out of the 8,400 a day average production, should fail quality standards. Your average percentage of failed units over the nine months is 1.9%. You feel this is excellent considering you are in a new department and on a new line.

Work Quantity and Quality schedule for Chris

Month	Average Units a Day	Average % Per Day Failing Quality Test
1	8290	1.8%
2	8300	1.9%
3	8390	1.9%
4	8400	1.9%
5	8400	1.9%
6	8500	1.8%
7	7900	2.0%
8	8000	2.0%
9	8150	1.9%
Average Over Nine Months	8259	1.9%

Absentee Rate -

Employees are allowed 5 days (or 40 hours) paid absences a year for illness without a doctor's excuse, and an additional 4 days (or 32 hours) paid absences with a doctor's excuse. They are allowed 2 personal days (16 hours). Employees are docked for late time up to one hour, on 3 occasions. After that disciplinary action may be determined by the immediate supervisor in the case. One option is to dock sick time on an hourly basis. You have been from 25 minutes to 40 minutes late four times. The fourth time your sick time was docked 30 minutes. In addition you have missed 2 days, or 16 hours sick time, in this 9-month period. You are a single parent and your child is in first grade. The school bus picks him up quite a ways from your house. You can't let him wait alone in this day and age, so when the bus is late you're late. That's just how it is as you see it. After all, your child comes first.

Cooperation -

Defined as the willingness of an employee to accept supervision and adapt to various situations. You have always been able to accept help and criticism very well, but with these new machines you reject the help of others because, quite frankly, they do not know any better than you how to operate this new line. You are frustrated because no hands-on training was offered.

Compatibility -

Defined as the ability of the employee to get along with others including supervisory personnel, peers, and subordinates. You get along well with fellow employees on breaks and in any situation where advice is not being given about those damn new machines. You just want to learn this new job so you can bring up those numbers that are so important to Sweetlane management.

Here are the results of your self-appraisal:

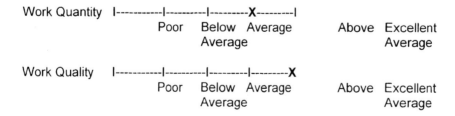

152

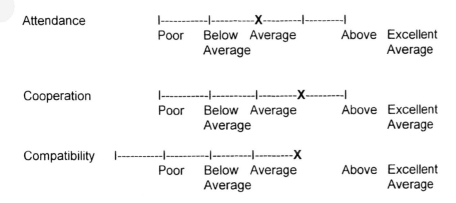

Attendance

Poor	Below Average	Average		Above Average	Excellent

Cooperation

Poor	Below Average	Average		Above Average	Excellent

Compatibility

Poor	Below Average	Average		Above Average	Excellent

Note: Before your performance appraisal interview, you see Pat talking to Sidney, and you wonder whether Sidney had his performance appraisal conducted this morning. You know Pat and Sidney are tight.

After the meeting...

1) Do you think Pat's original ratings were accurate?

2) Did the original rating change after your interview? Were Pat's final ratings of you fair?

3) Do you think they (the ratings) changed because of your self-appraisal?

4) What form of bias do you think Pat may have exhibited?

5) What active listening skills did Pat exhibit?

6) How could the appraisal have been more effective and useful?

Observer Questions

On another piece of paper answer the following questions.

1)   Did the supervisor give the employee sufficient time to present his or her self-appraisal?

2)   Did the supervisor use active listening skills, or did he or she do most of the talking?

3)   Did the supervisor create a nondefensive climate and refrain from becoming defensive himself or herself?

4)   Did the supervisor discuss training needs with the employee?

5)   What mistakes, if any, were made by either the supervisor or employee?

6)   What forms of bias should the supervisor be aware of when rating Chris?

7)   Were the supervisor's final ratings of Chris fair?

8)   Other comments:

In today's exercise...

You are Cary Dunn, and Bernie Tate is one the employees in the department you oversee.

Background...

You are one of eight Vice Presidents at Wayne Gaskets, the largest producer of gaskets in the United States and the second-largest producer of gaskets in the world. It is time for you to conduct your annual performance appraisals of the 22 employees in your department. You are Vice President of the Total Quality Department, which consists of 16 Quality Specialists and 6 support people. You are not looking forward to conducting the appraisals. You find it difficult to rate the specialists because: (1) many have become your friends over the years, and (2) the performance appraisal system at Wayne seems to ask you to wear too many hats at once. You feel pulled between acting as a coach and judge. After all, you are forced to suggest training and development needs, suggest raises, and evaluate performance all at once. A memo from management last month emphasized the importance of raters going over the employees' self-appraisal with them. In previous appraisals you have only devoted a minute or so to this, and are now uncomfortable with the thought of using it to any great extent. All you have wanted in the past is to assign employees ratings that make all parties happy.

Next Appraisal to be Conducted...

You have only conducted five appraisals so far. All of them have been with Quality Specialists. Your next appraisal is with Bernie Tate. You have known Bernie for seven years. You were there for only two and a half years when Bernie was hired. You worked side by side with Bernie as a Specialist for four years before you were promoted to Vice President. Bernie has an engineering degree from the same university as you. You are apprehensive about evaluating Bernie due to the new emphasis you must place on self-appraisal and because of your friendship with Bernie. Another concern you have is with the lack of definite guidelines for assessing a high score to an employee on a particular criterion versus a low one. Last but not least, you have to draw up those training and development needs.

How you see it...

You have evaluated Bernie's performance, knowing you can change the evaluation if you wish after your meeting.

Work Quantity -

Defined as the amount or volume of the work produced in terms of project starts, project completions, consulting services performed, and committee work. Bernie has started two new projects this year, one of which is to develop a computerized expertise index of company personnel. This project's estimated completion time was 8 months. It is now into the 11th month, and it is still not completed. The second project was to improve the current inventory system. It was projected to take 6 months. Bernie and another specialist completed it in 5 months. You as V.P. do not have the feedback on how the system is doing. Bernie consulted on 12 occasions in the last year.

Work Quality -

Defined as the reliability and accuracy of the work produced. You have no feedback on the inventory system project. On the consulting work Bernie performed, the company has received seven excellent reviews, two good reviews, two average reviews, and one below average review. Both the below average and average reviews cited Bernie's difficulty in communicating strategies and ideas as the main weakness of the consulting work.

Absentee Rate -

Employees are allowed 7 days paid absences a year for illness without a doctor's excuse, and an additional 9 days paid absences with a doctor's excuse. They are allowed 2 personal days per year. Bernie has 2 weeks vacation a year. One week (5-day period) must be taken together. The second may be taken only one or two days at a time. Employees here work on a flextime schedule allowing them to arrive from 7 A.M. to 9 A.M. and leave from 4 P.M. to 6 P.M. Bernie has missed six days this year. Bernie used all available vacation in July and August. You hardly saw Bernie in those two months. These 2 months were part of the 11 in which the expertise project was a priority. You also noticed Bernie's absence at both 8:45 A.M. and 5:45 P.M. You have begun to wonder what flextime schedule Bernie selected. Flextime to you means you select a schedule (a time to come in and one to leave) and stick to it. You must ask Bernie at the performance appraisal interview about this issue.

Cooperation -

Defined as the willingness of an employee to accept supervision and adapt to various situations. Bernie is open to constructive criticism from what you can see and has always accepted supervision well. Often Bernie invites you, as well as the specialists in the quality department, to get involved with a project that has been delegated to Bernie.

Compatibility -

Defined as the ability of the employee to get along with others including supervisory personnel, peers, and subordinates. Bernie's a team player from what you can see. Bernie invites the participation of others often and usually gets it. Bernie's easygoing and laid-back almost to a fault. Sometimes Bernie lacks motivation on different projects.

Here are the ratings you have come up with:

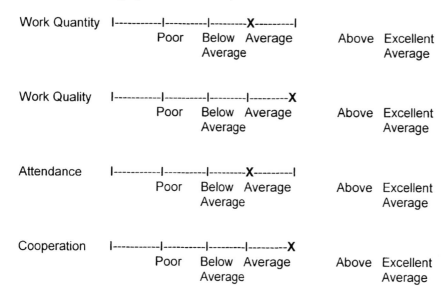

```
Work Quantity  |-----------|-----------|---------X---------|
                    Poor     Below   Average      Above  Excellent
                             Average                     Average


Work Quality   |-----------|-----------|---------|---------X
                    Poor     Below   Average      Above  Excellent
                             Average                     Average


Attendance     |-----------|-----------|---------X---------|
                    Poor     Below   Average      Above  Excellent
                             Average                     Average


Cooperation    |-----------|-----------|---------|---------X
                    Poor     Below   Average      Above  Excellent
                             Average                     Average
```

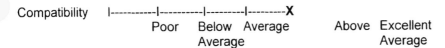

Compatibility |----------|----------|--------|--------**X**
                        Poor   Below   Average   Above Excellent
                                Average   Average

Note: You just finished rating Alex, the worst employee in the department, before deciding on Bernie's ratings. No one can figure out how Alex managed to get hired in the first place. As you began jotting down Bernie's ratings, another V.P. dropped by to complain about the conflict she was facing from employees who disagreed with their low ratings. You thought to yourself, "I don't need that hassle."

Final ratings for Bernie from you...

Note: You are not required to change the ratings from the previous page. Only do so if you feel the previous ratings were incorrect.

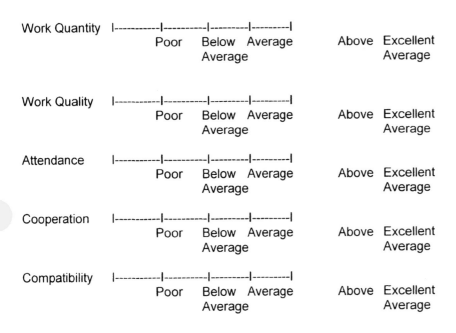

Work Quantity |----------|----------|--------|--------|
                        Poor   Below   Average   Above Excellent
                                Average   Average

Work Quality |----------|----------|--------|--------|
                        Poor   Below   Average   Above Excellent
                                Average   Average

Attendance |----------|----------|--------|--------|
                        Poor   Below   Average   Above Excellent
                                Average   Average

Cooperation |----------|----------|--------|--------|
                        Poor   Below   Average   Above Excellent
                                Average   Average

Compatibility |----------|----------|--------|--------|
                        Poor   Below   Average   Above Excellent
                                Average   Average

After the meeting...

1) Did your ratings of Bernie's performance change after the meeting? If so, how and why?

2) What have you determined to be Bernie's training and development needs, if any? Your company's needs?

3) What form of bias did you exhibit?

4) How could your company's performance appraisal system be improved?

5) What active listening skills did you use?

6) In retrospect, what would you do differently if you were to act as rater again?

In today's exercise...

You are Bernie Tate, and Cary Dunn is the Vice President of the department in which you work.

Background...

You are Quality Specialist at Wayne Gaskets, the largest producer of gaskets in the United States and the second-largest producer of them in the world. It is time for your annual performance appraisal. As a Specialist in the Total Quality Department, which consists of 16 Quality Specialists and 6 support people, you are not looking forward to your appraisal. You are uncomfortable with the idea of drawing up a self-appraisal this year, more than ever before. You feel burnt out at your job, though you do feel lucky to have it in this changing economy. You could have been more productive this year and you know it. But back to this appraisal, if you rate yourself completely honestly you'll be embarrassed first, and maybe out of a job second. After all, management doesn't want to hear excuses for slacking. Not even Cary Dunn, who is your friend and your boss, will be able to help you then. A memo from management last month emphasized the importance of employees developing an honest self-appraisal and sharing it with the rater.

Your appraisal...

You are apprehensive about this appraisal, and the fact that you and Cary are friends only makes it worse. You have known Cary for seven years. Cary had been there for only two and a half years when you were hired. You worked side by side with Cary as a Specialist for four years before Cary was promoted to Vice President. Cary has an engineering degree from the same university as you. You are worried about inflating your performance to Cary for two reasons: (1) you are friends, and (2) since Cary was at one time a Specialist, chances are this V.P. will be able to see through the desperate act of overestimating your own performance.

How you see it...

You have evaluated your own performance below, knowing Cary Dunn, your supervisor, probably has a different view.

Work Quantity -

Defined as the amount or volume of the work produced in terms of project starts, project completions, consulting services performed, and committee work. You have started two new projects this year. One project focuses on developing a computerized expertise index of company personnel. This project's estimated completion time was 8 months. It is now into the 11th month and it is still not completed. The second project was to improve the current inventory system. It was projected to take 6 months. You and another specialist completed it in 5 months. You consulted on 12 occasions in the last year.

Work Quality -

Defined as the reliability and accuracy of the work produced. On the consulting work you performed, the company received seven excellent reviews, two good reviews, two average reviews, and one below average review. You know your department receives feedback on these consulting jobs, but all you receive is a memo telling you how you were rated. No additional feedback is passed on to you. Just a few days ago you heard that the new inventory system you designed reduced stock outs by 12%, and cut inventory carrying costs by 20%. Your goal was to reduce stock outs by 18%, and cut carrying costs by 15%. The expertise project is still not finished. You lost your motivation working on it yourself. You finally see a trend in your performance. You perform better in a team environment.

Absentee Rate -

Employees are allowed 7 days paid absences a year for illness without a doctor's excuse, and an additional 3 days paid absences with a doctor's excuse. They are allowed 2 personal days per year. You have two weeks vacation a year. One week (5-day period) must be taken together. The second may be taken only one or two days at a time. Employees here work a flextime schedule allowing them to arrive from 7 A.M. to 9 A.M. and leave from 4 P.M. to 6 P.M. You have missed 6 days this year. You used all your vacation during the summer months. You avoided the office these months because it had just become too depressing. Same old job, same old people, same old everything. The expertise project just became a real downer to face every day. The flextime program was a lifesaver for you. On nice days you would start early and leave early. On ugly days, you started late and left late. After all, that's what flextime is for.

Cooperation -

Defined as the willingness of an employee to accept supervision and adapt to various situations. You always felt you were open to criticism and supervision, but you know you have a tendency to attempt to get others to "share the load" in work situations so to speak.

Compatibility -

Defined as the ability of the employee to get along with others including supervisory personnel, peers, and subordinates. You've always been a team player at the office. You invite the participation of others often and usually get it. You are easygoing and laid-back almost always.

Here are the ratings you have come up with:

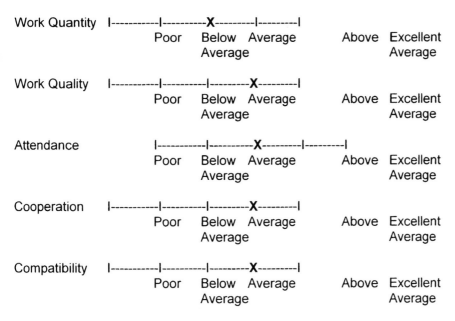

| | | Poor | Below Average | Average | | Above Average | Excellent Average |

Work Quantity — X at Average

Work Quality — X at Above Average

Attendance — X at Average

Cooperation — X at Above Average

Compatibility — X at Above Average

Note: Before deciding on your self-appraisal, you speak to another specialist in your department who has already been rated. You feel his performance is below yours, and his ratings were high. So you decide to go ahead and rate yourself somewhat better than you feel you deserve, but not as high as you were going to at first. Damn that conscience!

After the meeting...

1)   Did you think Cary's original ratings were accurate?

2)   Did the original rating change after your interview? Were Cary's final ratings of you fair?

3)   Do you think they (the ratings) changed because of your self-appraisal?

4)   What form of bias did Cary exhibit?

5)   What active listening skills did Cary exhibit?

6)   How could the appraisal have been more effective and useful?

Observer Questions

On another piece of paper answer the following questions.

1) Did the supervisor give the employee sufficient time to present his or her self-appraisal?

2) Did the supervisor use active listening skills, or did he or she do most of the talking?

3) Did the supervisor create a nondefensive climate and refrain from becoming defensive himself or herself?

4) Did the supervisor discuss training needs with the employee?

5) What mistakes, if any, were made by either the supervisor or employee?

6) What forms of bias should the supervisor be aware of when rating Bernie?

7) Were the supervisor's final ratings of Bernie fair?

8) Other comments:

APPENDIX M
GROUP PROJECT PEER EVALUATION

NAME: **Group Number:** _____

Please evaluate each member of your group in terms of their contribution to your group project. Rank everyone, **including yourself**, in each category using the following scale: 1=poor, 2=average, 3=excellent.

Group Members	Attendance (came to meetings, didn't miss for frivolous reasons)	Punctuality	Preparation (came to meetings prepared)	Overall knowledge and understanding of the group's task	Reliability (did assignment as promised and did his/her fair share)	Skill level/ quality of work (didn't need to be redone)	Attitude (positive attitude to task and others)	Communication (respectful, shared & fixed problems, helpful feedback)

GROUP PAPER: What percentage of your group grade does each person deserve, including yourself? (E.g., if a person did nothing, give them 0%; if a person made a major contribution, give them 100%.) Don't give 100% to every group member unless everyone made equal contributions. Please note that the percentages you give your group do not have to add up to 100. Please add any comments that explain your evaluations.

Group Members	Specific Contribution	Percentage of Grade Earned (0–100%)	Comments

Were there any extenuating circumstances that affected the performance of someone in your group?

Please explain extremely low ratings for teammates if there were any:

What did your group do well?

What could your group improve upon?

What could you personally do to be a more effective team member in your next group project? Write an action step for the behavior you want to improve.

THE DONOR SERVICES DEPARTMENT CASE
TEACHING NOTES

Case Overview

This case illustrates the effect of poor management and inadequate job design on the motivation of a Guatemalan office of translators. A vacuum of leadership and supervision allowed an informal group with poor work norms to take over, creating a climate that resulted in low productivity and morale. The protagonist, a consultant, must determine what recommendations to make about who should run the department and how the work should be structured.

Intended Audience

This case is appropriate for both undergraduates and MBAs. Although the setting is a nonprofit organization, the same problems can surface in a business context.

Discussion Questions and Answers

1. What was Joanna's diagnosis of the situation in the donor services department?
2. What should she recommend to Sam?
3. What are the cultural factors that influence this case? Would you expect any differences if it had taken place in the United States?

1. What was Joanna's diagnosis of the situation in the donor services department?

- All employees are committed to the overall goals of the organization and proud to work for the agency.
- The employees are conscientious about doing the work assigned to them but focus only on their tasks rather than the work of the department as a whole.
- There is an unequal distribution of work. The overloaded workers experience frustration and job stress, because it is impossible for them to finish their work while others have time to waste.
- There is a lack of cooperation and team spirit due to the unequal distribution of work and the presence of an exclusive subgroup. This results in low morale and low productivity.
- Productivity problems also stem from overly complicated work processes and a lack of attention paid to turnaround times and production goals.
- There are few standards or quality controls in place.
- The translators are overqualified for their job assignments, even though their level of English ability is not advanced. There is a lack of fit between the type of employees hired and the current job descriptions, which constitutes a motivation problem.
- Adding further insult to injury, the jobs are boring and repetitive. There is little variety in their work.
- The translators feel they cannot improve their English skills given their current tasks and a supervisor who is not bilingual.
- José promoted an employee (Elena) who is not suited for a supervisory role and put her in a no-win situation with regard to authority and discipline.
- The lack of attention on the part of Sam and José contributes to these problems. Because management has not established positive norms, the negative norms of the clique dominate the department.

2. What should Joanna recommend to Sam?

- Separate donor services from community services, making it a department in its own right at the same level on the organizational chart as Community Services and Accounting. Hire a department head who will ensure that donor services receives the attention, supervision, and importance it deserves. Hiring a department head will allow Elena to gracefully move from a supervisory position that does not suit her.
- Assign Elena a job that capitalizes upon her strengths—organization and diligence—and avoids her weaknesses—English and lack of supervisory interest or skills. Change her job title to Community Liaison and let her continue to work with the Spanish-speaking community

program representatives, which is a prestigious role in the department and suitable to her skills.

- If Magdalena, the most qualified internal candidate, will not accept the position, hire from the outside an experienced manager with excellent English and managerial skills.
- Reorganize the work on a geographical basis so that the four translators are responsible for entire gamut of work processes for a particular region. They would do enrollment figures, donor questions, gift registrations and acknowledgements, etc., giving them responsibility for both translations and clerical work. This would solve the problem of uneven work distribution, as all four would then have an equal and reasonable amount of work to do. The variety of tasks assigned would eliminate the boredom problem and the concern about not using their English skills. They would also have contact with community representatives from their region—their clients. Visitors who need the services of a translator would utilize those of the appropriate regional translator, a perk formerly enjoyed only by Juana.
- The two specialized jobs, which cannot be easily divided by region, should be assigned to the two most likely candidates. Marisol should continue preparing case histories, as it requires a customized computer and only one is available. Due to her superior English skills, Magdalena would take the senior translator job, which could include supervising the outsourced translations and answering difficult donor questions (formerly done by the director's secretary).
- Simplify the work processes to improve turnaround times and better utilize human resources.
- Encourage the department to work as a team by setting and posting departmental goals and output figures that would be updated daily and weekly. These goals would reflect the changing priorities in the department, and the translators would learn to help out other employees based on the needs of the workflow, rather than on friendships.
- Encourage teamwork by holding bimonthly meetings in which staff are kept informed of new developments and asked to problem-solve ways to streamline work processes and improve quality.
- Make the department a more pleasant place to work. Set norms that promote inclusion and mutual respect.
- Prepare a manual that explains how and why the work should be done that will be used in training and as a reference for current employees. Its purpose would be to supply clear work criteria and objectives.
- Provide equal opportunities for the translators to increase their English skills so their jobs have more meaning to them. A highly skilled bilingual department head should devote some time to coaching employees and upgrading the English work demanded of employees as much as possible.
- Redesign the office so that the traffic flow of visitors to Sam, José, and Elena does not disrupt the other workers. Use the file cabinets to form a hallway that leads to the back offices and place Elena in the front of the office rather than the back corner.

3. **What are the cultural factors that influence this case? Would you expect any differences if it had taken place in the United States?**
- Generally speaking, Central Americans expect to meet more of their social needs at work than Americans. Given a choice between locating their desk so it faces a wall or other employees, they will choose the latter so they can see and talk to other employees throughout the day. This may also be due to a polychronic orientation that allows them to focus on more than one activity at a time. Americans often prefer a quiet workstation that allows them to concentrate with fewer distractions on one task at a time, a monochronic orientation.
- In this culture, it is expected that people shake hands and inquire after families whenever they spot an acquaintance, regardless of the setting. Observing this etiquette is very important, so it was necessary to "hide" the translators from the foot traffic so they would have more time to focus on work and have fewer disruptions.
- The employees in this case were used to having decisions made for them by their superiors. An autocratic leadership style is still commonly found in this region (although recent research

indicates a trend towards more participation). Their lack of suggestions about how to make the necessary changes in the office does not indicate a lack of intelligence, but a lack of exposure to participative decision making.

- In a country characterized by high power distance and machismo, it is not surprising that Elena, rather than José or Sam, is the target of employee resentment. Elena is not an effective supervisor, but neither are her superiors. Because they are men and senior managers, however, the translators are more likely to overlook the flaws in their management style. Furthermore, José fits the Guatemalan image of a boss—articulate and forceful—while Elena does not.
- Gossip and pointed jokes are a means of social control in Latin America where there is more emphasis upon external controls (shame) than internal controls (guilt). This may explain why Juana might be slightly more powerful in this setting than in another culture.
- Although one finds cliques in many cultures, Latin American organizations tend to be more riddled with in-group/out-group factions.

Theoretical Analysis

Management Style: The managers and the supervisor in this case only performed some of the responsibilities in their job domain. Sam and José focused primarily on the parts of their jobs that interested them, and Elena mastered the paperwork but not the "people" part of her supervisor role. Although this type of behavior is commonplace and understandable, it does not result in an effective workplace.

The superiors' laissez-faire attitude and lack of interest in the translators' work and situation resulted in both low productivity and morale. In managerial grid terminology, the managers showed low concern for both the people and the task

In contrast, Joanna's management style indicated a high emphasis on both task and people. She provided structure, clear expectations, and removed obstacles that kept them from doing a good job. At the same time, however, she was concerned about their feelings and needs and tried to create a harmonious, inclusive workplace so that people looked forward to coming to work.

Although Joanna was limited somewhat by the cultural context and a hierarchical organizational culture, she tried to empower these employees. There are four aspects of empowerment: meaning, competence, self-determination, and impact (Spreitzer, 1992)

- *Meaning* (Employees see their jobs as having meaning when they care about their work and perceive it as important and meaningful): Joanna emphasized the importance of their role in retaining and attracting new donors and advocated for making the department of equal rank with the other departments.
- *Competence* (Employees are capable of performing all the work that must be done): Joanna placed the translators in jobs that suited their skills and worked to improve their English skills. She also set clear standards and procedures so workers knew what was expected of them.
- *Self-determination* (Employees have significant autonomy, considerable freedom and independence, and are able to use personal initiative in carrying out their work): The job redesign allowed the regional translators to choose which of their various tasks they would do each day, taking into consideration the departmental goals and priorities. The charts let them adjust work targets without having to be told by a supervisor (Mary Parker Follett's "the situation is the boss").
- *Impact* (Employees have some control and influence over what happens in their department): Although they seldom took advantage of the opportunity, Joanna asked employees frequently for their suggestions regarding policies and procedures and did not implement any without their approval (rubber stamp-like as it was).

Joanna's faux pas with the workstations is an example of an issue that fell outside the employees "zone of indifference" (Barnard, 1938). The new procedures and policies were within this zone, which lulled Joanna into making the mistaken assumption that the employees would accept almost anything she and Sam suggested or decided.

Motivation and Job Redesign: Many of the difficulties in this case can be traced back to selecting the wrong people for the job and job design errors. For example, José's personality and interests were more clearly suited for creative program work than the detail-oriented work of donor services. Finding those disparate orientations within the same person is usually a challenge.

Elena is a good example of what happens when the most dependable, competent employee is wrongly promoted to a supervisory position. In terms of McClelland's theory of motivation (1985), Elena had a high need for achievement, but virtually no need for power. She lacked the drive to learn to supervise, even if her superiors had taken the effort to teach her the necessary skills. Placing a less-educated person in charge of the bilingual secretaries was doomed to failure, given Elena's lack of supervision skills and retiring personality.

The bilingual secretaries were too well educated for their original jobs, another example of lack of fit that resulted in decreased motivation and frustration.

The uneven workflow also caused motivation problems. Expectancy theory can be applied to the overloaded translators who had no expectation of effort leading to performance. No matter how hard they worked, they could never clear away the backlog of work on their desks, which is demotivating.

A failure to understand social reinforcement theory explains some of the difficulties with Juana and her clique. Due to Elena's lack of leadership, there were no negative consequences for dysfunctional behaviors. Until Joanna, no one ever clarified for Juana that gossip and failure to act like a team player were not acceptable or explained that negative consequences would result (no chance of promotion, possible chance of termination). Elena did nothing when they wasted time, thereby reinforcing the negative behavior. In contrast, Joanna rewarded desirable behaviors both verbally and by assigning interesting special projects to people who had their work up to date.

The use of the chart showing goals and output is an example of the efficacy of goal setting as a motivational tool.

The switch to a regional division of work is an excellent example of job redesign (Hackman et al., 1975). Their previous jobs were simple and repetitive. The new, enriched jobs possessed the following characteristics of motivating jobs:
- *Skill Variety*—The new jobs combined several different tasks involving various skills.
- *Task Identity*—Translators were solely responsible for all the work processes done in their region, which made their job more meaningful.
- *Task Significance*—Joanna repeatedly explained the importance of donor services in the grand scheme of the organization and emphasized what good customer service meant to both donors and recipients.
- *Autonomy*—The regional translators had more discretion over scheduling their tasks as long as all were done in a reasonable time frame. Given the level of employee education, a procedures manual was necessary to set standards; the employees did, however, have a say (or veto) in developing the procedures.
- *Feedback*—The workstation cubbyholes allowed the employees to see at a glance their work progress. Joanna revised their work and gave them feedback on it. The praise or complaints about the work they did for their region went straight to them.

- *Customer contact*—The regional translators now dealt directly with two sets of customers—the community representatives and the donors who visited the programs—which further enriched their work.

Informal Structure vs. Team Approach

The lack of strong leadership created a power vacuum that Juana was quick to fill. She and her cronies created a we-they atmosphere with the rest of the department (in-group/out-group, leisure class/overworked class) that was fueled by gossip and pointed jokes. The informal structure was more powerful than a perceived need to work effectively as a department.

The lack of working meetings in the past also impeded teamwork. In the past, there was no superordinate goal (Sherif & Sherif, 1969) to unite the members into a team. Joanna set the superordinate goal of becoming a topnotch donor services department and structured cooperation into the department with the priorities chart, which made helpfulness a norm.

Organizational Culture: Pride in the organization, belief in its mission, and conscientiousness (to a degree) were the key values of the department's organizational culture. The values of the organization's religion were somewhat prevalent but did not always take precedence. Less-positive norms were passivity regarding problems, exclusion of certain members, unresolved conflict, and loafing on the job. Joanna tried to inculcate the following norms: efficiency, respectful treatment for all members, clear expectations, pride in achievement, and a focus on developing skills. In the past, no one had consciously managed the organizational culture or the socialization process by which members were brought into the organization.

EPILOGUE (IF PROFESSOR DECIDES NOT TO USE CASE B)
This is the report that Joanna sent to headquarters at the end of the four-month implementation period.

> "The major problems within this department were lack of supervision, unequal work distribution, narrow scope of work, absence of controls, and lack of cooperation among employees. During the next four months, I broadened the scope of the work by making employees responsible for geographical areas rather than one process. Staff were reassigned to jobs more in keeping with their skills. With the help of the employees, I wrote a procedures manual and designed new forms in order to streamline and control the processes. I revised the work daily and gave the employees immediate feedback, and quality improved noticeably. With the exception of the case histories sent to headquarters, no one had ever looked at their work before. I also redesigned the physical layout of the department to form workstations and eliminate traffic from certain areas. Lots of changes took place in a short period, and many hours were spent discussing them with staff. One employee quit, but the rest appeared to be happier with their jobs and more motivated. Looking back, I'd say it was a successful project, but I'd be less of a bulldozer if I had to do it over again."

Note: This type of job is not atypical for the educated spouses of expatriate managers on 2 to 3 year assignments in other countries. Although spouses are usually barred from official full-time work due to host country labor regulations, competent spouses are sometimes offered part-time jobs as a result of their social connections.

THE DONOR SERVICES DEPARTMENT (B)
EPILOGUE

Sam was pleased by the detail in Joanna's analysis of the department, but shocked by the findings. Joanna had compiled statistics on turnaround times and productivity levels for all the local sponsorship agencies, and Sam's office was the least efficient. Joanna went back to her other projects, but a week later Sam requested that she help him implement the recommendations. He was planning to run the department for two months to familiarize himself with its workings before hiring a department head. Because an invitation to implement is the dream (or nightmare) of all consultants, Joanna accepted—with the proviso that she could only spend two hours a day in the office given her other responsibilities. In actuality, Sam had no time to run the department, and Joanna ended up supervising the department two hours a day.

Joanna started out by having staff meetings with the translators. She told them she saw no reason why they could not be a topnotch donor services department and constantly stressed the importance of their role in retaining and attracting new donors. She told them that, as professionals who cared about the organization and its work, she expected them to work hard whether or not she or the other managers were present. She also asked them for suggestions on various changes. Although they were talkative in one-on-one conversations, they were generally very silent in these meetings. They were not used to being consulted, and they were not used to working on problems as a group. The only staff meetings they had attended in the past were inspirational talks from Sam who was stronger on vision than nuts and bolts. Joanna wrote up revised procedures for each work process and asked the translators for their approval before including them into a policy manual. There was no resistance to the policy changes.

Joanna redesigned the jobs of most of the translators. She split up all the community programs in the country and divided them into four geographic regions. Four translators were then named regional translators and made responsible for all the processes pertaining to their region. Juana and one of her cronies as well as the two newest translators were selected for these jobs, which were far more varied than the old jobs and included more opportunity to use their English and have contact with community personnel. This change eliminated the overload problem and gave the translators more control over the tasks they did throughout the day. As long as they met the needs of their region, they could decide what work needed to be done when. Magdalena, as senior translator, was relieved of translating greeting cards and simple queries from other countries, a task that now belonged to the regional translators. She continued to supervise the work of the external translators and assumed the difficult donor queries formerly handled by Sam's secretary, which resulted in speedier responses. Marisol continued to produce the case histories, but with help from the regional translators during crunch times. Because her work required a specialized computer, it was not possible to divide this task among the regional translators.

There was some jealousy regarding the two specialized jobs. The regional translators acknowledged that Magdalena's English was far superior to theirs. Some of them, however, coveted Marisol's job doing case histories, as they saw it as a more prestigious position. Even though her job was much more repetitive and boring than that of the regional translators, she had a special computer that symbolized status to the others. Furthermore, Sam frequently asked Marisol about her production because it related to his growth goals; the other translators were envious of the special attention she received from the director.

To deal with their perceptions, Joanna repeatedly reassured the regional translators that their job was equally important and they were not just a "pool" of clerical help. She focused on improving their English skills so they would eventually be in line for the specialized jobs should they become vacant. Joanna also assigned special projects that brought both status and growth opportunities to the regional translators who had their own work up to date. Although there was a little resistance to the reorganization, the jobs of the regional translators were so much more interesting that they accepted the changes fairly quickly.

Elena received a new title, "community liaison" and could focus on what she did best—keep track of communications to the communities. She was relieved to relinquish the headaches of supervision and became much more cheerful.

Joanna went over all the staff's work when she came to the office and answered their questions. She corrected their English and explained rules of usage so the translators not only improved their work but felt they were learning on the job. As she found fewer and fewer errors in their work, she checked it less and encouraged them to do their own quality control.

Joanna also posted two highly visible charts in order to motivate the employees and direct their efforts. One showed the priority tasks of the day, given the overall work of the department. This was done so that staff knew whether they should work on their own area or on special projects with a more pressing deadline. The other chart was a running total of the work produced compared with the set monthly quotas, so everyone could see the variance between the two and have something to aim for. She suggested a daily quota system for the employees, but there was so much resistance to that idea that she dropped it. Going from no supervision to a quota system was too great a leap for these employees and not an appropriate suggestion for their organizational culture.

Joanna made two changes in the office layout. She moved 20 file cabinets to form an aisle leading to the back offices. This separated the translators from all but the most garrulous and determined visitors. Elena's desk was moved to the entrance to the department, so visitors did not have to formally greet everyone else on their way to her desk.

Joanna's greatest implementation error involved the newly designed workstations. Joanna and Sam collaborated to make the best use of the available space; the result was partitions with cubbyholes that were both attractive and functional. However, they prevented the workers in the two back stations from seeing other people. There was one resulting casualty; a younger translator who reportedly had a volatile temper quit suddenly when her work area was reassigned to the far corner of the office. Apparently, the employee interpreted this location as the bottom of the totem pole. In reality, Joanna had placed her there because she trusted her to work with less supervision than some of the others (e.g., she put Juana smack dab in front of her own desk). There was a rumor that this employee had tried to poison Joanna's beverage out of vengeance; as the story went, Juana threw the beverage away before Joanna could drink it. One of the lessons Joanna drew from this incident (other than avoiding beverages at work) was that the physical setting had a different symbolic meaning to the Guatemalans than it did for her or Sam. She had underestimated the importance of social contact at work. And she realized in retrospect that although the staff was content to play a rubber stamp role in the reorganization decisions, Joanna should have involved them more in the decision about workstations. She tried to remedy the problem by having the regional translators pick up and deliver work to and from other areas, so they would have some opportunities for social contact built into their day, and the discontent eventually died down.

Juana never challenged Joanna's authority, but she did have a few run-ins with other people. In each instance, Joanna took Juana aside, informed her why this type of behavior was unacceptable, and coached her on how she could have handled herself more effectively. Joanna complimented Juana on her leadership potential and pointed out that she could use this strength to be either a negative or a positive force in the office. Juana would never, however, be promoted to a supervisory position until she showed the ability to get along with other people, whether she liked them or not. In a nonjudgmental way, Joanna explained that Juana's past actions had created a climate that was unpleasant for others and worked against the organization's mission. Fortunately, Juana chose to be a positive leader and became the most outstanding of the four regional translators. Joanna praised Juana for her change of attitude and assigned her special projects, like working on a training manual, to utilize her talents. The difficulties between the clique and the other employees disappeared almost completely.

Sam took four months to find a department head. To Joanna's surprise, he did not advertise the position; instead, members of the organization prayed for a candidate. Joanna acknowledged the wisdom of this method when they located an excellent woman with the age, experience, and language competence to inspire the respect of the translators. Joanna trained her, cleaned out her desk drawer, and gratefully returned to her research and her porch.

The production figures and turnaround times for the department improved significantly. The headquarters manager responsible for supervising donor services departments around the world was so amazed at the rapid improvement in the department that she came to visit the Guatemalan office. This further increased the morale of the staff—they had earned a reputation as "winners"!

Case Overview

This case provides students with an opportunity to understand and explore the complexity of a manager's job. The case, set in the semiconductor industry, describes a middle-level engineering manager's activities over the course of a day. Students see that this manager—Frank Question—is faced with a never-ending stream of organizational situations and opportunities to which he can respond. The primary issue in this case is Frank's effectiveness as a manager. The interplay of his personality, job requirements, and environment make the assessment of his effectiveness a challenging task for the students. The case also portrays aspects of meeting behavior, group conflict, differentiation and integration, and organization design.

Discussion Questions and Answers

1. **What are the key problems facing Frank?**
   - Dissension among departments holds back the work.
   - Lack of time, resources, and perhaps prioritizing is responsible for the lack of a crucial documentation.
   - Employee is burning out from chronic conflict among departments.
   - Employees can't respond quickly enough to production needs.
   - Poor relationship with key colleague harms collaboration of staff.
   - Unresponsive boss.

2. **What are the pros and cons of Frank's managerial style?**
   See the Mintzberg analysis below

3. **What is the source of conflict among the different departments? How could it be resolved?**
   Sources of conflict are: departmental design that prevents easy collaboration, attitude of Rod Cameron, different goals and time demands of the three departments involved, and lack of resources. (Use the differentiation and integration table to analyze the three departments.)

4. **What are the advantages and disadvantages of Custom Chip, Inc.'s organizational structure?**
   - Advantages—allows employees to work in their own functional area and profit from the opportunity to have staff meetings dedicated to their specific work. This allows them to deepen their professional skills. They benefit from the exposure to staff working on the same type of problems.
   - Disadvantages—The boundaries of each department and their varying goals and demands prevent a spirit of collaboration and quick responses to problems. The current design makes good customer service more difficult.

5. **What steps should Frank take to improve this situation?**
   - Make documentation a priority—consider forming an alliance with other department heads to obtain the necessary resources to make this happen.
   - Form a task force from the departments who are interdependent and ask them to devise solutions to coordination problems. Reengineering might be helpful in this case.
   - Work at improving his relationship with Cameron.
   - Study the costs and benefits of using a team structure that would combine the current departments.

Alternative Approach to Teaching the Case

Another alternative you can take with this case is to have students relate Frank's activities to Mintzberg's managerial role framework, which is found in his article in Chapter 2 of the *Reader*.

1. Figurehead—Although Frank was told about the fifth-year anniversary of Bill Lazarus, he did not acknowledge it.

2. Liaison—Frank established a good relationship with the head of applications engineering through formal and informal meetings. He attempted to do the same when meeting with Rod Cameron.

3. Leader—Frank has attempted team building in his regular weekly scheduled meetings with the product engineers. He also acted as a leader when he commended his engineers for quality work. His communication with Sharon exemplified the leader role.

4. Disseminator—First 30 minutes in weekly meeting to inform subordinates about upcoming company plans, projects, and other news that might be of interest to the group.

5. Monitor—He sought and received information and developed an understanding of issues when meeting in Rod Cameron's office.

6. Spokesperson—In the meeting one year ago with Sam Porter concerning the updating and standardization of all documentation for manufacturing products, Frank was speaking for and representing his department. He also was a spokesperson for his department during the conflicts with Rod Cameron.

7. Entrepreneur—Frank instituted regular weekly meetings (proactive). His idea to develop a proposal clearly outlining the benefits of a documentation program demonstrates the entrepreneurial role. Also, the proposal to Rod about pooling the efforts of manufacturing and the engineers was entrepreneurial in nature.

8. Disturbance handler—Bill Lazarus was not able to continue processing of 1210A work order because of the unhelpful attitude of the applications' engineer. Frank quickly resolved this in his meeting with Rita. Frank moved quickly to resolve the conflict between Sharon Hart and Brian Faber.

RUDI GASSNER AND THE EXECUTIVE COMMITTEE
OF BMG INTERNATIONAL (A) AND (B)[*]
TEACHING NOTES

Case Summary

BMG International was the international music subsidiary of the German media conglomerate Bertelsmann, the second-largest media enterprise in the world. In May 1993, CEO Rudi Gassner and the executive committee were gathered for one of their quarterly meetings. Arnold Bahlmann, a regional director and executive committee member, had recently negotiated a reduced manufacturing transfer price for the upcoming year's production of CDs, records, and cassettes. Because business plans for the year had been established in March based on the assumption of a higher manufacturing cost, the new price would realize an unanticipated savings of roughly $20 million. As a result, the executive committee was now faced with some tough decisions. It had to decide whether or not to change the business plans of each country and the managing directors' bonus targets (which were based primarily on their achievement of the targets) to reflect the new manufacturing price.

In Gassner's mind, the issues were clear. BMG International had achieved tremendous success and growth in its short lifetime of six years, and the team had every right to feel good about its performance. But now, Gassner wanted to guard against the company becoming a victim of its own success. He knew that they would have to monitor carefully the economics of the business and maintain their agility in order to meet future challenges. In light of these concerns, he felt that the managing directors should be held accountable for the savings. The executive committee, however, seemed unwilling even to entertain this possibility.

The (A) case describes the discussion during the quarterly meeting as well as the evolution of the executive committee from its inception. A short (B) case describes how Gassner decided to handle the issue of the reduced manufacturing price: when he sensed that the executive committee was not going to consider the possibility of changing bonus targets, he asked the group at least to agree to use the adjusted calculations as a reference for internally monitoring performance during the year, and then he tabled the discussion. The (B) case explains Gassner's rationale for his actions and his ultimate decision not to base bonuses on the adjusted targets.

To accompany the cases, we have prepared a video (HBS No. 494-524, 13:09 minutes) to be shown at the end of the class discussion. The video shows excerpts from a discussion with Rudi Gassner in an MBA classroom in February 1994. He elaborates on his decision and discusses the challenges and opportunities he faces in managing the top-management team of a global enterprise and the impact of his style on the team's culture.

Learning Objectives

This case was designed for the "Managing Your Team" module of the MBA second-year elective course Power and Influence. It highlights the role of the manager in designing and building an effective team[1] and the impact of the manager's style on the team's process and

---

[*] Professor Linda A Hill prepared this teaching note with the assistance of Research Associate Katherine Seger Weber as an aid to instructors in the classroom use of the cases "Rudi Gassner and the Executive Committee of BMG International" (A) and (B), HBS Nos. 494-055 and 494-056 respectively. A brief video, "Rudi Gassner at BMG International;" is also available, HBS No. 494-524.

[1] By managing a team, we mean managing the group performance of one's direct reports as opposed to managing their individual performance. Groups cannot be understood solely in terms of their collective

outcomes: These lessons are critical ones for MBA students. I found in my research that many new managers fail to recognize, much less address, their team-building responsibilities; they rarely understand the impact of their style on their team's process and outcomes.[2] In particular, this case provides an opportunity to analyze the issues of delegation and empowerment within the special context of a senior management team in a complex global organization.[3]

There are two levels of analysis to be considered in this case: (1) the specific question of how Gassner should handle the team meeting in which the group seems resistant to changing the bonus targets, and (2) the "bigger picture" analysis of the team's design, culture, and effectiveness. In teaching the case, I focus on the impact of Gassner's style on the evolution of the team over time. I use the instance of the executive committee meeting and the bonus question as one specific event that illustrates Gassner's options as the team manager and the impact of his actions on the team's process and outcomes.

The specific learning objectives for the case are:

1. To understand what an effective team is.

2. To consider the roles and responsibilities of the team manager and the impact of his or her style on the team's process and outcomes.

3. To explore the challenges of managing diversity—both interfunctional and international diversity—in a team context.

Assignment Questions

1. What should Gassner and the executive committee do about modifying the business plan and bonus targets of each country?

2. How effective has Gassner been in managing the executive committee?

3. What challenges lie ahead for Gassner and the executive committee?

Case Analysis

As discussed above, this teaching note focuses primarily on the role of the team leader and the impact of his or her style on the team. In managing the team, the leader has two sets of responsibilities: designing the team and facilitating the team's process (see **Exhibit 1**).[4] The

---

individual member characteristics. Groups have their own dynamics (e.g., stages of development, problem-solving processes, norms, cohesiveness) which have an impact-positive or negative—on group performance.

[2] See Linda A Hill, *Becoming a Manager: Mastery of a New Identity* (Boston: Harvard Business School Press, 1992), pp. 229-231.

[3] Although I use this case to study the role of the team manager, it is a rich case and could also be used effectively as a case on leadership in the special context of a large, highly-decentralized, global organization. It could also be used to highlight the specific nature of top management teams, transnational teams and cross-cultural, management, or performance measurement and incentives in a team context. For more information on these subject areas, see the References list at the end of this teaching note.

[4] For more elaboration on these responsibilities, see "Managing Your Team," HBS No. 494-081. Another responsibility of the team manager is managing the team's boundaries and relationships with external constituencies. For their teams to be effective, managers must understand the power dynamics of the larger organization, build relationships with those on whom the team is dependent, and negotiate their team's interests with others (see "Managing Your Team," p. 4). As manager of the executive committee, one area in which Gassner must manage the team's external relationship is with regard to the business targets and expectations of senior management (his boss, Michael Dornemann). The case does not contain much information with regard to Gassner's actions in this arena, but it is important for students

analysis below addresses each of these roles, examining how Gassner designed the team (set the agenda, decided what type of teamwork was needed, and defined the team's composition and structure) and his impact on the team's process and evolution. After this "big picture" diagnostic analysis, we then turn to the specific action questions of what Gassner should do in the future to improve the effectiveness of the team, and specifically, what he should do in the deadlocked executive committee meeting.

In order to fully understand the team and Gassner's role, however, it is useful first to study the context within which they operated. The analysis below therefore begins with a brief overview of the company context and the associated political dynamics.

Company Context

BMG International was a complex transnational organization composed of 37 local operating companies spread throughout the world and a corporate headquarters located in New York. From Bertelsmann, the company inherited a strong tradition of decentralization and delegation of operating responsibility and authority to local management. This culture was supported by Gassner's own personal style of delegating authority (He noted, "I liked the Bertelsmann style. It was very close to my own personal style.") as well as his strategy for the company, which emphasized the development of local repertoire ("I made it clear to the local managers that their foremost responsibility was developing domestic talent.").

Gassner's strategy, however, was not based solely on the development of local repertoire. Citing the global success of Whitney Houston as the ideal, his strategy was to develop acts locally and then launch them worldwide. He noted that "globalization allows you to serve a bigger market. Every time we add a new country, we would increase our revenue accordingly.... There's more money to be made outside the borders if you do it right." As Henn emphasized, the success of the strategy depended on the global coordination of the dispersed operating companies:

> You have to have coordination between the regions as far as marketing and promotion activities are concerned because recording and marketing expenses are far too great these days for any one [local] company to be able to earn back its investment in one country only.

BMG International, therefore, embodied a complex mix of decentralization and autonomy among the diverse operating units, combined with a centralized strategy which created interdependence among them.[5] In addition, the company was facing an environment of change that heightened the need for global coordination. In its short lifetime of six years, BMG International had achieved tremendous success and growth (revenues increasing 20% annually), but now there was evidence that some markets had matured and growth was leveling off. In this environment, efficiency and cost control were becoming highly important, and Gassner believed that "a regional focus alone would no longer be enough to guide BMG International through the uncertain and ever-changing terrain of the next five years." (Indeed, Gassner had begun to articulate a strategy for BMG International to serve as Bertelsmann's worldwide media distribution channel: "We're the only company in Bertelsmann that is really global; [w]e have something

---

to remember the team's external constituencies and Gassner's role in managing them as well as in managing the team itself.

5   For more on the complexities of establishing organizational forms and strategies for global companies, see, for example: J. A. Alexander, "Adaptive. Change in Corporate Control Practices," Academy of Management Journal, Vol. 34, No. 1, 1991, pp. 162-193; M. Goold and A Campbell, *Strategies* and Styles *The Role of the Centre in* Managing Diversified Corporations (Oxford: Basil Blackwell, Ltd., 1987); S. Goshal, and N. Nohria, "Horses for Courses: Organizational Forms for Multinational Corporations," Sloan Management *Review,* Vol. 34, No. 2, Winter 1993, pp. 23. 35; and W. C. Kim and R. A Mauborgne, "Effectively Conceiving and Executing Multinationals' Worldwide Strategies," *Journal of International Business Studio*, third Quarter, 1993, pp. 41948.

Bertelsmann can build on.")[6] The new emphasis on cost control was frustrating for local managers; they were skeptical about their ability to aggressively develop and market repertoire while also reducing costs.

These factors together—diversity, interdependence, resource scarcity, and a changing business environment—can heighten the potential for political conflict in an organization.[7] It is important to keep this context in mind when analyzing the goals, stakes, and pressures that Gassner and the executive committee faced in working together to lead BMG International and their individual regions.

Designing the Executive Committee

Setting the agenda. One of the first tasks a manager must address in designing his or her team is setting the team's agenda. Members need a clear and compelling sense of what is expected of the team. If the team does not know where it is going, its efforts will be fragmented, and team members will waste much of their energy trying to figure out how to spend their time. If team members do not know how their efforts fit into the broader organizational mission, they will not appreciate why their work is important. The agenda should be doable but challenging if it is to be engaging to team members.[8] Moreover, the manager needs to ensure that the members understand and perceive that they are in fact a "team"—that they share a common agenda and will benefit from their collective action. Simply because individuals are members of the same work unit or even share a joint task does not mean that they perceive themselves as interdependent or part of a team.

Gassner introduced his vision of the executive committee to the members as "the group, which will lead BMG International." He described his agenda for the team:

I always wanted to run a business on the basis of a European board system, like a vorstand:[9] although it is chaired by one person and members have their own portfolios [regions], the committee decides business issues jointly.

The way I see it, the board should decide about important issues strategically or from an investment point of view. And I wanted everybody to be involved in the process, despite the fact that some issues may not have a direct consequence for their region.

Gassner's description of how he wanted his executive team to operate included substantial delegation of authority and decision rights to the team. (On the continuum presented in **Exhibit 2,** his vision was of a team that operated with almost full delegation of decision-making authority by the leader.) In reality, however, the team did not operate in exactly this manner. Both Gassner and the team members recognized that the team did not have as much authority and control as his vision suggested.

---

[6] Indeed, in April 1994, BMG International moved ahead in this direction by agreeing to market and distribute multimedia CD-ROM products internationally for U.S: based Crystal Dynamics. Gassner commented on the deal: "This agreement represents an exciting first step in BMG International's effort to develop new multimedia markets throughout the world." 'Crystal Dynamics' CEO added, "BMG makes available to us their direct distribution system in 37 countries around the world, which overnight gives us one of the most powerful distribution systems in the business." See M. A. Gillen, "BMG Moves Into Multimedia with Pair of New Pacts," *Billboard,* April 9, 1994, p. 6.

[7] See J. P. Kotter, *Power and Influence: Beyond Formal Authority* (New York: The Free Press, 1985). For more on political conflict in organizations, see "Power Dynamics in Organizations," HBS No. 494-083.

[8] See the sections on managing teams in R. L. Hughes, R. C. Ginnett, and G. J. Curphy, *Leadership: Enhancing the Lessons of Experience* (Boston: Irwin/McGraw-Hill 1993).

[9] The case notes that a *vorstand was* a German managing board consisting of full-time executive members who carried out the day-to-day operation of a company.

Gassner's perspective was that the team members were not taking enough initiative at first. He commented that "everybody's too nice," and according to Gorman, desired more "strong dissenting opinions." Many of the team members, however, perceived that in fact, Gassner was not open to their opinions and that he did not delegate much authority. They described his style as "essentially autocratic" and like that of "a dictator." Although Gassner said he wanted the group as a whole to decide on strategic issues and investments even if they did not have direct consequences for some regions, some team members felt that in reality, he was not open to such broad-based decision making. One RD noted:

> Rudi usually does not allow himself in any way to be influenced by people who are not speaking directly about the areas for which they are responsible. In other words, he'll be very receptive to me for everything within my area, but when I stray into areas of the general good, I find him very unreceptive.

Indeed, there was some disparity between Gassner's stated agenda and the function of the team in the eyes of its members. (This issue of how much authority was delegated to the team is analyzed in greater detail below.) It is questionable, therefore, whether the team members felt bound to a common agenda or perceived themselves to be a team that benefited from collective action.[10]

Deciding what type of teamwork is needed. Closely related to defining the team agenda is the manager's decision about what type of teamwork is needed to fulfill that agenda. As Drucker points out, teams often fail because their managers are confused about which type of team they desire.[11] In an editorial in the *Wall Street Journal*, he makes a useful distinction between three kinds of, teams: baseball-type teams, football-type teams, and tennis doubles-type teams. Each type of team requires distinct behavior from the manager and its members and each has different strengths and limitations.

Drucker compares the baseball team to the surgical team performing an open-heart operation. He notes that on such teams the players "play *on* the team"; they do not "play *as* a team." They each have fixed positions that they rarely leave. The second baseman never pitches; the surgical nurse never does the anesthesiologist's job. Drucker notes that some of the advantages of such teams are that individual members can be clearly held accountable for their performance and trained and developed to the fullest extent of their individual potential. Each position can be staffed with a "star, no matter how temperamental, jealous or limelight-hogging each of them might be." The baseball team is inflexible, however; it only works well when the game has been played multiple times and when the sequences of its actions are thoroughly understood by everyone—circumstances seldom found in business today.

Drucker compares the football team to a symphony orchestra. Like those on the baseball team, the members of these teams have fixed positions. As Drucker puts it, "the oboe never comes to the aid of the violas, however badly they flounder." However, on these teams, players do play as a team. There is a common "score of music" which must be followed. If there are stars on the team, they are featured only if the score calls for a solo. Otherwise, team members must subordinate themselves to the team.

Finally, there is the tennis-doubles team, which Drucker compares to an improvisational jazz ensemble. On these teams, the players have a primary rather than a fixed position. As Drucker observes, in this kind of team "only the team performs; individual members contribute." Team members cover their teammates, adjusting as necessary to their teammates' talents and weaknesses and to the changing demands of the game. The requirements for tennis-doubles-type teams are quite stringent. They require intense commitment, trust, and collaboration on the

---

[10]   The individual performance-based incentive plan Gassner created supported this attitude (see discussion below).

[11]   P. Drucker, "There's More than One Kind of Team," *Wall Street Journal*, February 11, 1992, p. 16.

part of the team. Members have to be trained together and work together for some time before they can fully function according to this model. The managers of such teams must be quite comfortable with and skilled at empowering others; the members also have to be comfortable being empowered and must have substantial team management expertise.[12]

Gassner's vision for the executive committee team seemed to be closest to the "football" type team, in that each member would have his own portfolio (his "fixed position") but the group would work together to decide issues jointly (would "play *as* a team"). From the descriptions of the team members, however, it appeared that the group in fact functioned more as a "baseball" type team, composed of individual "stars" who were successful in their own regions and played *on* the team, rather than as a team. The European subcommittee, however, was evidence that team members were moving more toward the model of the "football team," in that this small group did decide certain issues jointly and they were largely self-managed.

Composition. Gassner composed the executive committee of the five Regional Directors and four senior staff members whom he had already placed in the senior positions of leadership at the company (see **Exhibit 2** of the case). Several aspects of the team composition are relevant for our analysis of the executive committee: that it is a senior team, and that it is a functionally and internationally diverse team.

Special characteristics of senior teams. As a team of senior managers, the executive committee had special characteristics that are unique to top management teams. In particular, Ancona and Nadler[13] identify the following characteristics of senior teams:[14]

- *Salience of the external environment.* The executive team is uniquely influenced by external forces such as customers, suppliers, competitors, financial markets, the board of directors, and shareholders.

  With responsibility for the operational success and strategic direction of their own region (or staff function) as well as for the strategic direction of the company as a whole, the executive committee members were highly focused on managing external forces. The issue of the reduced manufacturing price is just one example of an external event (albeit Sonopress was internal to Bertelsmann as a whole) to which the team had to respond.

- *Complexity of the task.* Executive teams must cope simultaneously with internal operations management, external relationship management, institutional leadership, and strategic decision making; these add up to more interrelated elements and higher levels of uncertainty than most teams face.

  With responsibility for their own "portfolios," special assignments (such as Bahlmann as head of central manufacturing), as well as for the company as a whole, executive committee members wore many "hats" and juggled, many responsibilities simultaneously. Hambrick notes that the danger with such multiple commitments is

---

12 For a discussion of the characteristics of self-managed work teams, see for example K. Fisher, *Leading Self-Directed Work Teams: A Guide to Developing New Leadership Skills* (New York: McGraw-Hill, 1993) and C. C. Manz and H. P. Sims, Jr., *Superleadership: Leading Others to Lead themselves* (New York: Prentice Hall, 1989).

13 D. G. Ancona and D. A. Nadler, "Top Hats and Executive Tales: Designing the Senior Team," *Sloan Management Review* (Fall, 1989).

14 Hambrick also offers a thorough analysis of senior groups and the "centrifugal forces" that tend to diminish their integration and team-like behavior. See D. C. Hambrick, "Top Management Groups: A Conceptual Integration and Reconsideration of the "Team Label," Columbia University Graduate School of Business Working Paper, January 1993. For more on top management teams, see the References list at the end of this teaching note.

that the team members could identify more strongly with the success of their individual region than with the executive team as a unit.

- *Intensified political behavior.* One of the executive team's key roles is to exercise power effectively. Consequently, for good or ill, politics are more pronounced and more frequent than in other teams.

  The evidence in the case suggests that the executive committee did not suffer much destructive political behavior. (See discussion below on political dynamics and "prevention factors.")

- *Fixed pie rewards.* While there are many rewards for executive team members, the ultimate reward is succession to CEO. By definition, succession created a zero-sum game, and thus a perception of a fixed pie of rewards. The question of succession may cause competition among team members that is detrimental to their working together effectively.

  As one team member noted, "there is a certain amount of jockeying for position within the executive committee" because of Bertelsmann's required retirement age and the possibility that Gassner could move on to other assignments within the company even before his retirement. The team members also wondered whether a non-German could ever be chosen to run the company—a question that presumably would be especially sensitive for the non-Germans on the team. The competition, however, did not appear to have a significant impact on the team's effective functioning to date, perhaps because Gassner's departure was not imminent.

- *Previous experience of members.* Executive team members tend to have histories of distinguishing themselves through individual achievement rather than through teamwork. Thus, they may be less prepared to participate effectively as team members. In addition, as Hambrick points out, individuals who have demonstrated significant and sustained accomplishments in their careers often expect a considerable degree of autonomy and discretion in the conduct of their affairs.

  Indeed, Gassner selected his committee members based on their track record of success in their regions (for the RDs) or for their functional expertise (for staff members). Bahlmann was the one exception, being selected as a regional director without previous experience in an operating company. Gassner chose him for his strategic experience and "because he had very good people skills." It is not known whether these individuals had much experience with teamwork, but presumably they did not. In terms of the expectation of autonomy and discretion on the part of senior individuals, the executive committee did display some of these attitudes. Gassner noted that the team members were somewhat resistant when he first formed the executive committee: "They had not been organized before in a way that had these limitations [to their autonomy], and they didn't like it."

- *CEO as team leader.* Because the leader of executive teams is typically the CEO, there may be more social distance between the leader and members of top teams than in other settings. The CEO determines rewards, including succession, and there is usually no recourse beyond the CEO if problems arise.

There was no question who was the boss in the executive committee—Gassner was clearly in charge, and had the ultimate authority. At the same time, however, there was a strong sense of camaraderie among Gassner and the team members. He promoted a culture in which the group frequently socialized and played sports when they were together. Their comfortable manner is evident in the group photograph, **Exhibit 7** of the case.

Functional diversity. The team comprised five regional directors who were line managers in charge of diverse regions, and four staff members responsible for different functional areas (finance, A&R marketing, human resources, and legal). Because of their responsibilities, the line managers and staff members each had different priorities, interests, and stakes. In addition, their physical locations helped to create a division between them. As is typical of many large organizations, the staff were located in New York headquarters with the CEO (Gassner), and the line managers were "in the field" spread throughout the world. To some extent, this structure created a natural connection between the senior staff executives and Gassner, which could potentially frustrate the RDs.

There was diversity *within* the line and staff groups as well. Certainly, for example, as head of A&R marketing, Henn had different priorities and concerns than CFO Gorman. And the RDs had different interests and priorities from one another because of their own different areas of expertise and the wide variations among their regions. As the case describes, Preston was seen as the "repertoire expert," Bahlmann was the "strategy expert," Stein was trying to carve out market share in a mature market, while Segura and Jamieson were concerned with establishing companies and developing talent in their relatively undeveloped markets.

As discussed above, the more diversity and interdependence in an organization, the more the potential for political conflict. (Just as diversity and interdependence were realities for BMG International on a company-wide basis, they were factors within the executive committee as well.) In terms of the line versus staff distinction, for example, Gassner noted that there was some political dissonance between the two groups in the initial executive committee meetings (ECMs). According to the RDs, they felt that "[a]t first there was no role for the RDs. . . The staff went into the meeting very well prepared and tried to establish a couple of policies with the help of Rudi in order to structure the business." The RDs were wary of the role of the staff, according to Gassner, and he had to explain to them: "You've got to see the staff as somebody helping you; it is not some governing body who tells you what to do."

For the most part, however, the executive committee did not seem to suffer from much destructive political conflict. A number of prevention factors were in place that ameliorated conflict, such as strong leadership by Gassner and a corporate culture that provided shared goals and values.[15]

For example, Bertelsmann's deeply rooted culture of decentralization and empowerment combined with team norms of "healthy competition" and mutual respect allowed each team member to be a "star" without the others feeling compromised. As Henn described it:

> Everybody in that room is the *best* at what he does. The absolute best, and we all know it . . . . We're also total egomaniacs, the whole group of us. But in this company, we still work as a team because we give each other the space to be the fool that everyone can be sometimes.

In addition, the executive committee had not been operating in an environment of financial resource scarcity. As Bahlmann insightfully noted, the group had been able to avoid a certain amount of political conflict because ample funding has been available to all of them: "[T]here has

---

[15]   For more on political conflict and prevention factors, see "Power Dynamics in Organizations," HBS No. 494-083, especially pp. 3–4.

always been money there to do what we wanted. So . . . the group has never been tested to see whether we can really work as a team under pressure when it comes to a fight over who will get funds for what investment."

International diversity. The executive committee was internationally diverse as well as functionally diverse. Including Gassner, the group comprised four Germans, three Americans, two from the U.K. (one Scottish, one English), and one Spaniard. (See **Exhibit 7** in the case for more demographic data about the team members.)

Nationality has been found to influence individuals' cognitive schema (e.g., assumptions, perceptions, knowledge), values, demeanor (e.g., preferred nonverbal communication patterns), and language—and consequently, their behavior on transnational teams. There is considerable debate, however, about the relative impact nationality plays in determining an individual's behavior and the group dynamics of a transnational team.[16]

Indeed, an individual's behavior on a team may be affected by a number of factors including his or her nationality, business/organizational experiences, and other, nonwork-related life experiences.[17] For example, it appears that organizational culture can reinforce or reduce the impact of nationality on an individual's behavior. In addition, there is some evidence that the more individuals have been exposed to other nationalities, the less likely they are to conform to the behavior associated with their own nationality. The careers of most of the executive committee members included extensive international experience, which, combined with Bertelsmann's corporate culture of "respect for the traditions of each country in which it operated," likely reduced the impact of each member's nationality on his interactions with the team.

Current research suggests that teams composed of individuals with diverse national backgrounds can face special challenges in functioning effectively on the one hand, since misperception and miscommunication can abound in such teams. On the other hand, they also have particular advantages that can enrich their performance, since more breadth of perspectives and experience can be brought to bear in culturally diverse teams and their diversity allows team members to avoid the trap of "groupthink." The executive committee did not appear to face inefficiencies due to its multiple nationalities. The common language of the group was English,[18] and the team members seemed comfortable communicating together effectively. The notable exception was Segura, of whom Gassner noted: "Segura . . . is an outstanding executive, but because he thinks his English is limited, he would rather discuss issues separately with me than in an open meeting." While Segura was highly successful in his own region, Gassner's model of the team deciding issues jointly surely suffered as a result of his reticence.

For a more elaborated discussion of transnational teams, see the **Appendix** and the References list at the end of this teaching note.

---

[16] For more information on transnational teams, see the References list at the end of this teaching note.

[17] See for example, D. G. Hambrick, S. G. Davison, S. A. Snell, and C. C. Snow, *When Groups Consist of Multiple Nationalities: Toward a New Understanding of the Implications*, and S. G, Davison, C: C. Snow, S. A, Snell, and D. C. Hambrick, *Creating High Performance Transnational Teams: Process, Phases, and Pitfalls*. Reports sponsored by and available from the International Consortium for Executive Development Research, Lexington, MA. Also, see R. M. Kanter and R. Corn, "Do Cultural Differences Make a Business Difference?: Contextual Factors Affecting Cross-Cultural Relationship Success," *Journal of Management Development,* Vol. 13, No. 2, pp. 5–23, special issue on cross-cultural management.

[18] It is interesting and significant that a German company made it policy to use English as the official company language. The purpose was to be all-inclusive, according to BMG International employees, if two German speakers were speaking together in German and a non-German speaker entered the room, "even a secretary," they would automatically switch to English. Within the executive committee, English was not the native tongue for the majority (Gassner and four of the others), and speaking English placed them all "on equal footing."

Structure. Gassner was very clear in defining the structural aspects of the executive committee. The group met four times per year at the New York headquarters to discuss current operating issues, and once a year outside of New York to examine long-term strategy. The agenda for each EMC was decided as follows: before each meeting, committee members were polled for items, and then Gassner "edited" the suggestions to create the agenda, which was circulated to the group.

The design of senior executive compensation and incentive systems is an area of much study and controversy. Certainly, the performance incentive system that a team manager puts in place has an impact on the behavior of the individual team members and how they function together as a group. The extent of the impact, however, is a much-debated subject. Most management theorists agree, however, that shared-fate economic incentives, in which every member of a team receives the same reward based on the overall performance of the team, tend to create more collaborative behavior than arrangements that tie rewards to individual performance.[19]

Gassner's system created individual performance incentives for each manager.[20] Consistent with Bertelsmann tradition, every manager at BMG International was rewarded with a performance-based bonus. Gassner's incentive plan was, as he described it, "very aggressive." Bonuses were based on each operating unit's *betriebsergebnis*, a German accounting term translated to mean *profit adjusted by imputed interest and imputed inflation* to account for cost of capital or opportunity costs.[21] Each year, business plans were agreed upon between the MDs, RDs, and Gassner, with specific targets set for *betriebsergebnis*. If managers exceeded their *betriebsergebnis* target by a certain percentage, they could receive up to half their salary as a bonus.[22]

For the managing directors in charge of local operating companies, their individual success in meeting their *betriebsergebnis* target seemed to be a logical basis on which to reward them; doing so encouraged them to focus on increasing their profits while using assets efficiently—just what Gassner, presumably, wanted them to do. The regional directors, however, were also rewarded by the same system: their bonuses were based on the achievement of the *betriebsergebnis* target for their region. The RDs, therefore, had a strong economic incentive to focus on the success of their individual region; they were not rewarded financially for their effective participation as members of the executive committee team. Students should note this disparity between Gassner's objectives for the team and the incentives he created for the team members.

---

[19] See, for example, D. C. Hambrick, "Top Management Groups: A Conceptual Integration and Reconsideration of the 'Team' Label, " Columbia University Graduate School of Business Working Paper, January 1993, p. 14. For more on incentive plans, see the References list at the end of this teaching note.

[20] According to the case, all Bertelsmann employees participated in profit-sharing, which certainly was a type of "shared-fate, group-based" performance incentive. It seems, however, that profit-sharing amounted only to a small portion of the managers' overall compensation; clearly it was the bonuses based on their individual *betriebsergebnis* target that was foremost in their minds.

[21] Using *betriebsergebnis* as the calculation for bonus criteria (rather than straight profit, for example) is a way of holding operating managers accountable for the "costs" of the capital and assets they use to generate profits. *Betriebsergebnis makes* managers responsible for the use of capital as if they were raising it from the market (with interest payments) instead of obtaining it from inside Bertelsmann. Accounting for the costs of these assets encourages managers to use them more efficiently.

[22] The specific structure, in terms of how much bonus managers receive based on certain levels of target achievement, is confidential information that we are not privileged to reveal in this case or teaching note.

Managing the Executive Committee: Rudi Gassner and the Evolution of the Team

The management style of Rudi Gassner had a significant impact on the development, culture, and process of the executive committee. In order to understand and evaluate his impact, however, it is useful first to analyze Gassner—his sources of power and management style.

Rudi Gassner. When he was chosen by Dornemann to be the CEO of BMG's international division, Gassner possessed many personal sources of power and credibility[23] that he continued to rely on as the head of BMG International. From his days at PolyGram, he had gained extensive expertise in the international music business and an impressive track record of success. Dornemann noted that he "had the right background in the music business and the right international experience. He best fit the leadership qualities we were looking for." The fact that he was handpicked by Dornemann was another source of power and credibility for Gassner within the organization.

As CEO of BMG International, Gassner had the most positional power (including formal authority and centrality in networks both internal and external to BMG International) of any individual in the organization, but in his role as leader of the executive committee, he relied heavily on his personal sources of power in order to exercise influence within the group. His personal sources of power included his:

- *Track record*. Gassner had continued to build his track record of success as CEO of BMG International. In only six years, he had grown the business from 17 to 37 countries, increased revenues annually 20%, and increased international market share from 11% to 17%.
- *Expertise*. Gassner arrived at BMG with substantial career expertise in the international music business and he continued to expand his knowledge within BMG. According to one MD describing Gassner during the business plan reviews, "Rudi knows the business inside and out, and he has an amazing grasp of the details. When he is going through these plans, he will go into particular line items if he wants to." Gassner's knowledge and grasp of the details earned him credibility with both the MDs and the members of the executive committee.
- *Effort*. The case describes Gassner's lifestyle of frequent travel and late nights spent at concerts viewing new talent with local operating managers (Gassner also alludes to this lifestyle in the video). **Exhibit 6** of the case shows his tightly-packed schedule of the business planning meetings he and Gorman attended. Another aspect of his effort is that Gassner always "did his homework." Before coming to the May ECM, for example, he had already discussed the reduced manufacturing price issue with Bahlmann and Gorman; as he noted, "[M]y opinions are not just invented on the spot. I usually discuss issues one-on-one with certain people beforehand. If I have a subject on the agenda, I almost always have an opinion on what I think the outcome should be." Gassner's effort and commitment were clear and earned him significant credibility.
- *Attractiveness*. Gassner had an easy, charismatic style that is best displayed in the group photo (**Exhibit 7** of the case) in which he stands smiling, dressed in blue jeans, arm-in-arm with the members of the executive committee. The video also reveals this manner. Gassner's attractiveness allowed him to develop easily another source of power—his strong network within the organization and industry. The case notes that he had cultivated the trust of managing directors and local employees and kept in touch with them frequently, "just to double check that my messages come through." He nurtured a similar network with artists, agents, and others throughout the music industry.

---

[23]   For more on individual sources of power, see "Power Dynamics in Organizations," HBS No. 494-083.

In addition to the above sources of power, other aspects of Gassner's personal style had an impact on his relationship with the executive committee. Committee members remarked, for example, that he had strong opinions and that it could be difficult to change his mind. They noted that "to influence Rudi, you have to convince him.... You have to be prepared to stand up for your argument." Jamieson observed that because Gassner usually had strong opinions, "I have never had an informal brainstorming session with him." Although Gassner's vision was for team members to share their opinions with the group and make decisions jointly, certain aspects of his personal style undermined his rhetoric, causing at least some committee members to feel that "Rudi is not a man who needs or wants many debates," and that he was the ultimate decision maker. Moreover, several committee members noted that it was especially difficult to influence him in a group setting; as Jamieson commented, his best opportunities to influence Gassner were not within the context of the team meetings but in separate, private meetings.

For the most part, Gassner's own influence style could be described as "push"—a style that earned him the reputation of being "tough." ("Push" influence strategies include proposing, reasoning, stating expectations, and using incentives and pressures.[24]) He stated his expectations strongly, for example, throughout the business planning process; one MD was so motivated by Gassner's expectations that he felt it was "a moral imperative to get it done." Certainly, the performance-based bonus system was an example of a powerful incentive Gassner used to motivate his team and the organization. His influence style in team meetings frequently relied on reason and logic (he had to be "convinced" in order to change his mind). Finally, he often proposed his ideas to the group as a way of influencing them. Sallen noted that "it is generally clear to all what his feelings are on most issues"; in the conversation at the May ECM, he alluded several times to his desire to change the bonus targets and finally proposed that he wanted the MDs "to be held accountable for the savings."

Although Gassner used "push" influence strategies most frequently, he had the ability to draw on a wide range of styles, and when circumstances called for it, he could also employ "pull" strategies. ("Pull" strategies include involving, listening, disclosing, visioning, and finding common ground.[25]) Sallen noted that "Rudi does a lot of consensus-taking" to find common ground within the group. Gassner was versatile in his use of different styles and was skilled at tailoring his approach to the individual and situation at hand.[26] As one RD explained, "Rudi plays a different role with each MD, depending on their personality and where he wants their country to go. Sometimes he plays the good cop, and other times he plays the bad cop. He's very versatile and very results-oriented."

A final strength of Gassner's that is important to note is his high level of self-awareness. He described aspects of his own style accurately and in detail, for example:

> [The team members] have a difficult time convincing me. I am a person who likes to win an argument....I think I know what is good for us. Therefore, when I'm convinced that that's the right way to go, it takes great effort to get me off that route.

Even more significant than his own self-awareness, however, is the fact that Gassner, seemed to understand how others perceived him. His comments in the case demonstrate that he had an accurate perception of what the executive committee members thought of his style; for example, he noted, "I think they feel a lot of things are a bit too prepared or precooked." He recognized his impact on the team, acknowledging that the way the team functioned "may very

---

[24]   See the *Influence Style Questionnaire*, copyright 1988 by Situation Management Systems, Inc., Hanover, MA.

[25]   Ibid.

[26]   For a discussion of the importance of tailoring one's influence style to the particular individual and situation at hand, see "Exercising Influence, "HBS No. 494-080, and "Broadening Your Influence Style Repertoire," HBS No. 494-077.

will have to do with me and the way I run things." The video shows Gassner reflecting further on his personal style and its impact on the team. Self-awareness and regular introspection are critical ingredients for successful management development and often distinguish executives like Gassner who reach the highest levels of corporate leadership from those who derail or stall in their careers.

Gassner's impact on the team. One of the key responsibilities of team leaders is managing the paradoxes and balancing the trade-offs inherent in team life (see Exhibit 3). The most significant trade-off for Gassner in managing the executive committee team was in balancing his managerial authority with the team's discretion and autonomy. Given that they were a team of senior executives in a highly decentralized and entrepreneurial organization, it is not surprising that the locus of authority and discretion would be a most challenging issue for this group. For teams to function most effectively, authority must be balanced between the manager and team members in ways best suited to the issue at hand. There are many ways decisions may be made by consensus. Some may be made through negotiations between the manager and those team members most directly affected by the outcome. Others may be made in a consultative manner, the manager gets input from the team members and discusses different alternatives with them, but retains the role of ultimate decision maker. And finally, some decisions may be made by the managers without consultation with team members. Managers cannot delegate final accountability for the team's performance, but they should strive to achieve a delicate balance between their authority and the discretion and autonomy of the team.

As discussed above, the reality of authority and discretion within the executive committee team diverged from the initial agenda Gassner outlined. Gassner conceived of the group deciding business and strategy issues jointly and he was frustrated that at first the RDs did not offer their opinions readily. Their initial reticence was understandable, however. Groups are inherently conservative at first, and until they have had time to establish trust and a comfortable way of working together, members tend not to be outspoken. The RDs offered this as one explanation for their initial lack of assertiveness; as Preston said, "It took us a certain amount of time to find a way of really working together." The RDs also noted, however, that during the early ECMs, they were somewhat overshadowed by Gassner and the staff, who were very active in seizing control of the meetings. According to Bahlmann, "Rudi needed to establish himself and the regional structure; it was like him telling us, via the [EMC] agenda, what we're going to do. It was our 'educational process.'"

In time, however, the RDs became more vocal, and according to Preston, their influence more balanced with that of the staff. Bahlmann explained that this shift in power was a result of the RDs' growing confidence and success in running their regions and that it reflected the realities of the business: "The regional directors and the managing directors make the decisions about the operating businesses and acquisitions."

However, even as the RDs began to assert their opinions more, they discovered that, in Jamieson's words, Gassner was "not a man who needs or wants too many debates," and was "essentially autocratic." Henn described Gassner as a "brilliant dictator." Although Gassner's vision for the team seemed to be that of a decision-making body, executive committee members instead described the team meetings as "an opinion-building exercise," and a forum for Gassner to test his ideas on the group. Consistent with the belief of several team members that they could influence Gassner more in a private meeting, they found that "real decisions" occurred outside of the ECMs.

Overall, the executive committee team seemed to work together effectively, agree on basic strategic goals, and avoid destructive political conflict. They successfully managed most of the paradoxes inherent in team life, including the need to embrace individual differences as well as collective goalsand the need to foster support as well as confrontation among members. In terms of their personal relationships with each other, team members seemed to like each other and be cohesive and comfortable working together. The question of balancing authority and discretion with Gassner, however, remained a challenge to be ironed out.

How Could Gassner Improve the Team's Effectiveness in the Future?

As discussed above, at the time of the case, BMG International was facing an environment of change. Previously, the strategic focus had been on growth and the development of local talent. But as some markets matured and competition intensified, Gassner had also begun to emphasize cost control, disciplined management, and an interest in capitalizing on BMG International's position as Bertelsmann's premier global distribution channel for new media and entertainment.

In this new context, the executive committee would have to work even more interdependently to achieve global operating efficiencies, capitalize worldwide on locally developed artists, and establish transnational marketing strategies. To meet these challenges, the team would have to take a more actively collaborative role in corporatewide strategic planning and business decisions; they would have to in fact make important decisions jointly. The type of teamwork the group engaged in would have to change; in Drucker's terms, they would have to move more in the direction of a "football team" or even a "tennis doubles team."

In order for the executive committee to enter this new phase, Gassner would have to alter his management style and allow the team more authority, discretion, and autonomy. His style was well-suited to turning around the organization and achieving significant growth, but the company was no longer in the turnaround stage it was in when he first took leadership. In addition, the organization had grown so large and complex that he could no longer manage the entire workload of leading the company himself (e.g., traveling to 37 countries on a regular basis to familiarize himself with the local situation and people was infeasible). Out of necessity and to meet the challenges of the future, Gassner would have to adjust his style to the new realities by delegating more authority and discretion to the team. He would have to send strong signals that he was willing to change his approach to encourage the group to become more of a collaborative decision-making body.

What Should Gassner Do during the Meeting?

There are solid arguments on both sides of the debate that arose during the May ECM over the question of whether to alter *betriebsergebnis* bonus targets to reflect the newly reduced manufacturing price. Gassner was concerned that without adjusting the bonus targets, the incentive plan he put in place would not have its intended impact; the new prices created "windfall profits," and he wanted the managers to be held accountable for them. The RDs, however, argued that business plans had never before been changed after being agreed upon, even though many unpredictable events happened during the year that affected the attainment of the original target.[27] They argued on the basis of consistency that the bonus criteria were never changed, even when the managers had been harmed as a result, and that it would be "unfair" to change them now, when the event could work in their favor. To alter the targets would be to go against well-established corporate culture and operating norms.

It is important to note that not all of the RDs were affected by this issue. The new manufacturing price applied only to those RDs who sourced their products from the European vendor (Bahlmann, Preston, Stein, and to a tiny—virtually insignificant—extent, Segura). However, they all agreed that the bonus targets should not be altered. Their consensus on this issue is an excellent example of their cohesion and lack of competitiveness. If they had been competing aggressively with one another, those who were not going to receive the "windfall"

---

[27] Indeed, the record industry was notoriously unpredictable. If a key artist did not release an album on time, for example, the entire year's business plan could be thrown off, and for smaller record labels, the financial viability of the operating company could even be jeopardized.

would presumably want the targets of the others to be adjusted accordingly so that the group would remain on "equal footing," and no one would have an "unfairly easy" time meeting their bonus target. It is highly significant, therefore, that no such suggestion ever arose.

During the meeting, Gassner became frustrated by the RDs' attitude, which to him seemed parochial—more like that of an MD than of a senior executive thinking about the good of the whole company. During the discussion at the end of the (A) case, he was considering two options for how to handle the RDs' resistance to his perspective: (1) he could table the issue for now, or (2) he could provoke them by saying what was on his mind.

Toward the end of class, I usually take a vote (see the teaching plan below), asking students what they think the team should do. The class is usually split fairly evenly on changing versus not changing the bonus targets. In terms of how Gassner should handle the impasse in the team meeting, some feel that this issue is an important one, and given his usual assertive style, he should tell the group what is on his mind, propose his plan, and lobby for buy-in. Others, however, believe that given the new direction Gassner and the team must set in order to meet the challenges of the future, he should seize this opportunity to demonstrate that he is willing to concede more discretion and authority to the group by backing down.

Students should note that Gassner's dilemma is an example of another paradox of team management that team leaders must balance and negotiate: they must focus both on performance and on the learning and development of the team. They must allow for trade making a particular decision "correctly" or using it as a developmental experience. "Mistakes" should be treated as sources of learning rather than reasons for punishment if risk taking (and thereby, development and innovation) are to be encouraged. Even if Gassner believed the team was making a suboptimal decision in leaving the bonus targets unaltered, he still might decide to let them have final discretion because he wanted to encourage their confidence and development as a decision-making body.

ANALYZING THE (B) CASE
To the surprise of many students[28] especially those who feel that Gassner was autocratic and unable to share power with others—that is exactly what he decided to do. As the (B) case reveals, he proposed that the group at least agree to use the adjusted calculations as a reference for internally monitoring performance during the year (no one opposed the suggestion), and then he tabled the discussion by asking the RDs to share the situation with their MDs and report back to him later. In doing so, he effectively turned over control for this decision to the committee members. As he later found out, in their various ways, they communicated to their MDs that despite the "windfall profits" for some, the original bonus targets would remain.

Teaching Plan

This teaching plan is designed for one 80-minute class session. There are many issues to discuss in this case, and with the video at the end, I find that it is a tightly packed class that moves very quickly.

Although the primary focus of the class is on the long-term evolution of the team and the impact of Gassner's style on the team's process and outcomes, I first pose the question of what Gassner should do in the meeting as a way of opening the discussion.

---

[28] Students often believe that managers cannot grow, develop, and change their management style later in their careers. In fact, however, many managers report that their styles do evolve over time. Furthermore, research shows that continuous growth and development through on-the-job learning experiences is a critical ingredient for managerial success.

I. Introduction (5 minutes)

This case offers us the chance to study the challenges and opportunities of designing and leading the senior executive committee of a complex global enterprise.

Our task today is twofold: (1) We want to step into Gassner's shoes to address his immediate concern: the committee has a delicate and important decision to make, and Gassner is not pleased with the way the discussion is going. What are his options for how to handle this situation? (2) We want to think more long term. How effective is the executive committee? What is working? What is not? What, if anything, should Gassner do to improve the effectiveness of the team?

II. What should Gassner do in the meeting? (10 minutes)

A. Should he table the discussion? Should he tell them what is on his mind? What are the pros and cons of each approach?

B. What does he want? What is the purpose of the discussion?

C. Why is the discussion going the way it is?

D. Why is he frustrated?

III. How effective is the executive committee? (20 minutes)

A. Why did Gassner create the executive committee?

B. What are the potential sources of political conflict?

    1. What are the natural tensions among the team members?

    2. What are the factors in place that prevent political conflict from disrupting the effectiveness of the team?

C. What works well about the team?

    1. Why does the team work together as well as it does?

    2. What impact does the team design have on how the team functions?

D. What does not work so well about the team?

E. What are the team's norms for dealing with conflict?

IV. How would you describe Gassner's influence style? (10 minutes)

A. What sources of power does he rely on?

B. What is the impact of his style on the team and its development?

V. What could Gassner do to improve the effectiveness of the team? (10 minutes)

A. What challenges will the team face in the future?

B. Will Gassner need to change his style in managing the team in the future? If so, will Gassner be willing and/or able to change?

VI. Let's find out what he did in the (B) case. (5 minutes)

A. Before reading the (B) case, how many of you think the team should change the bonus targets? (Take a vote.)

B. Take a few minutes to read the (B) case, which describes Gassner's decisionand his perspective on how the executive committee members approached the situation.

VII. Let's hear from Gassner himself by watching the video. (13 minutes)

VIII. Conclusion (5 minutes)

Because this class session is so tightly packed, there is no time at the end for a formal conclusion or even a "mini-lecture." I simply ask students to identify and reflect on the key lessons they can take from this case about (1) the critical ingredients for team effectiveness and (2) the balance between managerial control and delegating authority. In the subsequent class, I provide the students with an opportunity to share with each other any observations that they have about the Gassner video and what they have learned thus far about team management.

Rudi Gassner and the Executive Committee
of BMG International (B)

When he sensed that the executive committee was not going to consider the possibility of changing the bonus targets, Rudi Gassner decided to table the discussion. But before he did so, he said to the group: "OK, let's agree at least to use the adjusted calculations as a reference for internally monitoring performance during the year." No one openly, opposed the suggestion. Gassner continued, "This still leaves open the question of whether or not bonus targets will be affected. Go back to your people and speak to them about this. Think about what we should do, and get back to me as soon as you can with your recommendations."

Gassner explained later that he "wanted to send a message to the MDs, and also the RDs, about the need to stay focused on profitability and cost control:"

I wanted them to know that we still considered them accountable, even though there were these windfall profits.

I also wanted to test the RDs to see if they would go back to their MDs and say, "by the way, this is not just your new target, but also your new bonus target." I wanted to test who would really do that, and who would be hesitant.

I found two camps. I think Segura and Stein decided that they agreed with the logic, and they went to their people and told them that the targets and the bonuses were changed. Preston, Jamieson, and Bahlmann, on the other hand, said "hold it." With all their rationale, it boiled down to the fact that this was just one of those things they didn't want to do. They probably informed their MDs of what had happened "European style" with a phone call instead of a letter, although I know that Arnold sent a follow-up letter to his region. (See **Exhibit 1.**)

Gassner's Decision

In the weeks following the ECM, Gassner continued to think about this issue:

I analyzed the situation and tried to find the logic for why we should not base bonuses on the adjusted targets, and I found it. Over the years, we have never changed the targets—good times, bad times, rain or sun. And I felt that we would be opening a can of worms, because when you do it for this issue, you basically have to do it for all issues.

You can argue whether I came to this conviction because of these reasons, or because I wanted to solve the problem. But this is what I decided to do.

As soon as Gassner reached his decision, he told each member of the executive committee individually. He also began to think about the agenda for the upcoming ECM in September. Although he was comfortable with the outcome of the manufacturing price issue, he felt that it might be time to explore the larger question of whether the bonus system should be modified, given current business conditions and his goals for the future of the company.

Exhibit 1   Letter from Arnold Bahlmann to the MDs in his Region

22.06.93

TO: Central Europe Managing Directors

FROM: Arnold Bahlmann

SUBJECT: Manufacturing cost reduction effects

cc.   Rudi Gassner

Dear [MD],

Our manufacturing negotiations for the business year 93/94 have been quite successful. Meanwhile, you have got already the new price list effective July 1st and now attached please find the calculated impact for your territory based on the business plan.

Your internal Betriebsergebnis target for the business plan shall be corrected by the total impact of the manufacturing price adjustment in order to make sure that we do not lose this major advantage for 93/94. However, there is, with the approval of Rudi Gassner, no adjustment of your Bertriebsergebnis target for your bonus scheme.

Kind regards.

Yours,

Arnold

Enclosure

BESTFOODS AND GLOBAL LEADERSHIP
TEACHING NOTES

Case Overview

This case highlights the strategic importance of including the best people from around the world in a multinational corporation's senior leadership. The setting is Bestfoods International, one of the largest global food companies. The case describes the philosophy and approach of the CEO, Dick Shoemate, and of Laura Brody, a senior HR manager who strongly believes in the strategic function of Human Resources. Along with her bosses, Dick Bergeman, the senior VP of HR, and Shoemate, Brody is faced with the challenge of increasing business competitiveness by increasing the number of women in leadership positions around the world and making headway on an issue that is perceived differently in various parts of the world.

Brody frames this challenge as an organizational change effort and is herself a skillful change agent. She carefully lays the groundwork for change by developing the commitment of the Diversity Advisory Council and establishing training programs and Balanced Scorecard goals for diversity, including at the highest levels of global leadership. Brody is fortunate to have a supportive boss who grants her the autonomy to implement innovative programs. She also benefits greatly from having a CEO who is committed to promoting the best people, including both women and men, to top positions and who is a strong supporter of Brody's broader organizational change initiatives. She determines that the best way to speed up progress is to hold an action-learning meeting for the most senior and high-potential women from around the world. The case describes the planning phase, survey feedback process, design, and implementation of an innovative Women's Global Leadership Forum, which is apparently the first of its kind. A major challenge is ensuring that the Forum will serve as a catalyst for institutional change.

Case Themes

The primary topics portrayed in the case are global competitiveness, organizational change, strategic human resources, the role and experience of women, and global leadership.

Intended Audience

The case is appropriate for use with managers, MBA students, or undergraduates.

Discussion Questions and Issues

1. Given that diversity, especially as defined in the United States, is not a hot topic in most countries, should the headquarters of U.S.-based multinationals promote diversity initiatives in their worldwide subsidiaries? And if so, what's the best way to accomplish this?

This is a controversial issue. U.S. companies are obligated by law to refrain from discrimination in all countries in which they operate, regardless of local customs. Brody wisely insisted that diversity must be framed as a strategic issue, and that it has to be broadly defined so as to pertain to more than the common U.S. definitions of gender and ethnic status. The focus behind her formidable energy is neither "being nice to women" nor "evening up the score." Her driving force is making sure Bestfoods has the top-quality employees it needs for the future, especially in the company's senior leadership positions. Some of the Bestfoods affiliates initially took the position that diversity was only a U.S. issue. When they were exposed to diversity training programs, however, they recognized that they too had their own form of diversity challenges and opportunities, oftentimes in the form of religious, ethnic, or ideological diversity.

2. Do you agree with Brody's idea to hold the Forum? Why or why not? Can you suggest an alternative that would accomplish the same purpose or be even more effective?

Students may well have many different suggestions. A key lesson is that a sole intervention will not usually work. As Herb Shepard (1984) said, "Light many fires" and try to intervene on various levels in various subsystems. Brody recognized Shepard's advice in that the Forum was not a stand-alone event.

3. What challenges and problems do Brody and Shoemate face in getting their diversity strategy implemented?

- The previously mentioned disparate views on the relevance and strategic importance of diversity around the world.
- One of the largest obstacles relates to one of the historic strengths of Bestfoods—its highly decentralized structure. Neither the CEO nor corporate HR can send out edicts on diversity to the entire corporation and expect them to be adhered to by all the affiliates.
- The misleading illusion that all women do or should think and act the same. The high degree of cultural, and other forms of diversity within the company and even among the Forum participants, makes it difficult to reach to consensus on issues.
- There are always political issues to manage in a major organizational change effort like this. For example, some male managers viewed the forum as a threat. Corporate HR initiatives also sometimes run into resistance on the part of division-level HR departments.
- Attitudes are often a major obstacle to change. In many organizations, attitudes of both men and women can impede career progress of women. Harmful male attitudes are old-fashioned stereotypes about " a women's place," their supposed lack of capabilities, failure to understand that women may have a very different experience within the company, and perceiving inclusion efforts as threats. Potentially harmful female attitudes include unconscious preference for male bosses (who may in reality have more power in the system than a female boss), viewing other women as competitors, and blaming their failure to advance entirely on discrimination rather than holding themselves, in part, accountable.
- Similar to most companies, Bestfood's organizational culture has aspects that are both obstacles and aids to change. For example, the global action-learning task forces, which provide a model for accelerated learning and rapid change in the face of problems on an organizational level, are a positive force for change. While the conservative, sometimes change-averse nature of the overall organizational culture is an obstacle, the strongly held values of positive relations and mutual respect support the changes Brody is promoting. The company's propensity to promote from within has the benefit of fostering employee loyalty. One disadvantage of promoting with, however, is that this practice prevents management from simply hiring senior women from other companies into Bestfoods' leadership positions. Laterally transferring into senior leadership positions is, in fact, the single most common route for women into senior leadership positions (Adler, 1997). Another disadvantage is that there is less diversity in managerial styles and ideas when all employees are promoted from within.
- Confusion concerning the differences between women in general and women leaders, a mistake that is rarely, if ever, made with men. We never ask about the needs of male janitors and generalize to those of the male CEOs. However, some companies lump all women together when it comes to describing the condition of women and making policy.
-

4. Prior to the opening session of the Forum, what steps have Brody and her HR colleagues taken to promote diversity efforts throughout the company?

Brody carefully laid the groundwork for systemwide organizational change by:
- Linking diversity to the corporate vision, thereby recognizing it as a strategic business issue—not "reengineering society or changing attitudes," which would result in resistance
- Having the CEO send an annual "state of diversity" newsletter
- Gathering statistics on women and minorities within the company and their industry

- Providing decision makers with information about diversity challenges and opportunities and best practices of other companies
- Inviting HR professionals from leading companies to describe their best practices so that Diversity Advisor Council members could have direct, personal exposure to new ideas
- Planting seeds of ideas
- Taking a team-building approach with the Diversity Advisory Council, which involved them in crafting their own vision and strategic definition of diversity
- Defining diversity broadly enough so it would not exclude people, particularly white males, and would apply to the contexts of countries other than the United States
- Explicitly and publicly measuring and tracking progress on diversity goals
- Establishing the Cultural Connections program and the SOS program and continuing to sponsor the INROADS program
- Expanding diversity training programs to groups of managers in various countries and regions
- Gathering and communicating data from senior men and the most senior and high-potential women on their views of career and organizational opportunities and impediments, which highlighted differences in women's and men's understanding of the issues.
- Inviting nominations of Forum participants from the division presidents, which were then ranked by the Corporate Strategy Council. All of these senior executives thus became closely involved in the overall organizational change process and the planning for the Forum. The process forced them to recognize and carefully examine the career progress of their most senior and high-potential female managers.
- Including the most senior executives in the Forum—male and female—so they would become acquainted with the women and hear for themselves what the company's most senior and high-potential women thought and recommended

5. What actions or factors contributed to making this a successful change effort?
   - The survey-feedback process on women's and men's perceptions raised the level of dissatisfaction with the status quo and, along with some of the women's own experiences, served as a trigger event to promote change.
   - The change effort was initiated by and continuously supported from the top. The CEO remained a strong supporter and involved all the senior executives in the Forum.
   - The CEO sent clear messages about his goals regarding diversity, and the links between strategy, diversity, and increased competitiveness.
   - The senior executives responded quickly to the Forum recommendations and took immediate action wherever possible.
   - Bestfoods did not bring in a diversity expert to prescribe a strategy. Instead they relied on the women's recommendations, which gave the women a voice and a sense of ownership in the process. The suggested changes "fit" the culture and thus have a better chance of being successfully implemented.
   - Brody is a skilled change agent. For example, she used a vocabulary that the organization finds acceptable. She never pushed a more feminist rhetoric or her own strategies down the throats of senior executives. However, she continually pushed for progress, but in a way that was acceptable in Bestfoods' organization culture. Brody was careful to include others' ideas in the change process.
   -

6. What else should Brody and Bestfoods do to institutionalize the changes begun at the Women's Global Leadership forum? (See the Epilogue for other ideas.)

   - Report the Forum results immediately to the most senior leaders in the company at the WorldTeam meeting
   - Develop diversity councils in each division so they can respond to local diversity issues

- Add a target to the Corporate Balanced Scorecard to measure diversity progress
- Have the CEO report on the Forum to signal his continued support and interest in the outcomes
- Provide management development training for midlevel managers so women receive training before they arrive at senior levels
-

EPILOGUE

Brody returned to her office the day after the Forum to find a stack of messages from participants. A number of them had been asked by their bosses to report on the Forum at that Friday's Executive Committee Meetings and were hoping to borrow Brody's overheads summarizing the survey results and recommendations. While these requests for instant reports indicated the curiosity many nonparticipants felt about the Forum, Brody thought it was unreasonable to expect the participants to make presentations on their first day back on the job. At her request, Shoemate sent a cease-and-desist order to senior executives, asking them to hold off requesting formal reports until he had put an official communication strategy in place. A week later, Shoemate also sent a letter to participants and members of the DAC and CSC, thanking them for their input, complimenting them on the quality of their recommendations, responding in writing to each recommendation, and laying out the next steps that the company would be taking.

Meanwhile, Brody prepared a communication packet for each participant, including overheads they could use in their presentations to their colleagues "back home." Brody and Shoemate also circulated potential ideas for responding to the Forum recommendations that the Corporate Strategy Council (CSC) would be considering at their September meeting, just two months after the Forum. Brody discussed the recommendations with each Council member individually, so she could respond to any reservations they might have before the formal meeting. The CSC approved all the women's recommendations and even added two of their own. The council agreed to take responsibility for oversight of the company's global diversity strategy. In addition, the CSC members, as division presidents, as well as the unit presidents reporting to them, agreed to establish diversity councils in each of their respective businesses. Rather than simply adding international members to Brody's Diversity Advisory Council, they voted to establish local councils and invite the women who had attended the Forum to participate. This represented a major change from the previous attitude that "diversity is just a U.S. issue." The Forum had successfully demonstrated that diversity is a global challenge that appears in various forms throughout the world.

A month later at the October WorldTeam Meeting attended by the company's top 125 managers, Brody announced Shoemate's decision to establish a new Balanced Scorecard goal: By the year 2005, 25 percent of identified high potential employees will be women—an increase from the previous target of 16 percent. To Brody's pleasure, some male executives expressed their concern that the goal was still too low and recommended increasing it!

Changes occurred at an even faster pace after the WorldTeam Meeting. Local division councils were formed all over the world. Several Latin American countries—Argentina, Brazil, Colombia, and Mexico—began benchmarking themselves against other multinationals operating in their region. They discovered that Bestfoods is in the forefront in establishing diversity policies, measurable objectives, and meeting with employees about their performance and career enhancement opportunities. Both Argentina and Mexico held their own Women's Forums, modeled after the Arrowwood experience. Europe's newly formed diversity council created a regional strategy for retaining women and enhancing their development opportunities. Europe is also considering offering a training program for senior executives on managing inclusion.

The Women Leaders Network established at the Forum quickly became a very active conduit for communications and change. Immediately following the Forum, the women shared their reentry stories via e-mail or phone. They continue to use the network for coaching, disseminating information about career opportunities, professional support, and strategizing.

Even though the Forum was designed to benefit the company by focusing on women, other groups have also profited from increased attention to the concerns the women raised. For example, Bestfoods is now providing management development training for both male and female midlevel managers to ensure that more formal development opportunities occur before employees attain senior management positions. The recommended more flexible work options and assignments have also benefited a broader group of employees than those specifically targeted at the Forum.

References

Adler, N. (2000 in press). Coaching global executives: Women succeeding in a world beyond here. In M. Goldsmith, L. Lyons, and A. Freas (eds.). *Beyond Executive Coaching: Helping Learners Learn.*

Adler, N. (1994). Competitive frontiers: Women managing across borders. In N. Adler and D. Izraeli (eds.). *Competitive Frontiers: Women Managers n a Global Economy.* Cambridge, MA: Blackwell, pp. 22–40.

Adler, N., Brody, L., & Osland, J. (2000 in press). The women's global leadership forum: Enhancing one company's global leadership. *Human Resource Management.*

Adler, N., Brody, L., & Osland, J. (2000 in press). Advances in global leadership: The women's global leadership forum. In W.H.Mobley (ed.). *Advances in Global Research*, Vol. 2 (Greenwich, CT: JAI).

Ragins, B. R., Townsend, B., and Mattis, M. (1998). Gender gap in the executive suite: CEOs and female executives report on breaking the glass ceiling.

Shepard, H. (December 1984). Rules of Thumb for Change Agents, *OD Practitioner*, Organization Development Network, Portland, Oregon.

Wellington, S. W. (1996). "Women in Corporate Leadership: Progress and Prospects." New York City: Catalyst.

Course Objectives

- To increase your self-awareness

- To help you become more skilled at analyzing
  behavior in organizations

- To help you learn what actions are appropriate
  for different situations

- To help you acquire a larger repertoire of
  behaviors or skills

- To teach you to think like an organizational
  behavior expert

Organizational Behavior: An Experiential Approach 7/E
Joyce S. Osland, David A. Kolb, and Irwin M. Rubin

T1.0

Characteristics of OB

- Multidisciplinary Nature

- Three Levels of Analysis: Individual, Group, and Organizational

- Acknowledgement of Environmental Forces

- Grouped in the Scientific Method

- Performance Orientation

- Applied Orientation

- Change Orientation

Organizational Behavior: An Experiential Approach 7/E
Joyce S. Osland, David A. Kolb, and Irwin M. Rubin   T1.1

Model for Managing Psychological Contracts

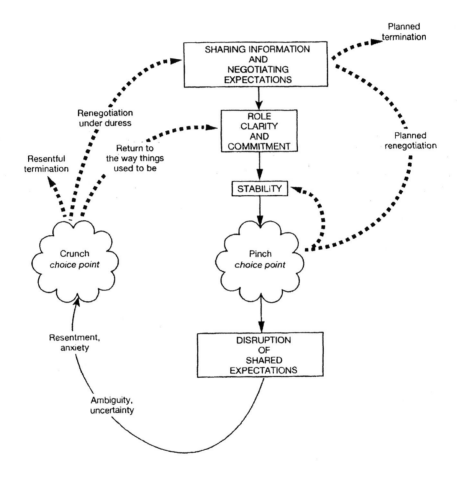

Common Sources of Contract Violation

Sources	Violations
Recruiters	• Unfamiliar with actual job
	• Overpromise
Managers	• Say one thing, do another
Coworkers	• Failure to provide support
Mentors	• Little follow-through
	• Few interactions
Top management	• Mixed messages
Compensation	• Changing criteria
	• Reward seniority, low job security
Benefits	• Changing coverage
Career paths	• Dependent on one's manager
	• Inconsistent application
Performance review	• Not done on time
Training	• Skills learned not tied to job
Documentation	• Stated procedures at odds with actual practice

Organizational Behavior: An Experiential Approach 7/E
Joyce S. Osland, David A. Kolb, and Irwin M. Rubin

How to Manage Generation X^{ers}

- Vary their assignments

- Teach them new skills

- Teach them some manners

- Keep them in the loop

- Tie praise for a job well done to a

  concrete reward

- Keep it fun

T1.4

Organizational Behavior: An Experiential Approach 7/E
Joyce S. Osland, David A. Kolb, and Irwin M. Rubin

Committed Employees

- Have the self-control required for teamwork, empowerment, and flatter organizations
- Display organizational citizenship behavior that benefits the organization
- Are "willing to help"
- Adapt better to unforeseeable occurrences
- Perform better
- Have better attendance records
- Stay with the company longer
- Work harder at their jobs

T1.5

Organizational Behavior: An Experiential Approach 7/E
Joyce S. Osland, David A. Kolb, and Irwin M. Rubin

Earning Employee Commitment

- **Commit to people-first values**:
  - Put it in writing; hire right-kind managers; walk the talk
- **Clarify and communicate your mission**:
  - Clarify the mission and ideology; make it charismatic; use value-based hiring practices; stress values-based orientation and training; build the tradition
- **Guarantee organizational justice**:
  - Have a comprehensive grievance procedure; provide for extensive two-way communications
- **Create a sense of community**:
  - Build value-based homogeneity; share and share alike; emphasize barn-raising, cross-utilization, and teamwork; get together
- **Support employee development**:
  - Commit to actualizing; provide first-year job challenge; enrich and empower; promote from within; provide developmental activities; provide employee security without guarantees

Organizational Behavior: An Experiential Approach 7/E
Joyce S. Osland, David A. Kolb, and Irwin M. Rubin

T1.6

Robert Quinn's Completing Values Model of Leadership

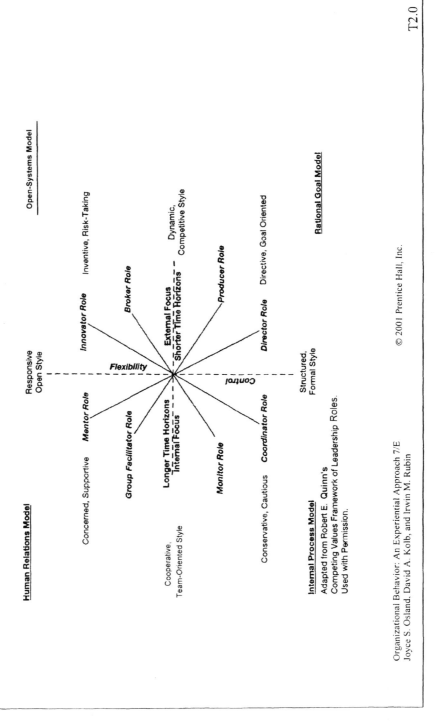

Human Relations Model

Concerned, Supportive

Cooperative,
Team-Oriented Style

Open-Systems Model

Inventive, Risk-Taking

Dynamic,
Competitive Style

Innovator Role

Broker Role

Mentor Role

Responsive
Open Style

External Focus
Shorter Time Horizons

Flexibility

Group Facilitator Role

Longer Time Horizons
Internal Focus

Producer Role

Director Role — Directive, Goal Oriented

Structured,
Formal Style

Control

Monitor Role

Coordinator Role

Conservative, Cautious

Rational Goal Model

Internal Process Model

Adapted from Robert E. Quinn's
Competing Values Framework of Leadership Roles.
Used with Permission.

Organizational Behavior: An Experiential Approach 7/E
Joyce S. Osland, David A. Kolb, and Irwin M. Rubin

© 2001 Prentice Hall, Inc.

T2.0

The Positive and Negative Zones

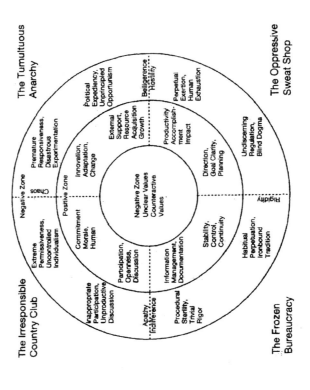

The Irresponsible Country Club

The Tumultuous Anarchy

The Oppressive Sweat Shop

The Frozen Bureaucracy

Organizational Behavior: An Experiential Approach 7/E
Joyce S. Osland, David A. Kolb, and Irwin M. Rubin

© 2001 Prentice Hall, Inc.

T2.1

Managerial Work: Folklore and Fact

Folklore

— Managers are reflective, systematic planners

Fact

— Their fast-paced activities are brief, varied, and discontinuous.

Folklore

— Effective managers have no regular duties to perform.

Fact

— They perform regular duties in addition to handling exceptions.

Folklore

— Senior managers need aggregated MIS information

Fact

— Managers favor verbal media—phone calls and meetings.

Folklore

— Management is becoming a science and profession.

Fact

— Managers' programs are locked in their heads.

Organizational Behavior: An Experiential Approach 7/E
Joyce S. Osland, David A. Kolb, and Irwin M. Rubin

Kolb's Experiential Learning Model

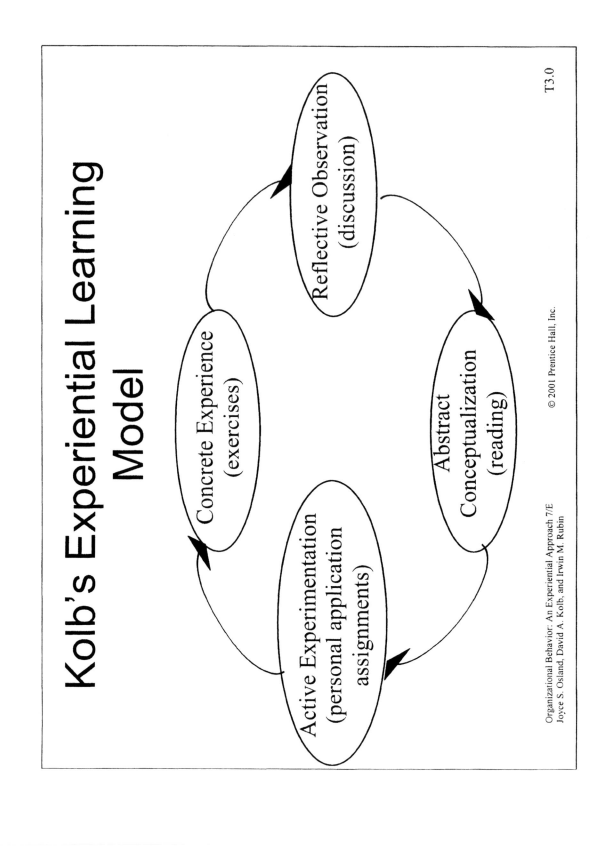

Concrete Experience (exercises)

Reflective Observation (discussion)

Abstract Conceptualization (reading)

Active Experimentation (personal application assignments)

Organizational Behavior: An Experiential Approach 7/E
Joyce S. Osland, David A. Kolb, and Irwin M. Rubin

T3.0

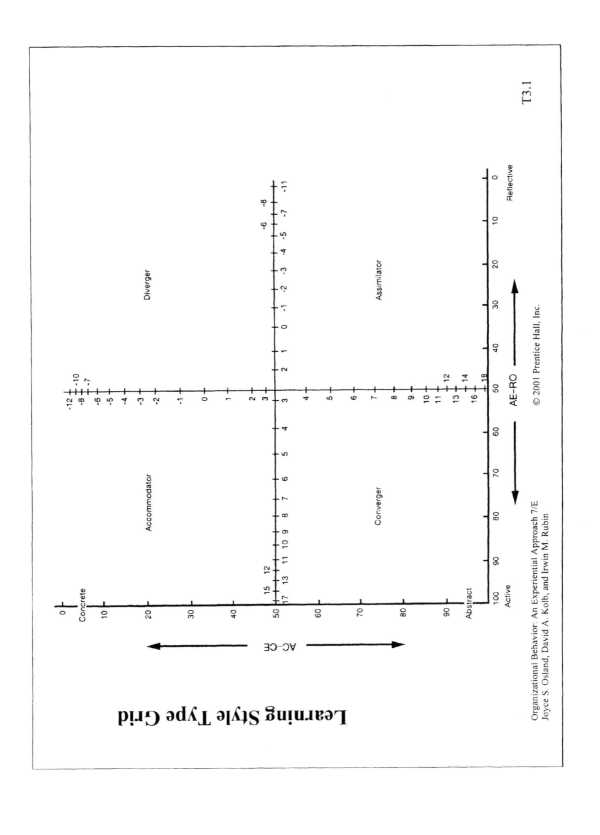

Learning Style Type Grid

Concrete

Diverger

Accommodator

Assimilator

Converger

Active

Reflective

Abstract

AC–CE

AE–RO

© 2001 Prentice Hall, Inc.

Organizational Behavior: An Experiential Approach 7/E
Joyce S. Osland, David A. Kolb, and Irwin M. Rubin

T3.1

Characteristics of a Learning Organization

- Systematic problem solving

- Experimentation

- Learning from past experience

- Learning from others

- Transferring knowledge

T3.2

Organizational Behavior: An Experiential Approach 7/E
Joyce S. Osland, David A. Kolb, and Irwin M. Rubin

Argyris's Types of Learning

- ADAPTIVE
- Single-loop learning
- Refine prevailing mental models
- Coping orientation
- Problem solving

- GENERATIVE
- Double-loop learning
- Question assumptions underlying mental models
- Creative orientation
- Analysis of the process

Organizational Behavior: An Experiential Approach 7/E
Joyce S. Osland, David A. Kolb, and Irwin M. Rubin

David McClelland's Major Motives

Motive	Need	Typical Behavior	Typical Roles
(n-Ach) Need for Achievement	To improve, do better: • Achieve personal and others' standard of excellence • Unique accomplishment • Long-term career involvement	• Set goals and measures outcome • Takes calculated (moderate) risks • Likes immediate, concrete feedback • Takes responsibility for own success or failures • Likes to work alone	Entrepreneurs
(n-Aff) Need for Affiliation	To have warm, close relationships: • Have friends • Establish friendship • Sustain relationships • Avoid conflict	• Prefers to work with others • Holds meetings • Participates in friendly activities • Writes letters, sends cards, and calls	Supervisors
(n-Pow) Need for Power	To impact others: • Influence others • Impress others • Lead others • Control others	• Seeks leadership • Seeks prestige of self and organization • Gives unsolicited help and advice • Displays strong, forceful behavior • Competitive	Middle- or Upper-Level Managers

Organizational Behavior: An Experiential Approach 7/E
Joyce S. Osland, David A. Kolb, and Irwin M. Rubin

T4.0

Expectancy Theory

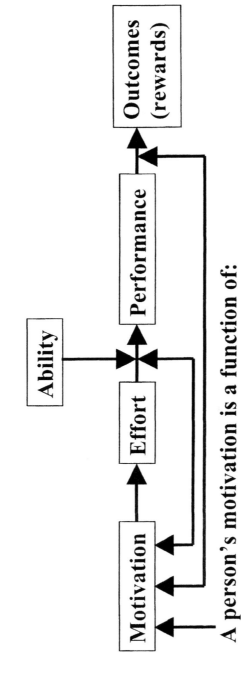

A person's motivation is a function of:

    A. Effort-to-performance expectations
    B. Performance-to-outcome expectancies
    C. Perceived valence of outcomes

Organizational Behavior: An Experiential Approach 7/E
Joyce S. Osland, David A. Kolb, and Irwin M. Rubin

T4.1

Job Characteristics Model

| Core Job Characteristics | Critical Psychological States | Personal Work Outcomes |

Core Job Characteristics

Skill variety

Task identity

Task significance

Autonomy

Job feedback

Critical Psychological States

Experienced meaningfulness of the work

Experienced responsibility for outcomes of the work

Knowledge of the actual results of the work

Personal Work Outcomes

High internal work motivation

High-quality work performance

High satisfaction with the work

Low absenteeism and turnover

Individual Differences

• Knowledge and skill
• Growth-need strength
• Satisfaction with contextual factors

Organizational Behavior: An Experiential Approach 7/E
Joyce S. Osland, David A. Kolb, and Irwin M. Rubin

Kohlberg's Three Levels of Moral Development

Stage	What is considered to be right
Level—One-Self-Centered (Preconventional)	
Stage One—obedience and Punishment Orientation	Sticking to rules to avoid physical punishment Obedience for its own sake
Stage Two—Instrumental Purpose and Exchange	Following rules only when it is one's immediate interest; right is an equal exchange, a fair deal
Level Two—Conformity (Conventional)	
Stage Three—Interpersonal Accord, Conformity, Mutual Expectations	Stereotypical "good" behavior Living up to what is expected by peers and people close to you
Stage Four—Social Accord and System Maintenance	Fulfilling duties and obligations of social system; upholding laws except in extreme cases where they conflict with fixed social duties Contributing to the society, group
Level Three—Principled (Postconventional)	
Stage Five—Social Contract, Individual Rights	Being aware that people hold a variety of values; that rules are relative to the group upholding rules because they are the social Contract; upholding nonrelative values and rights regardless of majority opinion
Stage Six—Universal Ethical Principles	Following self-chosen ethical principles of justice and rights; when laws violate principles, act in accord with principles

Organizational Behavior: An Experiential Approach 7/E
Joyce S. Osland, David A. Kolb, and Irwin M. Rubin

T5.0

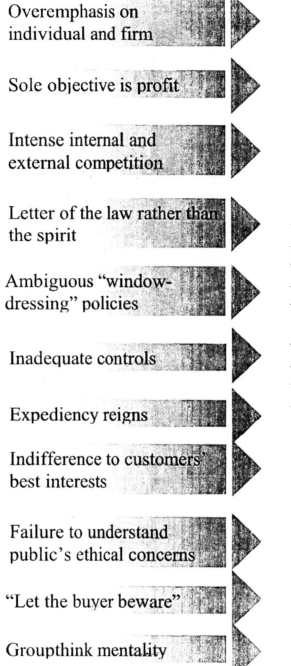

Overemphasis on individual and firm

Sole objective is profit

Intense internal and external competition

Letter of the law rather than the spirit

Ambiguous "window-dressing" policies

Inadequate controls

Expediency reigns

Indifference to customers' best interests

Failure to understand public's ethical concerns

"Let the buyer beware"

Groupthink mentality

Factors That Foster Unethical Business Practices

T5.1

Organizational Behavior: An Experiential Approach 7/E
Joyce S. Osland, David A. Kolb, and Irwin M. Rubin

Tripod of Life Plan Perspectives

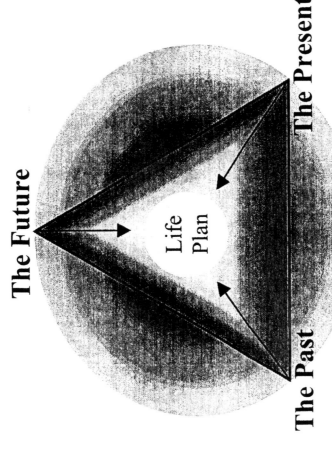

The Future

The Past

The Present

Life Plan

Organizational Behavior: An Experiential Approach 7/E
Joyce S. Osland, David A. Kolb, and Irwin M. Rubin

T6.0

Transactional Model of Career Stress

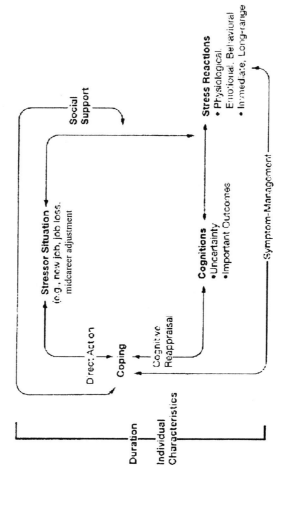

Organizational Behavior: An Experiential Approach 7/E
Joyce S. Osland, David A. Kolb, and Irwin M. Rubin

Arc of Distortion

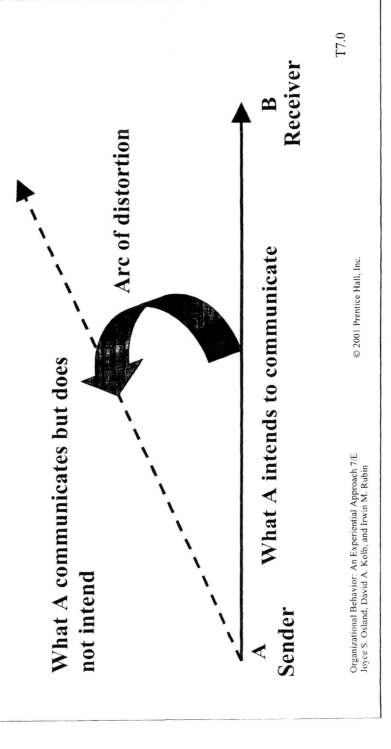

What A communicates but does not intend

Arc of distortion

What A intends to communicate

A
Sender

B
Receiver

Organizational Behavior: An Experiential Approach 7/E
Joyce S. Osland, David A. Kolb, and Irwin M. Rubin

T7.0

Transactional Model of Communication

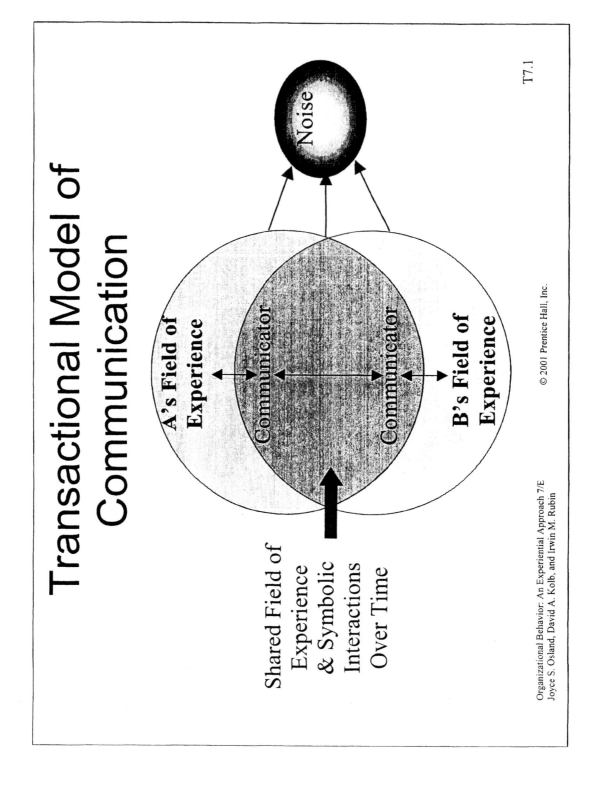

Organizational Behavior: An Experiential Approach 7/E
Joyce S. Osland, David A. Kolb, and Irwin M. Rubin

T7.1

Defensive/Nondefensive Communication Climates

Defensive Climates	Supportive Climates
1. Evaluation	1. Description
2. Control	2. Problem orientation
3. Strategy	3. Spontaneity
4. Neutrality	4. Empathy
5. Superiority	5. Equality
6. Certainty	6. Provisionalism

Organizational Behavior: An Experiential Approach 7/E
Joyce S. Osland. David A. Kolb. and Irwin M. Rubin

© 2001 Prentice Hall, Inc.

I-Statements

Behavior	Effect	Feelings
When you come to class late	it disrupts what's going on and we have to stop to orient you and figure out what group you should join	and that's annoying.
When you don't turn in your part of the project on time	we can't proceed with our work, and we have to work overtime to make the deadline	and we're irritated about this.

Organizational Behavior: An Experiential Approach 7/E
Joyce S. Osland, David A. Kolb, and Irwin M. Rubin

T7.3

Circle Limit IV (Escher)

Organizational Behavior: An Experiential Approach 7/E
Joyce S. Osland, David A. Kolb, and Irwin M. Rubin

T8.0

Johari Window

	Known to Self	Not Known to Self
Known to Others	Arena	Blindspot
Not Known to Others	Facade	Unknown

Organizational Behavior: An Experiential Approach 7/E
Joyce S. Osland, David A. Kolb, and Irwin M. Rubin

Punctuated Equilibrium Model of Group Development

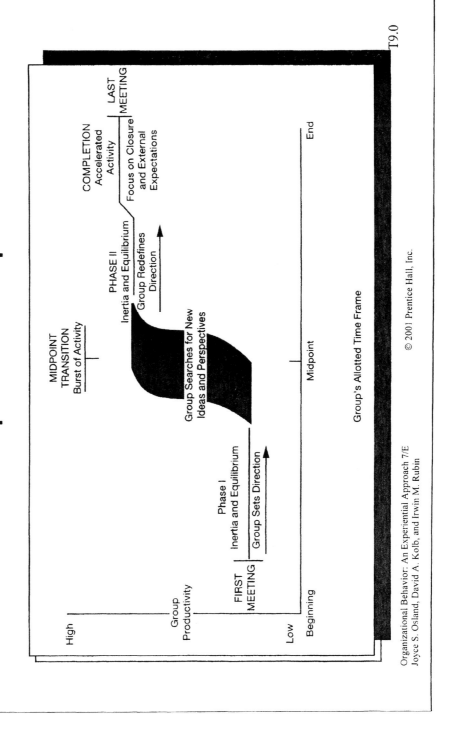

Organizational Behavior: An Experiential Approach 7/E
Joyce S. Osland, David A. Kolb, and Irwin M. Rubin

© 2001 Prentice Hall, Inc.

T9.0

Five-Stage Model of Group Development

- Forming
- Storming
- Norming
- Performing
- Adjourning

Organizational Behavior: An Experiential Approach 7/E
Joyce S. Osland, David A. Kolb, and Irwin M. Rubin

Content and Process

- Content issues refer to the task, the group's raison d'être, the WHAT

- Process issues refer to HOW the group is functioning.
  - Task process—how groups accomplish their work
  - Maintenance process—how groups meet psychological and relationship needs

Organizational Behavior: An Experiential Approach 7/E
Joyce S. Ostland, David A. Kolb, and Irwin M. Rubin

T9.2

Problem Solving as a Dialectic Process

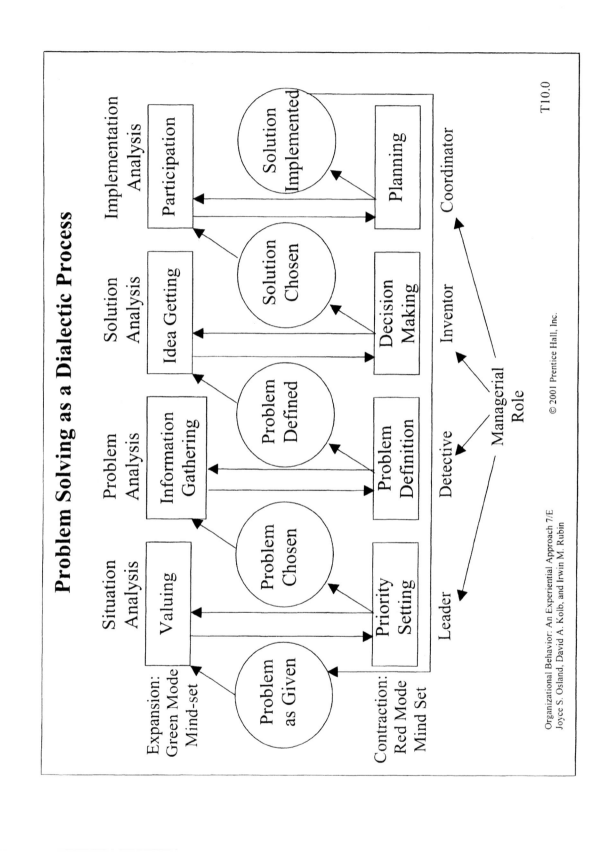

Organizational Behavior: An Experiential Approach 7/E
Joyce S. Osland, David A. Kolb, and Irwin M. Rubin

T10.0

The Learning Model and the Problem-Solving Process

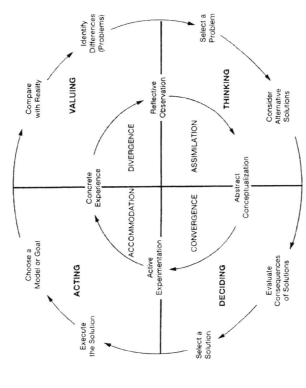

PROBLEM FINDING

- Compare with Reality
- Identify Differences (Problems)
- Select a Problem
- Consider Alternative Solutions

VALUING

THINKING

- Concrete Experience
- Reflective Observation
- Abstract Conceptualization
- Active Experimentation

DIVERGENCE

ASSIMILATION

ACCOMMODATION

CONVERGENCE

ACTING

DECIDING

- Choose a Model or Goal
- Execute the Solution
- Select a Solution
- Evaluate Consequences of Solutions

PROBLEM SOLVING

Organizational Behavior: An Experiential Approach 7/E
Joyce S. Osland, David A. Kolb, and Irwin M. Rubin

T10.1

Five Conflict-Handling Orientations

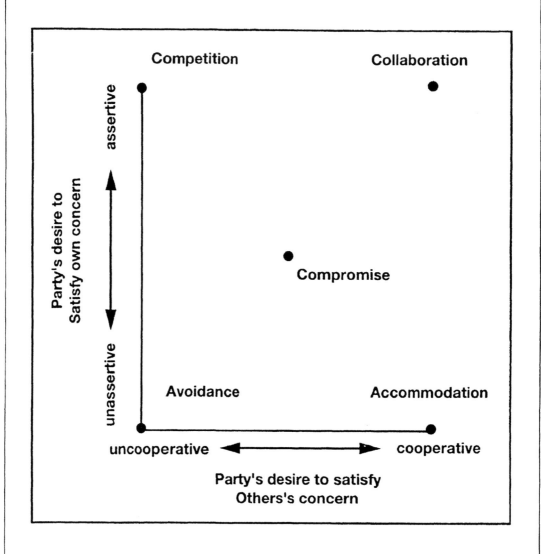

Competition

Collaboration

Party's desire to
Satisfy own concern

assertive

unassertive

Avoidance

Accommodation

Compromise

uncooperative ⟷ cooperative

Party's desire to satisfy
Others's concern

T11.0

Organizational Behavior: An Experiential Approach 7/E
Joyce S. Osland, David A. Kolb, and Irwin M. Rubin

Principled Negotiation

- Separate the people from the problem
- Focus on interests, not positions
- Invent options for mutual gain
- Insist on objective criteria

BATNA

Best **A**lternative **t**o a **N**egotiated **A**greement

- Determine your BATNA and that of the other party beforehand.
- Compare offers to your BATNA during the negotiation

Organizational Behavior: An Experiential Approach 7/E
Joyce S. Osland, David A. Kolb, and Irwin M. Rubin

Hofstede's Value Dimensions

A. Power Distance Dimension

<u>**Large**</u>

Unequal Distribution
of Power

<u>**Small**</u>

Equal Distribution
of Power

B. Uncertainty Avoidance Dimension

<u>**Strong**</u>

Avoidance
of
ambiguity and risk

<u>**Weak**</u>

Acceptance
of
ambiguity and risk

C. Individualism Dimension

<u>**Individualist**</u>

Loose social
framework
(self and immediate
family)

<u>**Collectivist**</u>

Tight social
framework
(relatives, clan,
in-groups)

D. Masculinity Dimension

<u>**Masculinity**</u>

Extreme
assertiveness,
materialism,
independence

"Androgyny"

<u>**Feminine**</u>

Nurturance,
quality of life,
interdependence

Organizational Behavior: An Experiential Approach 7/E
Joyce S. Osland, David A. Kolb, and Irwin M. Rubin

© 2001 Prentice Hall, Inc.

T12.0

Continuum of Leadership Behavior

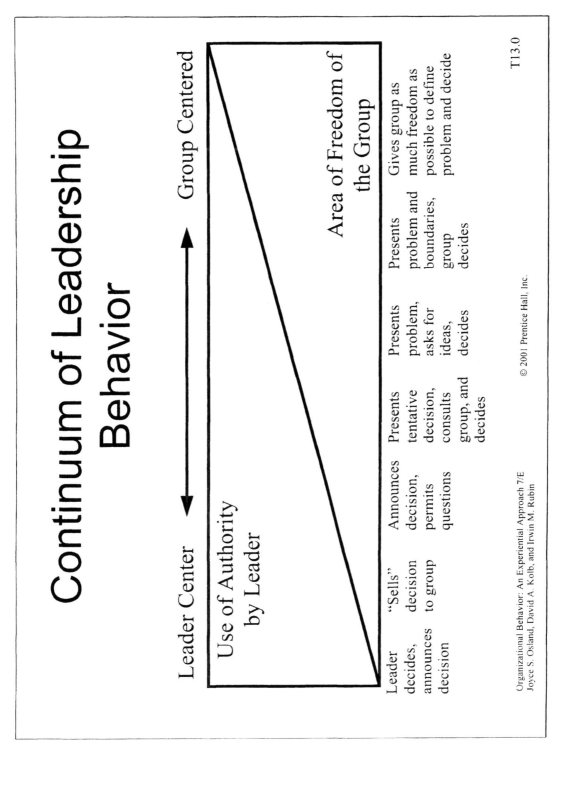

Leader Center ← → Group Centered

Use of Authority by Leader

Area of Freedom of the Group

| Leader decides, announces decision | "Sells" decision to group | Announces decision, permits questions | Presents tentative decision, consults group, and decides | Presents problem, asks for ideas, decides | Presents problem and boundaries, group decides | Gives group as much freedom as possible to define problem and decide |

Organizational Behavior: An Experiential Approach 7/E
Joyce S. Osland, David A. Kolb, and Irwin M. Rubin

© 2001 Prentice Hall, Inc.

T13.0

The Path Goal Theory

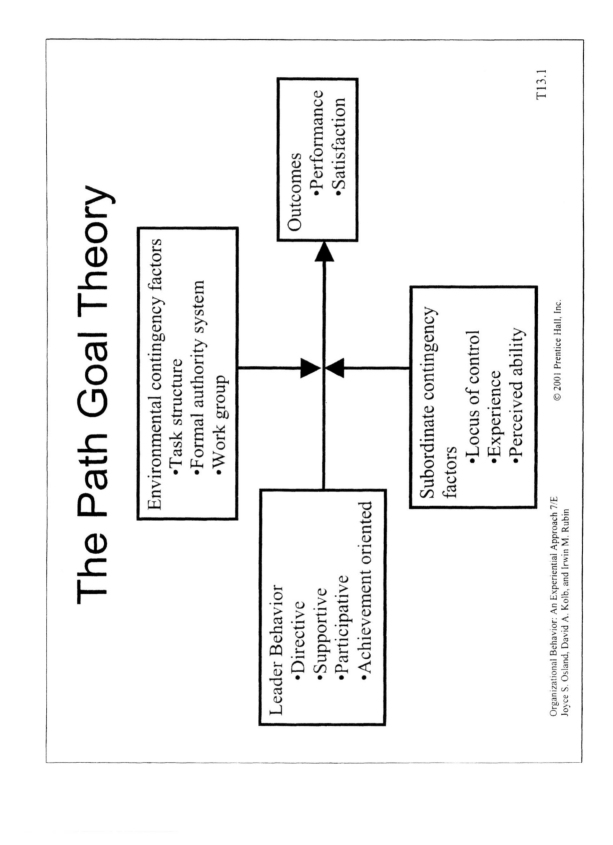

Environmental contingency factors
- Task structure
- Formal authority system
- Work group

Outcomes
- Performance
- Satisfaction

Leader Behavior
- Directive
- Supportive
- Participative
- Achievement oriented

Subordinate contingency factors
- Locus of control
- Experience
- Perceived ability

© 2001 Prentice Hall, Inc.

T13.1

Organizational Behavior: An Experiential Approach 7/E
Joyce S. Osland, David A. Kolb, and Irwin M. Rubin

Uncovering Levels of Culture

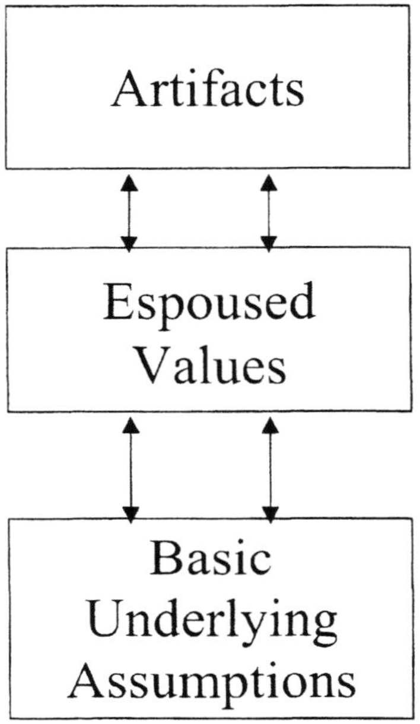

Artifacts	Visible organizational structures and processes (hard to decipher)
↕	
Espoused Values	Strategies, goals, philosophies (espoused justifications)
↕	
Basic Underlying Assumptions	Unconscious, taken-for-granted beliefs, perceptions, thoughts, and feelings (ultimate source of values and action)

Organizational Behavior: An Experiential Approach 7/E
Joyce S. Osland, David A. Kolb, and Irwin M. Rubin

T14.0

Five Phases of Growth

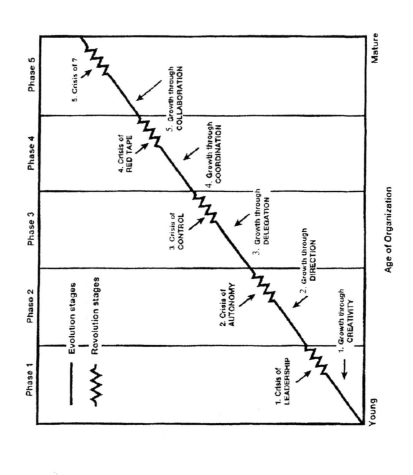

Phase 1 | Phase 2 | Phase 3 | Phase 4 | Phase 5

—— Evolution stages
〰〰 Revolution stages

1. Crisis of LEADERSHIP

2. Crisis of AUTONOMY

3. Crisis of CONTROL

4. Crisis of RED TAPE

5. Crisis of ?

1. Growth through CREATIVITY

2. Growth through DIRECTION

3. Growth through DELEGATION

4. Growth through COORDINATION

5. Growth through COLLABORATION

Young

Mature

Age of Organization

Organizational Behavior: An Experiential Approach 7/E
Joyce S. Osland, David A. Kolb, and Irwin M. Rubin

Leadership Styles

AI You solve the problem or make a decision for yourself, using whatever facts you have at hand.

AII You obtain any necessary information from those who report to you and then reach a decision alone. You only seek relevant facts, not advice or council.

CI You consult one-on-one with those who report to you, describing the problem and asking for each person's advice and recommendations. The final decision, however, is yours alone.

CII You consult with those who report to you in a meeting, describing the problem, and request their collective advice and recommendations. The final decision is yours.

GII You share the problem with your subordinates as a group. Your goal is to help the group concur on a decision. Your ideas are not given any greater weight than those of others.

Organizational Behavior: An Experiential Approach 7/E
Joyce S. Osland, David A. Kolb, and Irwin M. Rubin

T15.0

QR **Quality Requirement:** How important is the technical quality of this decision?
CR **Commitment Requirement:** How important is subordinate commitment to the decision?
LI **Leader's Information:** Do you have sufficient information to make a high-quality decision?
ST **Problem Structure:** Is the problem well structured?
CP **Commitment Probability:** If you were to make the decision by yourself, is it reasonably certain that your
   subordinates would be committed to the decision?
GC **Goal Congruence:** Do subordinates share the organizational goals to be attained in solving the problem?
SC **Subordinate Conflict:** Is conflict among subordinates over preferred solutions likely?
SI **Subordinate Information:** Do subordinates have sufficient information to make a high-quality decision?

The Revised Leadership—Participation Model

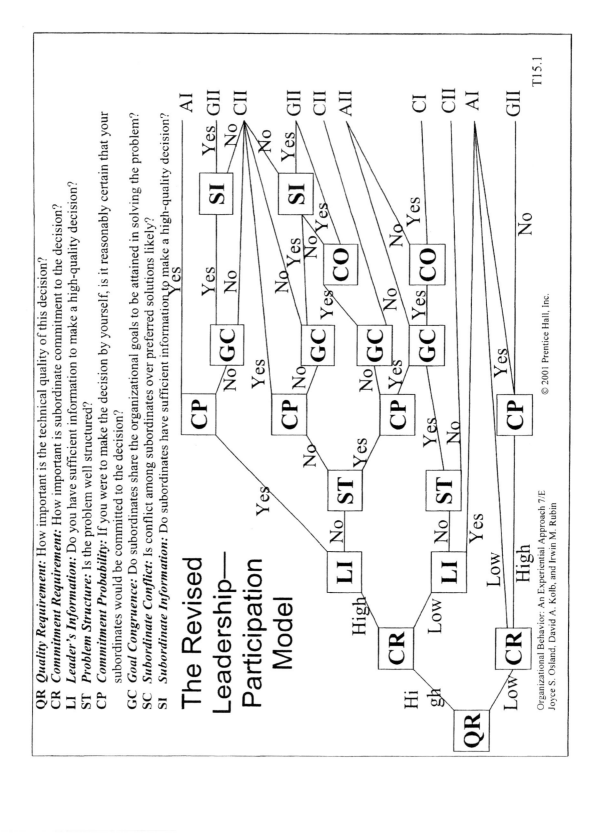

Organizational Behavior: An Experiential Approach 7/E
Joyce S. Osland, David A. Kolb, and Irwin M. Rubin

T15.1

Recognition-Primed Decision Model

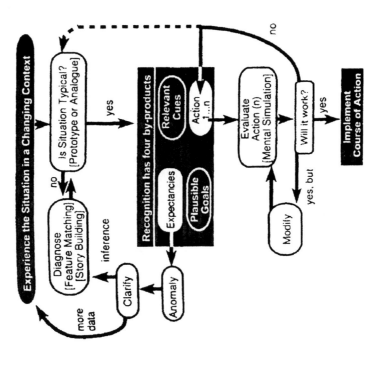

Organizational Behavior: An Experiential Approach 7/E
Joyce S. Osland, David A. Kolb, and Irwin M. Rubin

Influence Tactics

Type

Rational persuasion

Inspirational appeals

Consultation

Ingratiation

Personal appeals

Exchange

Coalition tactics

Legitimating tactics

Pressure

Tool

Logical arguments and facts

Target's values, ideals, and aspirations

Inclusion of target in planning

Praise, flattery, friendly, helpful behavior

Target's loyalty and friendship

Reciprocated favors

Seek aids of others

Claim authority or right, point to policy, tradition

Demands, threats, frequent checking

T16-0

Organizational Behavior: An Experiential Approach 7/E
Joyce S. Osland, David A. Kolb, and Irwin M. Rubin

Influence Styles

Assertive Persuasion   Facts, logic, rational argument, persuasive reasoning

Reward/Punishment   Bargaining, incentives and pressures, stating expectations

Participation/Trust   Involve others, active listening, personal disclosure, admit mistakes

Common Vision   Articulate goals, seek common ground, enthusiasm, expressive, vivid imagery

Organizational Behavior: An Experiential Approach 7/E
Joyce S. Osland, David A. Kolb, and Irwin M. Rubin

Command-and-Control vs. Involvement

	COMMAND AND CONTROL	INVOLVEMENT ORIENTED
Best Way to Organize	Hierarchy and vertical relationships	Employee self-management
Role of Managers	Make decisions, give orders, ensure that subordinates obey	Share power and information Listen to employees
Role of Employees	Obey orders	Carry out thinking and controlling functions of their job Make decisions
Required Employee Skills	Job skills	Basic problem solving, communication, quantitative techniques, commitment to learning and self-development

Organizational Behavior: An Experiential Approach 7/E
Joyce S. Osland, David A. Kolb, and Irwin M. Rubin

Four Aspects of Empowerment

- Meaning—their work is important

- Competence—confidence in their ability, self-efficacy

- Self-determination—autonomy on how to do the work

- Impact—influence in their work unit

© 2001 Prentice Hall, Inc.

Organizational Behavior: An Experiential Approach 7/E
Joyce S. Osland, David A. Kolb, and Irwin M. Rubin

Effective and Ineffective Feedback

Effective

Descriptive

Specific and data based

Directed toward
controllable behaviors

Solicited

Close to the event

Occurs when receiver is
ready to accept it

Suggests

Is intended to help

Ineffective

Evaluative

General

Personality traits

Imposed

Delayed

Occurs at convenience of
sender

Prescribes

Is intended to punish

Organizational Behavior: An Experiential Approach 7/E
Joyce S. Osland, David A. Kolb, and Irwin M. Rubin

Appraisal Process

- Review legal requirements
- Translate organizational goals into job descriptions
- Set clear job expectations
- Provide job training or coaching to meet expectations
- Supply adequate supervision
- Acknowledge accomplishments, diagnose strengths and weaknesses in interview
- Establish performance goals and development plan

Organizational Behavior: An Experiential Approach 7/E
Joyce S. Osland, David A. Kolb, and Irwin M. Rubin

T18.0

The 7-S Model

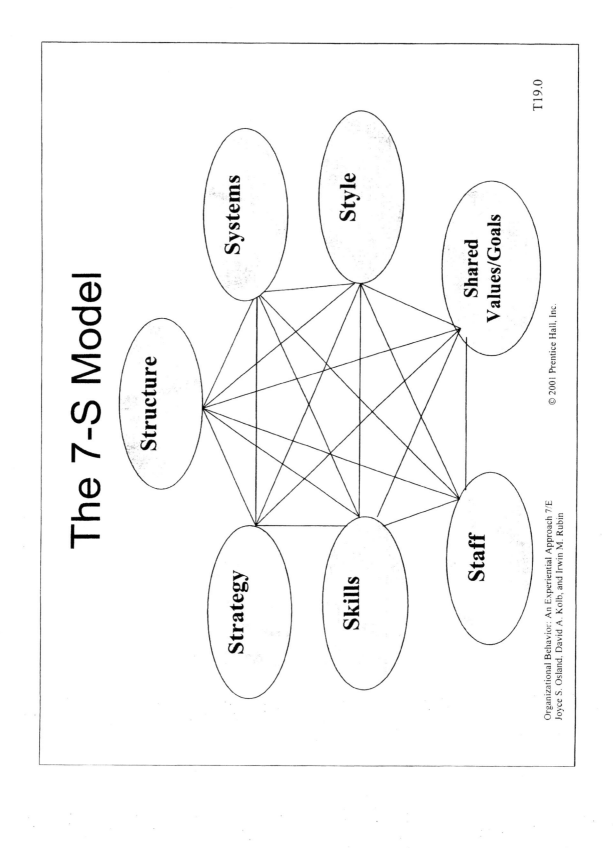

Organizational Behavior: An Experiential Approach 7/E
Joyce S. Osland, David A. Kolb, and Irwin M. Rubin

T19.0

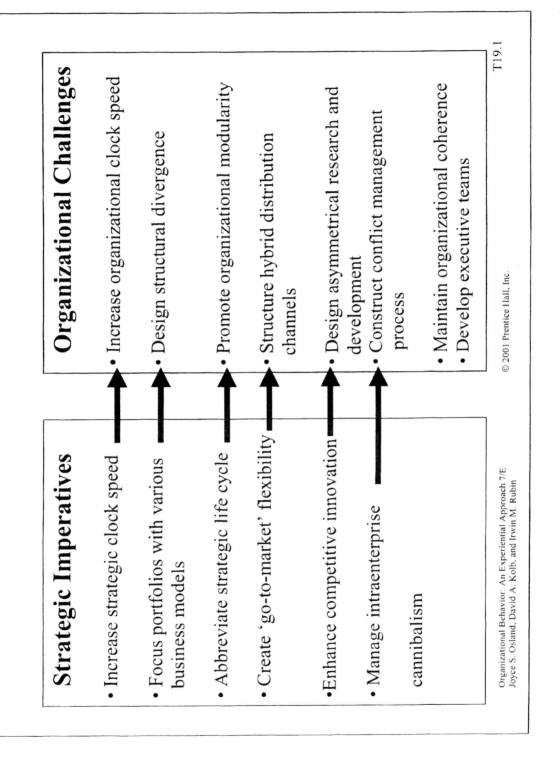

Strategic Imperatives

- Increase strategic clock speed
- Focus portfolios with various business models
- Abbreviate strategic life cycle
- Create 'go-to-market' flexibility
- Enhance competitive innovation
- Manage intraenterprise cannibalism

Organizational Challenges

- Increase organizational clock speed
- Design structural divergence
- Promote organizational modularity
- Structure hybrid distribution channels
- Design asymmetrical research and development
- Construct conflict management process
- Maintain organizational coherence
- Develop executive teams

Organizational Behavior: An Experiential Approach 7/E
Joyce S. Osland, David A. Kolb, and Irwin M. Rubin

T19.1

E. ORG DIMENSIONS

	1990s	E. Org
Organization Structure	• Hierarchical • Command-and-control	• Centerless, networked • Flexible structure that is easily modified
Leadership	• Selected "stars" step above • Leaders set the agenda • Leaders force change	• Everyone is a leader • Leaders create environment for success • Leaders create capacity for change
People & Culture	• Long-term rewards • Vertical decision making • Individuals and small teams are rewarded	• "Own your career" mentality • Delegated authority • Collaboration expected and rewarded
Coherence	• Hard-wired into processes • Internal relevance	• Embedded vision in individuals • Impact projected externally
Knowledge	• Focused on internal processes • Individualistic	• Focused on customers • Institutional
Alliances	• Complement current gaps • Ally with distant partners	• Create new values and outsource uncompetitive services • Ally with competitors, customers, and suppliers
Governance	• Internally focused • Top-down	• Internal and external focus • Distributed

Organizational Behavior: An Experiential Approach 7/E
Joyce S. Osland, David A. Kolb, and Irwin M. Rubin

Steps in the Change Process

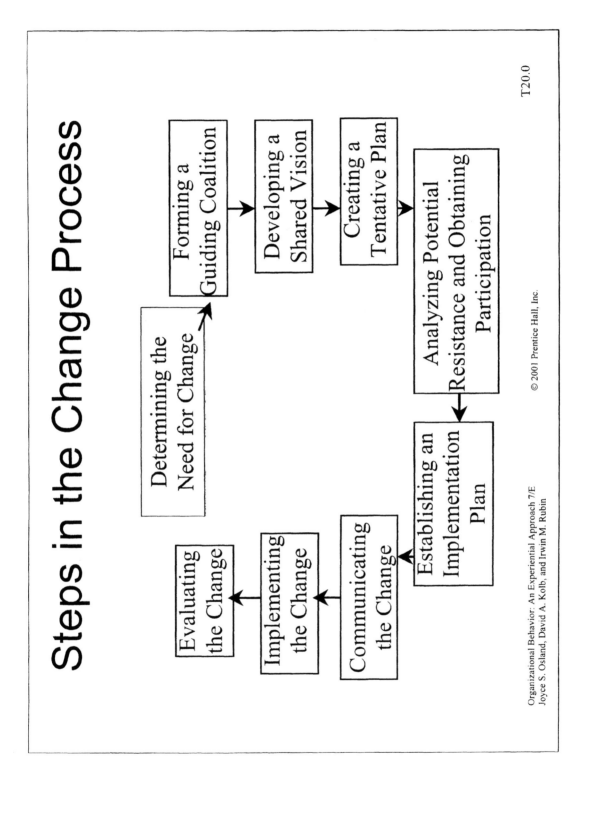

Determining the Need for Change → Forming a Guiding Coalition → Developing a Shared Vision → Creating a Tentative Plan → Analyzing Potential Resistance and Obtaining Participation → Establishing an Implementation Plan → Communicating the Change → Implementing the Change → Evaluating the Change

Organizational Behavior: An Experiential Approach 7/E
Joyce S. Osland, David A. Kolb, and Irwin M. Rubin

T20.0